D1521650

A Kingdom of Stargazers

A KINGDOM OF STARGAZERS

Astrology and Authority in the Late Medieval Crown of Aragon

MICHAEL A. RYAN

CORNELL UNIVERSITY PRESS
ITHACA AND LONDON

Publication of this book was made possible, in part, by a grant from the Program for Cultural Cooperation between Spain's Ministry of Culture and United States Universities.

First published 2011 by Cornell University Press
Printed in the United States of America

Library of Congress Cataloging-in-Publication Data

Ryan, Michael A.
    A kingdom of stargazers : astrology and authority in the late medieval crown of Aragon / Michael A. Ryan.
        p. cm.
    Includes bibliographical references and index.
    ISBN 978-0-8014-4984-0 (cloth : alk. paper)
    1. Astrology, Spanish—History—To 1500.   2. Divination—Spain—Aragon—History—To 1500.   3. Prophecies (Occultism)—Spain—Aragon—History—To 1500.   4. Astrology and politics—History—To 1500.   5. Aragon (Spain)—Kings and rulers.   I. Title.
    BF1714.S65R93 2011
    133.50946—dc22   2011001002

Cornell University Press strives to use environmentally responsible suppliers and materials to the fullest extent possible in the publishing of its books. Such materials include vegetable-based, low-VOC inks and acid-free papers that are recycled, totally chlorine-free, or partly composed of nonwood fibers. For further information, visit our website at www. cornellpress.cornell.edu.

Cloth printing   10 9 8 7 6 5 4 3 2 1

I dedicate this book to the memory of my grandfather,
Ferdinand Charles Mariano (1922–2001), whose resonant voice
now echoes among the stars.

Men at some time are masters of their fates. The fault, dear Brutus, is not in our stars, but in ourselves.

—William Shakespeare, *Julius Caesar*

The historian does for the past what the necromancer and fortuneteller pretend for the future, but the latter, in contrast to the historian, are exposed to verification.

—Paul Valéry

Contents

Acknowledgments

By their very nature, the stars elicit wonder and fascination in those who view them. They also provide hope. In studying the individuals who were interested in sidereal matters in the later Middle Ages, it struck me how much they invested their hopes in the stars. In their reckonings, the stars, although remote, could still provide answers to uncertain events that were far beyond their control. The stars could thus soothe from afar. It is no coincidence that Dante Alighieri's final line from the thirty-fourth, and final, canto of the *Inferno* states, "*e quindi uscimmo a riveder le stelle.*" After witnessing the countless horrors of hell, the first thing the author and his guide, Virgil, saw after leaving the Underworld was the comforting sight of the stars. More than seven hundred years later, in September 2005, at least one man, known only as Strangebone, echoed Dante's sentiment in the drowned city of New Orleans a week after Hurricane Katrina slammed into the city, devastating it and creating a veritable hell on earth. Those who did not or could not evacuate the city before Katrina's arrival and survived had to face the additional horrors of chaos and destruction that erupted around them. As New Orleans became a place described by Dan Barry, a reporter from the *New York Times,* as dwelling "in the post-apocalypse, half baked and half deluged: pestilent, eerie, unnaturally quiet," things were dire indeed. Nevertheless, Strangebone was able to find hope. With the absence of electricity, the streetlights were dark, permitting him to remark about the nighttime sky, "You're able to see the stars. It's wonderful."

This book has been a labor of love, and in writing it I have incurred many personal, professional, and financial debts. First I must first thank my former advisers from the University of Minnesota, William D. Phillips Jr. and Carla Rahn Phillips, for their continuing advice regarding this project, other scholarly projects, and academic life in general. They have always been helpful, sage, patient, and in good cheer, and I am blessed to count them as both colleagues and dear friends. Another colleague and dear companion from Minnesota, Ruth Mazo Karras, always provided significant help, support, laughter, and friendship, and I thank her from the depths of my heart.

Financial support my research came from many sources. I received generous funding from the University of Minnesota's Center for Early Modern History, especially in the form of the Union-Pacific Fellowship and Microfilm Grants. Funds provided by the Program for Cultural Cooperation between Spain's Ministry of Culture and United States' Universities, helped toward the research and publication of this book, as did a short-term fellowship from the Newberry Library. After arriving at Purdue University in 2005, I was able to conduct research at the Hill Monastic Manuscript Library at St. John's University in Collegeville, Minnesota, thanks to a Heckman stipend, and I thank the library's staff and librarians, especially Theresa Vann and Matthew Heintzelman, for all of their assistance. A Library Scholars Grant from Purdue permitted me a month's sojourn at Yale University's Beinecke Rare Book and Manuscript Library in the summer of 2006. I thank Bartow Culp and Larry Mykytiuk, librarians at Purdue University, as well as Robert Babcock, at the Beinecke, and the staff of the Beinecke, for their assistance in procuring valuable catalogs and primary sources affiliated with the Mellon Collection of Alchemy and the Occult. Purdue University's Department of History provided me an invaluable semester research leave to transcribe Nicolau Eymerich's treatise *Contra praefigentes certum terminum fini mundi,* a copy of which the helpful staff at the Biblioteca Nacional de España in Madrid readily and conscientiously provided me, and to travel to Barcelona to conduct additional research at the Archivo Diocesano de Barcelona, the Biblioteca de Catalunya, and the Archivo de la Corona de Aragón. The staff at all of these institutions, especially Jaume Riera i Sans, was incredibly helpful at all times and patiently answered my questions, provided me with registers and manuscripts when I requested them, and offered me their own thoughts regarding the parameters of this project. Last-minute research conducted at the Bibliothèque nationale de France, made possible by funds provided by a Research Incentive Grant provided by Purdue University's College of Liberal Arts, was both helpful and necessary, and I extend my thanks to the staff at the Bibliothèque nationale as well.

I have had many hours' worth of conversation with different scholars during the research and writing of this project. Discussions with Ann Astell, Raymond Clemens, Adam Franklin-Lyons, Tom Barton, Michelle Herder, Beth Duncan, Barbara Weissberger, Ronald Surtz, José Enrique Ruiz-Domènec, Christian Sheridan, Donald Kagay, Joel Kaye, William Chester Jordan, David Nirenberg, Brian Catlos, Núria Silleras-Fernández, Anne Marie Wolf, Ian Lekus, Leah DeVun, Dyan Elliott, Richard Emmerson, Jöelle Rollo-Koster, Renate Blumenfeld-Kosinski, Paul Freedman, Richard Kieckhefer, Marie Kelleher, Michael D. Bailey, Anthony Grafton, and, above all, Laura Ackerman Smoller were always illuminating, helpful, and most enjoyable. Derek Rivard was kind enough to share with me a copy of a medieval liturgical source that relied heavily on sidereal imagery and rhetoric when our sojourns at the Hill Monastic Manuscript Library overlapped. Participants in the Premodern Spanish History Association of the Midwest meeting held on the campus of Kenyon College included Lucy Pick, Lisa Voigt, Rowena Hernández-Múzquiz, Miriam Shadis, Jeffrey Bowman, Olivia Remie Constable, and Gretchen Starr-LeBeau, all of whom offered helpful criticism, germane suggestions, and enthusiastic support.

Many of my colleagues and friends at Purdue also were generous with their time and assistance. From Purdue's History Department, Tithi Bhattacharya, Neil Bynum, John Contreni, Susan Curtis, Charles Cutter, Alicia Decker, Joseph Dorsey, Jennifer Foray, William Gray, Sally Hastings, Carrie Janney, Rebekah Klein-Pejšová, Dawn Marsh, Bob May, Gordon Mork, Whitney Walton, and Melinda Zook frequently offered critical readings and discussions, as well as great support, of my work. Members of the staff in the History Department at Purdue, including Fay Chan, Nicole Federer, Tami Johnson, and Rebecca Gwin, were unflagging in their help. Scholars in other departments at Purdue, Dorsey Armstrong, Patricia Boling, Ayse Çiftçi, Angelica Duran, Dan Frank, Geraldine Friedman, Ana Gómez-Bravo, Brian Kelly, Yonsoo Kim, Michael Johnston, Paula Leverage, Jackie Mariña, Robyn Malo, Bill Mullin, Tom Ohlgren, Aparajita Sagar, Marcia Stephenson, and Paul White, were always helpful and generous with their energy and knowledge.

Other individuals also offered their thoughts and expertise in discussing and reading over portions of the manuscript. D. Jack Norton and Andrea Burns, colleagues and very dear friends from our shared time at the University of Minnesota, read over drafts of the prospectus and introductory chapters. Discussions over the years with Char Aloisio, Mark Aloisio, Ellen Arnold, Bridget Bentz-Sizer, Matt Desing, Doris Dirks, Chris Freeman, Greg Gidden, James Kinane, Don Leech, Arnold Lelis, Spencer Lucas, Larry Mott, Troy Osborne, April Pickrel, Eric Richtmyer, Heidi Sherman, Jason Smith, Kate Staples, Nancy Stone, Marynel Ryan Van Zee, Emily Weglian, and, particularly, Karolyn Kinane were always inspiring and crucial to the conception and writing of this study.

I must give special recognition to the members of my faculty cohort, Darren Dochuk, Stacy Holden, Kevin Vaughn, and Juan Wang, who arrived at Purdue the same year as I did. Along with their partners and spouses, Debra Dochuk, Mark Bernstein, Dawn Vaughn, and Peter Lichtenstein, we have read and criticized each other's works, spent many hours discussing matters scholarly and not, and watched each other grow and develop as we transitioned to Purdue. I thank them for their thoughts, suggestions, support, and friendship. A better group of people with whom to be part of a cohort I would be hard-pressed to find.

To the undergraduate and graduate students whom I had the honor of teaching at both the University of Minnesota and Purdue University, I thank you for your own thoughts and questions regarding some of the trickier issues surrounding medieval magic and the occult. Your ideas and suggestions have always been helpful and most welcome, and my interactions with you have helped me grow as a scholar and a teacher. The teaching assistance provided over the years by graduate students Heather Akin, Shawn Bennion, Hira Bhattacharyya, Dorothée Bouquet, Elise Dermineur,

Joshua Flanery, Angela Ghionea, Amy Harris, Tim Olin, David Schlosser, Pierre Schmitt, Luo Wang, James Williams, and, crucially, Amy Bosworth, was invaluable, and your labor helped provide me substantial time to work on this manuscript. I am grateful to each of you.

Half of chapter 5 previously appeared as "To Condemn a King: The Dream of Bernat Metge and King Joan's Ties with the Occult," *Magic, Ritual, and Witchcraft* (Winter 2008): 158–86, and the other half appeared as a book chapter, "Nicolau Eymerich and Discerning the End of Days," in *The Devil in Premodern Society* (Toronto: CRRS Publications, 2010). These selections are reprinted here courtesy of the editorial board of *Magic, Ritual, and Witchcraft,* published by the University of Pennsylvania Press, and my thanks go to the journal's then editor, Michael D. Bailey, and to Richard Raiswell and Peter Dendle, coeditors, for the collection of essays published by the Centre for Reformation and Renaissance Studies at Victoria University in the University of Toronto.

Special thanks go to my faculty mentor at Purdue, James R. Farr, and to Mike Sizer, both of whom generously spent significant amounts of their own time and energy reading over and critiquing the entire first draft of my manuscript. Their suggestions were invaluable and helped me clarify my arguments and avoid potential pitfalls. I thank Angelika Paraßl, Peter Prokop, and Ernst Gamillscheg of the Österreichische Nationalbibliothek in Vienna for granting me permission to use the image of "The Influence of the Planets," which comes from the *Losbuch in deutschen Reimpaaren,* for the cover of my book. Although of Austrian provenance, the image is contemporary with the events that occurred in the Crown of Aragon, hailing from the fourteenth century, and exemplifies graphically the many themes that I discuss throughout the course of this book. I extend my deepest thanks to Peter Potter, editor in chief at Cornell University Press, who, along with his assistant, Rachel Post, as well as Karen Laun and Jill Hughes, helped a new author navigate the world of monograph publishing. They patiently answered all of my many questions. It was a true honor and pleasure to work with such a conscientious, caring, thoughtful, and supportive editor as Peter. I also give heartfelt gratitude to the two anonymous readers of the drafts of this manuscript provided by Cornell University Press. Their suggestions improved my manuscript considerably, and I am most grateful for all the time and effort they invested in reading over the drafts and for providing me with richly detailed suggestions and comments. Any

remaining infelicities in transcription, translation, or analysis remain mine
alone.

My family, whom I define as such through ties of both biology and
companionship, has been my pillar throughout this entire process. To my
mother, Doretta Ryan-Sutton, and grandmother, Loretta Bland, I thank
you for your lifetime of constant love and support. I recognize all the sacrifices you both made for me, and I am indebted. Lora and Nancy Pelligrino,
although not biologically related, are nevertheless very much a part of my
family, and I consider myself lucky to have grown up under their care
as if they were beloved aunts. Margaux Barclay, Tiffany Barclay, Christine Barclay, and the late, great John Barclay comprise my surrogate family in Barcelona. Colleen Bos, Jeannine Bos, Colby Mills, Eric Owen, and
Mike Sizer occupy a very special place in my heart as if they were siblings.
I would be remiss if I failed to thank the cats in my life, the departed Bear,
the lovely Gracie, and, of course, the inimitable Slim, who has been with
me through thick and thin. Finally, to my partner, Gary Massey, I say that
the twinkling of the stars is nothing next to the glittering beauty of your
laughing, blue eyes. You came into my life when I was suffering a particularly bleak period, but the radiance of your smile and warmth of your heart
dispelled the darkness. Your love, patience, and devotion have sustained
me always, and I could not have completed this work without you by my
side and in my life. To you I give my unending gratitude, devotion, and all
the love that is in my heart, which is greater than the number of stars in
the nighttime sky.

When I was a young boy, the night would sometimes scare me. When
the darkness closed in and my imagination ran wild, I would call out for
my grandfather, and he would come to my bedroom, place his rough hand
on my head, and, while singing softly, soothe me back to sleep. Ferdinand
Mariano could be a gruff, but also gentle, man and instilled in me from a
very early age the importance of education. He was proud I was the first
member of the family to study at a university, let alone to go on to graduate
school, and he encouraged me throughout all of my academic endeavors.
He died in 2001, when I was first conceptualizing this project, and his loss
was immeasurable. I like to think he would have enjoyed reading about
these prophets, magicians, and astrologers who did not fear the night, but
instead sought to unlock its mysteries. It is to his memory that I dedicate
this book.

A KINGDOM OF STARGAZERS

INTRODUCTION

Traveling South

Gerbert d'Aurillac (ca. 945–1003) had a well-earned reputation as a first-rate mathematician. During his years as a teacher at the cathedral school of Rheims, he contributed significantly to the development of mathematic and scientific studies in transalpine Europe with his work on the abacus, his encouragement of using Arabic numerals for calculation, and his writings on the operating principles of the astrolabe.[1] But Gerbert had gained much of his knowledge of math and science before his days at Rheims. A peripatetic scholar, he traveled far in his quest for knowledge. For three years, from 967 until 970, he had sojourned in Catalonia studying mathematics in Vic, where he encountered Arabic manuscripts from the nearby monastery of Santa Maria de Ripoll.[2] Gerbert's encounter with

---

1. Brian Stock, "Science, Technology, and Economic Progress in the Early Middle Ages," in *Science in the Middle Ages*, ed. David C. Lindberg (Chicago: University of Chicago Press, 1978), here 37.

2. Ricard Torrents Bertran, "La peregrinatio accademica de Gerbert d'Orlhac (Silvestre II)," in *Actes del Congrés Internacional Gerbert d'Orlhac i el seu temps: Catalunya i Europa a la fi del*

these texts fueled a passion for Arabic science that would endure throughout his life.

Gerbert did not remain ensconced in the cloistered world of academic study for long. In 999 he ascended to the papal see as Sylvester II, capping a remarkably swift rise to the top of Christendom—a rise that astonished many of his critics. Men such as Adhemar of Chabannes, Orderic Vitalis, Walter Map, and Vincent of Beauvais were deeply skeptical of Gerbert's affinity for Arabic scientific works. Some, for instance, suggested that he had traveled farther south during his time in Iberia, visiting the cities of Toledo, Córdoba, and Sevilla in the Muslim region of Spain called al-Andalus. The early twelfth-century *Chronicle* of William of Malmesbury painted an especially nefarious picture of Gerbert, suggesting he had left for Spain "fleeing by night . . . chiefly designing to learn astrology and other sciences of that description from the Saracens."[3] To his detractors, Gerbert's awe-inspiring scientific knowledge and ascent to the highest levels of influence and power could only have been gained through a pact with the devil, and such a pact must have been forged while he was in Spain.

The medieval perception of the Iberian Peninsula as a domain of magic and the occult was widespread and would continue long after Gerbert's death.[4] Some medieval scholars saw the city of Toledo, the historic seat of the Visigothic kings located in the heart of the medieval kingdom of Castile-León, as a famous center of magical and astrological study. Legend had it that the *ars notoria* (notorious art) was "revealed by God through an angel to [King] Solomon who in a very short time was able to acquire all the liberal and mechanical arts."[5] For the fifteenth-century critic

I^r mil·leni, Vic-Ripoll, 10–13 de novembre de 1999, ed. Imma Ollich i Castanyer (Vic, Spain: Eumo Editorial, 1999), 13–16.

3. Oscar G. Darlington, "Gerbert, the Teacher," *American Historical Review* 52, no. 3 (1947): 456–76, here 462 n28. Darlington explains how Gerbert acquired magical abilities with which he "got into and out of a series of exciting scrapes." See also Owen Davies, *Grimoires: A History of Magic Books* (Oxford: Oxford University Press, 2009), 35.

4. This reckoning of Iberia as such continued well into the early modern era, especially in the world of theater. See, among others, Augusta Espantoso Foley, *Occult Arts and Doctrine in the Theater of Juan Ruiz de Alarcón* (Geneva: Droz, 1972); John S. Mebane, *Renaissance Magic and the Return of the Golden Age: The Occult Tradition and Marlowe, Jonson, and Shakespeare* (Lincoln: University of Nebraska Press, 1989); and Robert Lima, *Stages of Evil: Occultism in Western Theater and Drama* (Lexington: University Press of Kentucky, 2005).

5. Jan R. Veenstra, trans. and ed., *Magic and Divination at the Courts of Burgundy and France: Text and Context of Laurens Pignon's "Contre les devineurs" (1411)* (Leiden: Brill, 1998), 293 n.239;

of astrology Laurens Pignon, who also referred to the *ars notoria* as the "*art de Tolede*," the city was a veritable haven for the study of the occult:

> as a center of learning Toledo had considerable reputation in the Middle Ages. Apart from the more regular studies in theology and philosophy, its academies also harboured the study of magic, kabbalah, astrology and alchemy. Arabic and Hebrew works in these fields were there translated into Latin. It is this that gave Toledo a reputation for being a city of magicians and sorcerers. . . . There also was] a still very common sentiment [of] Toledo as a sorcerer's capital . . . in the works of the demonologists during the great witch craze.[6]

Gerbert's supposed nefarious and demonic pact and Pignon's opinion of Toledo as a center for the study of magic are but two examples of this premodern perception of Iberia as a land of the occult. Gerbert, of course, studied in Catalonia, while Toledo was part of Castile-León by the time of Pignon's writing, but for many it was clear that these ideas extended to all of the Iberian Peninsula. Even if the legends and ideas are fanciful, they nevertheless hint at an interesting question regarding the place of magic in medieval Iberia, one that has not been adequately explored before now.

In this study I investigate the liminal status that occult practices, especially those involving astronomy and astrology, occupied in the late Middle Ages. I use the term "liminal" because attitudes toward the occult, including its legitimacy, were never stable or fixed during the Middle Ages. I focus my investigation on one particular geographic region, the coastal Iberian kingdom of the Crown of Aragon, during the late fourteenth and early fifteenth centuries. In this kingdom, as in much of late medieval Europe, the occult held an important place in people's conception of the world. Derived from the Latin adjective *occultus*, meaning hidden, occult matters were those that involved secret powerful information.[7] Medieval

---

and Gerd Mentgen, *Astrologie und Öffentlichkeit im Mittelalter* (Stuttgart: Hiersemann, 2005), 28; Davies, *Grimoires*, 26–28.

6. Veenstra, *Magic and Divination*, 293 n239.

7. Karen Jolly, "Medieval Magic: Definitions, Beliefs, Practices," in *Witchcraft and Magic in Europe: The Middle Ages*, ed. Bengt Ankarloo and Stuart Clark, 6 vols. (Philadelphia: University of Pennsylvania Press, 2002), 3:1–71, provides a detailed introduction to the variety of methods used by sociologists, historians, and anthropologists in understanding the breadth of magical experiences.

interest in the occult centered on the promise of accessing a body of hidden and privileged knowledge and a battery of arcane disciplines, including astrology, that constituted the occult and magical arts.[8] Clerical authorities might construct precise definitions and explanations as to the nature of magic, future insight, prophetic revelation, and their roles within a Christian framework, but for the vast majority of people, who lacked systematic and rigorous intellectual training, such rigid thinking did not necessarily apply.[9] It is no surprise that a common miller from Friuli named Menocchio, when pressed by an inquisitor in 1599 to elaborate upon his reckoning of the world and his unorthodox visionary experiences, described himself in the same breath as a "philosopher, astrologer, and prophet."[10] For Menocchio, all three professions occupied the same space in his mind, regardless of any denunciations the inquisitor ultimately wrested from him. Such reckonings suggest that the definitions used to categorize the occult disciplines were far from "watertight" and that the arts themselves resisted easy taxonomy.[11]

---

8. Astrological and prophetic discourses also occupied the realm of medieval magic, as I address throughout this book. For introductions to the study of medieval magic, see Lynn Thorndike, *The History of Magic and Experimental Science*, 8 vols. (New York: Macmillan, 1932–1958) (hereafter referred to as *HMES*); Richard Kieckhefer, *Magic in the Middle Ages* (Cambridge: Cambridge University Press, 1989); and Michael D. Bailey, "The Meanings of Magic," *Magic, Ritual, and Witchcraft* 1 (Summer 2006): 1–23, who discusses the inherent instability of magic. For early modernity, see Keith Thomas, *Religion and the Decline of Magic: Studies in Popular Beliefs in Sixteenth and Seventeenth Century England* (New York: Oxford University Press, 1971). Jean-Patrice Boudet, *Entre science et* nigromance: *Astrologie, divination et magie dans l'Occident médiéval (XIIe–XVe siècle)* (Paris: Publications de la Sorbonne, 2006), provides a monumentally important survey of astrology and its role in medieval thought.

9. See, for instance, Thomas Aquinas's discussion of the magical arts in chapter 1. In 1395 Nicolau Eymerich, the inquisitor general of the Crown of Aragon, wrote a treatise against astronomers in which he spent extensive time railing against astrology and the occult. Heavily influenced by Aquinas, Eymerich identified and outlined twenty specific occult arts. Bibliothèque nationale de France (hereafter referred to as BnF), MS lat 3171, ff. 87v.-95v.

10. Carlo Ginzburg, *The Cheese and the Worms: The Cosmos of a Sixteenth-Century Miller*, trans. John and Anne Tedeschi (Baltimore: Johns Hopkins University Press, 1980), 107; and Stephen Pumfrey, Paolo L. Rossi, and Maurice Slawinski, eds. *Science, Culture and Popular Belief in Renaissance Europe* (Manchester: Manchester University Press, 1994). See also the collection of essays by William R. Newman and Anthony Grafton, eds. *Secrets of Nature: Astrology and Alchemy in Early Modern Europe* (Cambridge, MA: MIT Press, 2001).

11. Renate Blumenfeld-Kosinski, *Poets, Saints, and Visionaries of the Great Schism, 1378–1417* (University Park: Pennsylvania State University Press, 2006), 15.

One of the most powerful bodies of privileged knowledge that individuals hoped to access through the occult arts was the unfolding of future events. Astrological, astronomical, and divinatory works were written, read, adhered to, expounded upon, or rejected outright across late medieval Europe. Hundreds of such documents circulated among and within European royal and noble courts as well as among the mercantile and ecclesiastical elite. They were housed in archives and university libraries, their very plurality speaking to their popularity. The increased production of such texts during this period coincided with major political, economic, social, and religious upheavals taking place throughout Europe, including the Crown of Aragon, and the few literate medieval Europeans who wrote and read these texts did so to better understand these events.[12] Many of them viewed astrology and the occult as indispensable tools for comprehending the past, understanding the present, and predicting the future. It is these people's receptivity to astrology and the occult arts, which straddled the borders between heresy and orthodoxy, secular and ecclesiastical authority, and science and religion, that I investigate throughout this book.

The problematic, ill-defined space that the occult occupied in late medieval Europe poses many intriguing questions. Why, for example, did people believe in the existence of a body of hidden knowledge? Why did some view themselves as having a special ability or position in society that permitted them to access this hidden knowledge whereas others were denied that same privilege? What happened when powerful individuals—those who considered themselves wholly orthodox in their religious beliefs and practices—chose to engage in actions viewed by others as highly suspect if not outright heretical?

To answer such questions, I explore the interest in occult practices, especially the sidereal arts of astrology and astronomy, in the Crown of Aragon

---

12. Veenstra, *Magic and Divination*, 22. Jacques d'Avout, *La querelle des Armagnacs et de Bourguinons* (Paris: Gallimard, 1943); George K. Park, "Divination and Its Social Contexts," *Journal of the Royal Anthropological Institute of Great Britain and Ireland* 93, no. 2 (1963): 195–209; Mircea Eliade, "Some Observations on European Witchcraft," *History of Religions* 14, no. 3 (1975): 149–72; Richard Kieckhefer, *European Witch Trials: Their Foundations in Popular and Learned Culture, 1300–1500* (Berkeley: University of California Press, 1976); Guy Thompson, *Paris and Its People under English Rule: The Anglo-Burgundian Regime, 1420–1436* (Oxford: Oxford University Press, 1991); and Walter Stephens, *Demon Lovers: Witchcraft, Sex, and the Crisis of Belief* (Chicago: University of Chicago Press, 2002), have also addressed aspects of people's interest in the divination and the occult in response to various crises.

during the reigns of Pere (Peter) *el Cerimoniós*, the Ceremonious (r. 1336–1387); Joan (John) *el Caçador*, the Hunter (r. 1387–1396); and Martí (Martín) I, *l'Humà*, the Humane (r. 1396–1410).[13] I focus on these three kings because they are the last three kings from the original House of Aragon, established by Guifré (Wilfred) *el Pelòs*, the Hairy, in the ninth century, and because their markedly different personalities and regnal styles colored their attitudes toward, and approaches to, the occult. Put simply, Pere and Joan were deeply interested in the occult arts whereas Martí came to reject them (at least partially). Moreover, the degree to which occult practices flourished in the Crown of Aragon was directly related to the power and authority each monarch exhibited and applied.

As Thomas Aquinas (d. 1274) recognized in his *Summa Theologiae*, the lure of divination was universal because people had a "natural inclination" to attempt to know the future before it happened.[14] Nevertheless, attempting to divine the future was fundamentally problematic in that it inevitably required the summoning of forces that religious authorities deemed diabolic. The Church, therefore, believed it was absolutely necessary to restrict people's access to the reservoirs of power and knowledge that the occult, by its very nature, promised. By engaging in occult practices, the kings of the Crown of Aragon were operating in defiance of centuries-old theological restrictions against divination and the occult. In their eyes, however, they were monarchs, the supreme representation of medieval secular authority outside of emperor, and thus they had the right to engage in such activities regardless of the Church's view on the matter. On the other side, Church officials such as the inquisitor general of the Crown of Aragon, Nicolau Eymerich (d. 1399), believed that the very act of ascertaining what the future held was a damnable one, regardless of the practitioner's station in life.

---

13. Although I have Anglicized the name of the *Corona de Aragó*, referring to it throughout this book as the Crown of Aragon, I nevertheless have maintained the Catalan names of the sovereigns and their contemporaries. In addition to those being the names with which they were born and to which they would have answered, I reinforce the linguistic and political divisions between the various kingdoms that comprised the political landscape of late medieval Iberia.

14. Thomas Aquinas, *Summa Theologiae*, trans. Blackfriars, 61 vols. (London: Eyer and Spottiswoode, 1964–). This point appears in volume 40, on "Superstition and Irreverence," 2a2ae, 95.1: "Ad tertium dicendum quod homo habet naturalem inclinationem ad cognoscendum future secundum modum humanum: non autem secundum indebitum divinationis modum." I discuss Aquinas further in chapter 1.

It is well known that the medieval Inquisition failed to make significant inroads in the Crown of Aragon during these years relative to, say, Italy and France. I do not believe one can draw a causal relationship between the kings' interest in the occult and the relative lack of inquisitorial power in the Crown of Aragon. That is, I do not argue that the papal inquisitorial apparatus failed to take root in the kingdom directly because of the monarchs' heretical behavior. And yet at some level the kings' interest in the occult, especially astrology and alchemy, challenged the legitimacy of the inquisitorial enterprise and drew concern from contemporary ecclesiastical and secular authorities alike, further evidencing the flexible definitions and context-bound uses of magical and occult arts within society.

Compounding the matter further were the contradictory personalities of the monarchs themselves. Pere was a powerful sovereign who enforced his claims to authority through traditional means, including military conquest, and thus he was not an easy target for criticism. When Joan, his eldest son, ascended to the throne in 1387, he undermined Pere's hard-earned authority by frittering away the resources of the royal coffers on perceived frivolities, which earned him the less than flattering sobriquet *el Descurat*, or "the Negligent." After Joan's premature death in 1396, his younger brother, the stoic and pious Martí, ascended the throne, ushering in a markedly different era. In contrast to Pere and Joan, Martí focused on enforcing religious orthodoxy, both in his realms and in the culture of his court. Yet the new king did not entirely reject all things occult; he kept certain occult texts owned by his father and brother in his royal library, and he maintained at least one occult project commissioned by Joan.

When considering the importance of occult matters within the royal court of the Crown of Aragon, it is important to remember the broader culture of secular courts in the late Middle Ages. As Edward Peters and others have demonstrated, the medieval royal court functioned as an independent demimonde, one populated by the king, the queen, mistresses, ladies-in-waiting, legitimate heirs, bastard children, emissaries, bureaucrats, and various courtiers and hangers-on of all stripes.[15] It was also a

---

15. Edward Peters, *The Magician, the Witch, and the Law* (Philadelphia: University of Pennsylvania Press, 1978), 112–25; Peters, "The Magical Church and State on Superstition, Magic and Witchcraft: From Augustine to the Sixteenth Century," *Witchcraft and Magic in Europe: The Middle Ages*, 3:175–272; and Bailey, "Meanings of Magic," 10 n16. For a comparative glimpse into the

shadowy, frightful world for anyone who occupied a tenuous position within it—made worse because of the speed and randomness with which one's personal fortunes could rise and fall according to the caprices of the monarch. In such an environment, it is not difficult to imagine the appeal of the magical arts, offering courtiers a modicum of control over highly changeable circumstances. Dabbling in the magical arts could potentially bolster one's personal fortunes in the ongoing competition for the monarch's patronage and affection.

Courtly culture in the Crown of Aragon during these years was splendid, comparable to those of other great medieval kingdoms. An economic and diplomatic powerhouse, Aragon interacted with all other major European states and principalities and with the competing papacies of Rome and Avignon during the period of the Great Western Schism (1378–1417). Moreover, many of these other royal courts, such as those of the kings of France and counts of Burgundy, and the respective papal curiae in Avignon and Rome, had their own thriving occult cultures. As such, the royal court in Barcelona was no more astrologically obsessed than others. However, the reigns of the three kings of the House of Aragon provide a unique perspective on the constantly shifting world of divination, magic, and astrology and how they join with the construction and legitimization of power in the late medieval world.

Most studies of courtly culture recognize that the principal authoritative figure, the king or noble patron, was the engine for cultural development and change within the royal court. Court styles and fashions changed with sometimes dizzying speed, based on the whims of the monarch in power. Hilary Carey has argued that in the hands of the English kings, astrology was "an exotic game, a pretty ornament, something to pass the time, like listening to romances, or playing chess."[16] However, it was also true that certain members of the English landed aristocracy exploited astrology and astrologers for their own political machinations. Jan Veenstra has elaborated further on this point in his analysis of astrology in the royal and

---

fiscal, cultural, and social expenditures of other medieval monarchs' courts, see Malcolm Vale, *The Princely Court: Medieval Courts and Culture in North-West Europe* (Oxford: Oxford University Press, 2001).

16. Hilary Carey, *Courting Disaster: Astrology at the English Court and University in the Later Middle Ages* (New York: St. Martin's, 1992), 22–23.

noble courts of France in the fourteenth and fifteenth centuries. Veenstra focused on Laurens Pignon, a cleric who was troubled by the increasing rise of magic, sorcery, divination, and astrology and the growing influence of these disciplines among courtiers and nobility alike within the French demimondes.[17] In this respect, the relationship between the French kings and the clergy, in which theologians from the University of Paris wielded enormous power in their condemnation of marginal behavior, was different from the situation that existed in the Crown of Aragon. There is no doubt that the Catalan kings were aware of theological restrictions against magic and the occult, but King Pere especially was secure enough in his authority to define his interest in astrology as he saw fit. The situation was not the same for Joan and Martí. In short, the particular stance that Pere and each of his sons would take toward astrological matters and the occult must be seen in the context of court politics, monarchical authority, and religious orthodoxy—something I try to bear in mind throughout this book.[18]

The title I have chosen for the book, *A Kingdom of Stargazers*, has a dual meaning. On one level it refers to the proliferation of sidereal-themed texts in the Crown of Aragon. During the fourteenth and fifteenth centuries, Aragon was a vibrant center for the production of astrological and astronomical works (many of which still require editing and analysis).[19] In that sense, *A Kingdom of Stargazers* refers to the collective of people who wrote, read, and commented upon astrological and astronomical works during this period. The title's other meaning evokes the kings' own interest in,

---

17. Veenstra, *Magic and Divination*, 2.

18. John Scott Lucas, "Tempting Fate: The Case against Astrology and the Catalan Response," *Catalan Review* 17, no. 2 (2003): 123–37, although quite useful, briefly touches upon the count-kings' interest in astrology.

19. John Scott Lucas, *Astrology and Numerology in Medieval and Early Modern Catalonia: The Tractat de prenostication de la vida natural dels hòmens* (Leiden: Brill, 2003), 3–30. On pp. 28–29 Lucas discusses the importance of the *Bibliografia de Textos Catalans Antics* (BITECA) section of the *PhiloBiblon* (http://sunsite.berkeley.edu/PhiloBiblon, accessed 1 June 2010). For an introduction to the premier scholar of medieval Iberian sidereal matters, see José María Millás Vallicrosa, *Assaig d'història de les idees físiques i matemàtiques a la Catalunya medieval* (Barcelona: Institució Patxot, 1931); Millás Vallicrosa, *Estudios sobre historia de la ciencia española* (Barcelona: Consejo Superior de Investigaciones Científicas, 1949); and Millás Vallicrosa, *Nuevos estudios sobre historia de la ciencia española* (Barcelona: Consejo Superior de Investigaciones Científicas, 1960). For a more recent study, see Aurelio Pérez Jiménez, ed. *Astronomía y astrología: de los orígenes al Renacimiento* (Madrid: Ediciones Clásicas, 1994).

or rejection of, astrology and divination. The right to see that which was meant to be unseen was no small component in the application of royal secular authority.[20]

Astrology and the occult were not the only domains through which the Catalan monarchs sought information and power. They actively appropriated apocalyptic rhetoric and imagery in a propagandistic manner to construct a larger notion of a providential destiny and thus fulfill aspects of their secular program.[21] In fact, a large part of the interest in divination during this period was apocalyptic in nature and in direct response to a perceived threat: that of the imminent arrival of the Antichrist and the fulfillment of history. Magical and astral imagery were linked closely with apocalyptic expectations, as some people viewed their surrounding crises as harbingers of the Antichrist. Some of them thus turned to the stars to help perceive the future. According to the Gospel of Matthew, nobody knows the day and hour of the arrival of the Antichrist, "not even the angels of the sky," but this did not prevent people from attempting to know.[22] Some might reject the use of ancient sidereal insight in Christian prophecy, but the stars, their images, and their symbols continued to occupy an important place in Christian teleology, offering the prospect of decipherable signposts that would usher in the fulfillment of history.[23]

For biblical precedents, one needed to look no further than the book of Revelation 12:1 and 3–4, speaking of the role that heavenly bodies would play in the drama of the Apocalypse: "And a great sign appeared in heaven: A woman clothed with the sun, and the moon under her feet, and on her head a crown of twelve stars. . . . And there appeared another wonder in

---

20. Lucas, *Astrology and Numerology*, 21–28; and Carey, *Courting Disaster*, 93–106.

21. Martin Aurell, "Prophétie et messianisme politique: La Péninsule ibérique au miroir du *Liber ostensor* de Jean de Roquetaillade," *Mélanges de l'Ecole Française de Rome. Moyen Age* 102 (1990): 317–61; Aurell, "Eschatologie, spiritualité, et politique dans la confédération catalano-aragonese (1282–1412)," *Cahiers de Fanjeaux* (1992): 191–235; Aurell, "La fin du monde, l'enfer et le roi: une prophétie catalane du XVe siècle," *Revue Mabillon* (1994): 143–77; Aurell, "Messianisme royal de la Couronne d'Aragon (XIVe–XVe s.)," *Annales. Histoire. Sciences Sociales* 52, no. 1 (1997), 119–55; Aurell, "Les Prophétes de la fin du monde," *L'Histoire* 206 (Jan. 1997): 50–54; and, most recently, Aurell, ed. *Convaincre et persuader: communication et propagande aux XII et XIIIe siècles* (Poitiers, France: Université de Poitiers, 2007).

22. Matt. 24:37: "De die autem illa et hora nemo scit neque angeli caelorum."

23. Jacques Chevalier, *A Postmodern Revelation: Signs of Astrology and the Apocalypse* (Toronto: University of Toronto Press, 1997).

heaven: and behold a great red dragon, having seven heads and ten horns, and seven crowns upon his head. And his tail drew the third part of the stars of heaven, and did cast them to the earth."[24] Other references could be found in the Gospels. Citing Matthew again, upon the arrival of eastern pseudo prophets and the Antichrist, "the sun will be obscured and the moon will not give its light and the stars will fall from the sky," and Luke writes that the heavenly bodies will manifest the imminent end of the world: "And there will be signs in the sun and the moon and the stars."[25] The stars were therefore closely connected with people's expectations of the End Times, and some very powerful people in the Crown of Aragon sought answers from those remote, glittering bodies.

Historians have at times overemphasized the fourteenth century as a period of crisis, but there is no doubt that Europe experienced significant tumult and upheaval during the later Middle Ages.[26] Whether we can, or even should, investigate the medieval past through the prism of crisis is a point of contention. Jacques Verger has argued that using the word "crisis" to describe what happened across late medieval Europe is "liable to facile analogies" without contextualizing it within medieval peoples' notions of what actually constituted those crises.[27] Mindful of

---

24. See also Blumenfeld-Kosinski, *Poets, Saints, and Visionaries*, 169–72, where she discusses the connection of Pope Urban VI with the terrible beast of the book of Revelation. She reprinted an image from a sixteenth-century collection of pope prophecies in which Urban VI is depicted as a horrific monster, "the last beast, terrible to look at, which pulls down the stars" (171). In the picture, a waning crescent moon supports five stars, while the scaled and serpentine tail of the monstrous pope encircles seven of ten stars.

25. Matt. 24:29: "Statim autem post tribulationem dierum illorum sol obscurabitur et luna non dabit lumen suum et stellae cadent de celo et virtutes caelorum commovebuntur." Luke 21:25: "Et erunt signa in sole et luna et stellis et in terries pressura gentium prae confusione sonitus maris et fluctuum"; and Andrew Cunningham and Ole Peter Grell, *The Four Horsemen of the Apocalypse: Religion, War, Famine and Death in Reformation Europe* (Cambridge: Cambridge University Press, 2000), 73 and 77. See also Hilary Carey, "Astrology and Antichrist in the Later Middle Ages," in *Time and Eternity: The Medieval Discourse*, ed. Gerhard Jaritz and Gerson Moreno-Riaño (Leiden: Brepols, 2002), 477–535; and Jean-Patrice Boudet, "Simon de Phares et les rapports entre astrologie et prophetié à la fin du Moyen Âge," *Mélanges de l'École Française de Rome: Moyen Âge* 102 (1990): 617–48.

26. The book that popularized the notion of a fourteenth-century crisis is Barbara Tuchman, *A Distant Mirror: The Calamitous 14th Century* (New York: Knopf, 1978).

27. Jacques Verger, "Different Values and Authorities," *The Cambridge Illustrated History of the Middle Ages III, 1250–1520* (Cambridge: Cambridge University Press, 1986), 119–91. Howard Kaminsky has argued that scholars who interpret the events of the fourteenth and fifteenth centuries through the lens of crisis are bound by, and within, a periodization established by Johan

Verger's admonition, I would nonetheless maintain that the fourteenth and fifteenth centuries were in fact marked by very real crises that shook the foundations of Western Europe, leading some individuals to turn to the words of seers, magicians, and astrologers alike. Two events in particular that had a profound impact were the Black Death and, more significantly for the history of apocalypticism, the Great Schism of the Western Church.

The great European pandemic of bubonic plague known as the Black Death was staggering in its impact, killing an estimated one-third to one-half of Europe's population in the span of about three years, from 1347 to 1350.[28] The plague followed European maritime and terrestrial trading routes and penetrated the interior of the continent from cities and towns located along the maritime coasts and on the banks of major rivers. This geographic pattern of contagion was mirrored in the Iberian Peninsula. In March 1348 the plague first hit the Balearic Islands and then appeared in the coastal cities of the Crown of Aragon, including Barcelona, Valencia, and Tarragona. After it struck those cities, the disease penetrated the interior of the peninsula with devastating consequences. By October 1349 the city of Zaragoza reported some three hundred monthly deaths by plague.[29]

Huizinga in his *The Waning of the Middle Ages:* "From Lateness to Waning to Crisis: The Burden of the Later Middle Ages," *Journal of Early Modern History* 4, no. 1 (2000): 85–125, here 94. Richard K. Emmerson has elaborated upon the issues surrounding the study of apocalyptic and millenarian matters in "The Secret," *American Historical Review* 104 (1999): 1603–14. Other scholars who have addressed the issue of crisis as a category for historical inquiry include Eric Aacheson, *A Gentry Community: Leicestershire in the Fifteenth Century, c. 1422–c. 1485* (Cambridge: Cambridge University Press, 1992); Aileen Kraditor, "American Radical Historians on Their Heritage," *Past and Present* 56 (Aug. 1972): 136–53; Randolph Starn, "Historians and 'Crisis,'" *Past and Present* 52 (Aug. 1971): 3–22; František Graus, *Pest—Geissler—Judenmorde: Das 14. Jahrhundert als Krisenzeit* (Göttingen: Vandenhoeck and Rupprecht, 1994); Peter Schuster, "Krise des Spätmittelalters: Zur Evidenz eines sozial—und wirtschaftsgeschichtlichen Paradigmas in der Geschichtsschreibung des 20. Jahrhunderts," *Historisches Zeitschrift* 269 (1999): 19–56; and, most recently, Michael D. Bailey, "A Late-Medieval Crisis of Superstition?" *Speculum* 84, no. 3 (2009): 633–61. For late medieval Spain, see Teofilo Ruiz, *Spain's Centuries of Crisis, 1300–1474* (Malden, MA: Blackwell, 2007).

28. Rosemary Horrox, ed., *The Black Death* (Manchester: Manchester University Press, 1994), 3. For a comprehensive survey, see Ole Jørgen Benedictow, *The Black Death, 1346–1353: The Complete History* (Woodbridge, Suffolk: Boydell Press, 2004).

29. See William D. Phillips Jr., *"Peste Negra:* The Fourteenth-Century Plague Epidemics in Iberia," *On the Social Origins of Medieval Institutions: Essays in Honor of Joseph F. O'Callaghan,* eds. Donald Kagay and Theresa Vann (Leiden: Brill, 1998), 47–62, especially 49–50, for the geographic

The appearance of the Black Death contributed to the rise of apocalyptic expectations, from which the Crown of Aragon was not exempt.[30] As the specter of pestilence initially loomed across Europe, it was reported that members of the Medical Faculty of the University of Paris had astrologically predicted its arrival. The Parisian physicians observed a great conjunction of Saturn, Jupiter, and Mars that occurred on March 21, 1345, a cosmological event that would portend imminent and widespread pestilence, destruction, and death.[31] As the disease spread, its relentless presence and horrific effects contributed to people's fears and speculations about the End Times. They contextualized the plague within an apocalyptic framework and utilized apocalyptic imagery to further reinforce the disease's devastation. Some argued that rains of vermin and the appearance of comets in the heavens presaged the plague, and that stinking, miasmatic clouds and physical traumas of all stripes, especially monstrous births, were heralds of the disease.[32] In some cases the disease was contextualized apocalyptically, as seen in the 1350 account of William Dene of Rochester, who wrote that because of the plague, "it is therefore much to be feared that Gog and Magog have returned from hell," and rumors swirled in Rome that the Antichrist had been born and was already a beautiful ten-year-old boy.[33]

Another major event, or series of events, facing late medieval Europeans was the Great Western Schism (1378–1417).[34] The Schism was a

spread of the disease in Iberia; and Charles Verlinden, "La Grande Peste de 1348 en Espagne: Contribution à l'étude de ses conséquences économiques et sociales," *Revue belge de Philologie et d'Histoire* 17 (1938): 101–46; Richard Gyug, *The Diocese of Barcelona during the Black Death: The Register Notule Communium 15 (1348–1349)* (Toronto: Pontifical Institute of Mediaeval Studies, 1994).

30. Robert Lerner, "Aspects of the Fourteenth-Century Iconography of Death and the Plague," in *The Black Death: The Impact of the Fourteenth-Century Plague: Papers of the Eleventh Annual Conference of the Center for Medieval and Renaissance Studies*, ed. Daniel Williman (Binghamton, NY: Center for Medieval and Early Renaissance Studies, 1982), 77–105, especially 98 n20; Lerner, "The Black Death in Western European Eschatological Mentalities," *American Historical Review* 86 (1981): 533–52.

31. S. Jim Tester, *A History of Western Astrology* (Woodbridge, Suffolk: Boydell Press, 1987), 185.

32. Laura Ackerman Smoller, "Of Earthquakes, Hail, Frogs, and Geography: Plague and the Investigation of the Apocalypse in the Later Middle Ages," *Last Things: Death and the Apocalypse in the Middle Ages* (Philadelphia: University of Pennsylvania Press, 2000), 156–87.

33. Horrox, *Black Death*, 99–100.

34. For introductions to the Great Schism, see the works of Walter Ullmann, *The Origins of the Great Schism: A Study in Fourteenth-Century Ecclesiastical History* (London: Oates and

fundamental rupture in the foundation of Western Christendom, pitting two (and eventually three) papal claimants against each other—one based in Avignon and the other in Rome. Secular rulers throughout Europe took sides, aligning with one or the other of the popes, thus dividing Western Europe. Laura Ackerman Smoller has described the religious and intellectual tumult engendered by the Schism as the "salient crisis" of the later Middle Ages.[35] As Renate Blumenfeld-Kosinski has shown, the Schism provoked a large outpouring of visionary, prophetic, and occult literature.[36] Dating back to the twelfth century, certain medieval exegetes, especially the group of twelfth-century theologians who worked with Anselm of Laon to produce the *Glossa ordinaria*, had localized religious discord within an apocalyptic teleology based on Paul's second letter to the Thessalonians. In it Paul wrote that the "son of perdition," the Antichrist, would not come "except there first come a falling away" of the Church.[37] By the fourteenth century the events of the Great Schism led many to believe that the drama they were experiencing was in fact the "falling away" that Paul had predicted. They argued, in turn, that the arrival of the Antichrist was nigh.[38]

Washbourne, 1948); Guillaume Mollat, *Les Papes d'Avignon, 1305–1378* (Paris: Letouzey and Ané, 1949); Étienne Delaruelle, *L'Église au temps du Grand Schisme et de la crise conciliaire*, 2 vols. (Paris: Bloud and Gay, 1962); Noël Valois, *La France et le Grand Schisme d'Occident*, 4 vols. (Paris: A. Picard et fils, 1896–1902); Bernard Guillemain, *Les Papes d'Avignon 1309–1376* (Paris: Les Éditions du CERF, 2000); Robert Norman Swanson, "A Survey of Views on the Great Schism, c. 1395," *Archivum Historiae Pontificae* 21 (1983): 79–103; and *La papauté d'Avignon et le Languedoc, 1316–1342*, Cahiers de Fanjeaux 26 (Toulouse: Édouard Privat and Centre d'études historiques de Fanjeaux, 1991).

35. Laura Ackerman Smoller, *History, Prophecy, and the Stars* (Princeton, NJ: Princeton University Press, 1994), 4; and Hélène Millet, "Le grande schisme d'Occident selon Eustache Deschamps: un monstre prodigieux," *Miracles, prodigès et mervielles au Moyen Age: Actes du XXVe Congrès de la Société des Historiens Médiévistes de l'Enseignement Supérieur Public Orleáns, juin 1994* (Paris, 1995), 215–26.

36. Blumenfeld-Kosinski, *Poets, Saints, and Visionaries*, 11–17. See also Marjorie Reeves, *The Influence of Prophecy in the Later Middle Agés: A Study in Joachimism* (Oxford: Clarendon Press, 1969), 416–28.

37. Smoller, *History, Prophecy, and the Stars*, 87. 2 Thess. 2:3. See also Roberto Rusconi, *L'attesa della fine: crisi della società, profezia ed Apocalisse in Italia al tempo del grande scisma d'Occidente* (Rome: Istituto storico italiano per il Medio Evo, 1979); Eugenio Dupré Theseider, "L'attesa escatologica durante il periodo Avignonese," *L'attesa dell'età nuova nella spiritualità della fine del medioevo* (Todi, Italy: Presso l'Accademia Tudertina, 1962); and also Kevin L. Hughes, *Constructing Antichrist: Paul, Biblical Commentary, and the Development of Doctrine in the Early Middle Ages* (Washington, DC: Catholic University of America Press, 2005).

38. Richard K. Emmerson, *Antichrist in the Middle Ages: A Study of Medieval Apocalypticism, Art, and Literature* (Seattle: University of Washington Press, 1981), 38–39; André Vauchez, "Les

Scholars and theologians alike turned to biblical exegesis in tandem with astrology and other occult practices for purposes of divining future events, but of course they read their results through a particularly Christian lens. The French cardinal and theologian Pierre d'Ailly, for example, relied on astrology in just this manner. Convinced that the end of the world was not imminent and that the crisis of the Great Schism could be resolved through a council, he marshaled all the evidence he could in favor of his own reading of the End Times. D'Ailly was deeply conversant with apocalyptic rhetoric. While a student at the University of Paris in October 1380, he preached a sermon before the faculty and students in which he discussed the importance of persecutions to both the past and the future of the Church. He explained that there were a total of seven periods of persecution that the Church would have to endure. Up to that point the Church had already suffered three of them. The Great Schism represented the fourth, and current, trial; three more future persecutions were yet to come. Eventually these future persecutions would culminate in the arrival of the Antichrist and the fulfillment of history.[39]

To prove his point d'Ailly used sidereal imagery. Drawing upon Revelation 8:12, in which the fourth angel sounds his trumpet, thereby lessening the light of the sun, the moon, and the stars by one-third, d'Ailly argued that these heavenly bodies represented respectively the ecclesiastical prelates, the secular princes, and the lower clergy of the world.[40] The dimming of the celestial luminaries signified the loss of these leaders' moral integrity.[41] For d'Ailly, even though the prior persecutions had wrought significant harm to Christendom, no other age could surpass the wickedness of his own, which could be seen in "its spirit of

---

théologiens face aux prophéties à l'époque des papes d'Avignon et du Grand Schisme," *Mélanges de l'Ecole Française de Rome: Moyen Age* 102, no. 2 (1990): 577–88.

39. See Pierre d'Ailly's Advent Sermons and his *De falsis prophetis II*, both of which hail from the 1380s. Smoller, *History, Prophecy, and the Stars*, 50–51. See also Alan E. Bernstein, *Pierre d'Ailly and the Blanchard Affair: University and Chancellor of Paris at the Beginning of the Great Schism* (Leiden: Brill, 1978).

40. Rev. 8:12: "et quartus angelus tuba cecinit et percussa est tertia pars solis et tertia pars lunae et tertia pars stellarum ut obscuraretur tertia pars eorum et diei non luceret pars tertia et nox similiter."

41. Louis B. Pascoe, S.J. *Church and Reform: Bishops, Theologians, and Canon Lawyers in the Thought of Pierre d'Ailly (1351–1420)* (Leiden: Brill, 2005), 14; and Smoller, *History, Prophecy, and the Stars*, 34–35.

rebellion, its advocacy of evil, and its adherence to heretical beliefs."[42] According to d'Ailly, therefore, the prophets of doom were wrong in their predictions concerning the end of the world and the arrival of the Antichrist.

In the mind of Pierre d'Ailly, as with others of his day, astrology could be understood within a Christian framework, offering the promise of powerful knowledge that could be used toward beneficent ends. A more mundane example of this can be seen in a fourteenth-century spell that was part of a homiletic rite used to remove worms from a vegetable garden. Speaking directly to the worms, the practitioner adjures them, "through the Father, Son and Holy Spirit, one God, living and true, omnipotent, creator of heaven and earth, of the sea and of all things which are in them . . . through the name of the eternal God Adonay, tetragrammaton and through the other names of the same ones, through the Sun and the Moon and the other planets, through the stars and the sydera of heaven," to abandon the garden and perish.[43]

Just as prophecy, divination, and astrology were all part of larger intellectual constructs, so too can we see in them cultural indicators of society revealing contemporary concerns and preoccupations. Astrology was only one of multiple occult disciplines believed to operate along comparable sidereal principles. As evidence of this, medieval astrological and divinatory texts were frequently bound within compendia that included alchemical and other kinds of magical works.[44]

Taken together, the documents I rely upon for this study (theological treatises, literary works, archival documents, and occult writings) portray a society in which divination via the occult and astrology occupied a powerful, yet ultimately nebulous, space in late medieval reckoning that resists

---

42. Pascoe, *Church and Reform*, 25.

43. Adolf Franz, *Die kirchlichen Benediktionen des Mittelalter*, 2 vols. (Freiburg: M. Herder, 1909), 2:169. My thanks go to Derek Rivard for sharing this reference with me.

44. See the entirety of documents compiled within BnF lat. 3171, which also includes a copy of Eymerich's treatise *Contra praefigentes terminum fini mundi*, ff. 64–81. I discuss this document in chapter 5. The particular version that I analyze comes from Biblioteca Nacional de España (hereafter referred to as BNE) register 6213, ff. 217–42, the incipit of which is *Incipit tractatus contra alchimistas*. See also Claudia Heimann, *Nicolaus Eymerich (vor 1320–1399)—praedicator veridicus, inquisitor intrepidus, doctor egregius: Leben und Werk Eines Inquisitors* (Münster: Aschendorff, 2001), 145–51.

easy categorization.[45] There is an inherent difficulty in working with these texts, however, for they often reference names, events, and issues in an intentionally obscure manner. Deliberately employing obfuscatory language to write magical and occult texts had a dual purpose: it prevented the uninitiated from unlocking the secret information contained within them and hindered authorities inimical to their messages from understanding them. Divination resists absolute precision, for these texts could be, and were, read in a multiplicity of ways. That variability is part of the strength of these sources, but it also is one of the methodological challenges inherent in any interpretation of these sources.[46] Further complicating matters, medieval prophetic texts are filled with allusions that contemporary readers might have understood but which modern readers, many centuries removed, have difficulties unraveling. As Robert Lerner has put it, "The modern commentator . . . has no touchstone for distinguishing the originally intelligible from the eternally unintelligible."[47]

Whatever else one might say about the later Middle Ages, they were a time of considerable uncertainty and uneasiness. Visions of the Apocalypse and debates over the end of the world were rampant throughout centers of learning across the continent. Some people understandably responded with fear and trepidation; others, searching for answers, turned their eyes to the night skies and to the words and spells of magicians and astrologers. Knowledge of future events was powerful information in a time

---

45. Paul Edward Dutton, *Charlemagne's Mustache and Other Cultural Clusters of a Dark Age* (New York: Palgrave MacMillan, 2004), xiii: "The whole of a culture may never exist in any comprehensible form, since transience, ill-defined borders, shifting ideas, and a continually changing cast of characters make any larger cultural entity as difficult to grasp as a slippery and wriggling brook trout in a swift flowing stream." See also Dutton, *The Politics of Dreaming in the Carolingian Empire* (Lincoln: University of Nebraska Press, 1994). For the variability inherent to cultural history, see Peter Burke, *Varieties of Cultural History* (Ithaca, NY: Cornell University Press, 1997); and Burke, *What Is Cultural History?* 2nd ed. (Cambridge: Polity Press, 2008).

46. See Blumenfeld-Kosinski, *Poets, Saints, and Visionaries*; and Barbara Newman, *God and the Goddesses: Vision, Poetry, and Belief in the Middle Ages* (Philadelphia: University of Pennsylvania Press, 2003), 300. One way to bypass these problems is to use the approach used by Robert Lerner in which one prophetic text is parsed and its later variants identified in order to trace the dissemination and elaboration of the original strain of prophetic thought and to track their changes over time. See Robert Lerner, *The Powers of Prophecy: The Cedar of Lebanon Vision from the Mongol Onslaught to the Dawn of the Enlightenment* (Berkeley: University of California Press, 1983; rprt. Ithaca, NY: Cornell University Press, 2008).

47. Lerner, *Powers of Prophecy*, 8.

of insecurity. In the fourteenth and fifteenth centuries, the kings of the Crown of Aragon tapped into the power behind astrology and the occult in the hope of discovering future events, understanding them, and manifesting yet another aspect of their royal authority. In the divinatory works and astrological visions of astrologers and seers lay the answers, they hoped, to the questions posed by such tumultuous times.

Part I

Positioning the Stars, Divining the Future

1

Prophecy, Knowledge, and Authority

Divining the Future and Expecting the End of Days

In the modern world we have all but banished the supernatural to the margins of intellect, to the realm of superstition. Yet during the Middle Ages the spiritual and supernatural worlds were of unquestioned importance to the vast majority of people. Soldiers entered the battlefield only after having been blessed for protection from harm and for salvation should they fall. Families preparing to buy property or arrange for the marriage of a child needed the spiritual guidance and approval of patron saints. The ravages of war, famine, and disease—perceived by some as the deeds of malevolent forces or punishment from an angry God—could be mitigated by praying to benevolent spiritual guardians and intercessors. For the clergy and others in the literate minority, the Bible and the writings of the Church fathers spoke of a vengeful God who had no qualms about punishing mankind for its sins, sometimes by spectacular means. They wrote, edited, analyzed, and disseminated these lessons to the illiterate majority of medieval Christendom.

The decorative arts of cathedrals and churches, their stained-glass windows and stone sculptures, also illustrated the effects of leading a sinful life. The Last Judgment series of stained-glass windows in the fifteenth-century Catalan Gothic church of Santa María del Mar in Barcelona, for instance, horrifically depict the torments of hell that awaited a sinful populace. Created by the master Severí Desmanes de Avignon, the images are chilling, as demons prod and push a group of damned souls, glowing red as hot coals, into the mouth of hell while directing their gazes to the congregants who might behold them.[1]

To soothe a wrathful God, mortals needed spiritual intercessors, beings who knew firsthand the temptations that humans faced and who resisted them successfully. After these holy people died, the surviving members of the Christian community recognized them as saints—individuals whose prior lives attested to humanity's ability to overcome carnal enticements. During times of crisis, Christians remembered the pious actions of saints, invoking their protection and drawing inspiration for strength to press on. Saints were thus vital for the living world, responding "to the spiritual needs of a generation."[2]

Saints were not the only ones who were able to act as intermediaries with the supernatural. Among the living, visionaries and magicians were blessed with extraordinary powers to see beyond the present moment, revisiting the past and even glimpsing the secrets of the future. Not everyone, of course, could claim such abilities, and those who were seen to be genuine visionaries occupied a special but precarious place within society, because the medieval general populace regarded them with both awe and fear. In short, these individuals were both part of and separate from their larger community.

In Jewish and Christian reckoning, the ability to comprehend future events dated back to the biblical prophets. Daniel, Ezekiel, Isaiah, Ezra,

---

1. Xavier Barral i Altet, *Vidrieras medievales de Cataluña* (Barcelona: Institut d'Estudis Catalans, 2000), 93–95.

2. See André Vauchez, *Sainthood in the Middle Ages*, trans. Jean Birrell (Cambridge: Cambridge University Press, 1997), 7 n16; Vauchez, *Saints, prophètes et visionnaires: Le pouvoir surnaturel au Moyen Age* (Paris: Albin Michel, 1999); and Richard Kieckhefer, "The Holy and the Unholy: Sainthood, Witchcraft, and Magic in Late Medieval Europe," in *Christendom and Its Discontents: Exclusion, Persecution, and Rebellion, 1000–1500*, ed. Scott L. Waugh and Peter D. Diehl (Cambridge: Cambridge University Press, 1996), 310–37.

and Enoch of the Old Testament and Jesus and John of the New Testament were granted insight into the unfolding of the future. Their abilities, however, were understood to be a divine gift from God. The biblical prophets and Christian saints received their skills because of their holiness. Not surprisingly, the early Church fathers were especially careful to condemn sinister aspects of divination—those that relied on astrological or geomantic principles—to distinguish them from divinely inspired prophetic insight. This same concern persisted throughout the Middle Ages, as evidenced by the Church's continued condemnation of divination achieved through occult practices. Indeed, the Church was forced to reckon with suspect practices even within monastic and clerical circles.[3] By the fourteenth and fifteenth centuries, ecclesiastical authorities had become so wary of the occult that any claims whatsoever to divinatory insight were inherently suspect.

The theological logic behind the Church's suspicion rested largely on three principles: the Bible already revealed any information about the course of the future that God wanted people to know; God had granted prophetic insight to the biblical prophets and saints but had ceased this practice in the present age; and, finally, "whereas at present the Lord seldom, if ever, communicated prophetic visions, the devil was only too happy to take advantage of human weakness by deceiving the gullible with false visions."[4] Clerical authorities argued that humans' vanity made them susceptible to demonic wiles and thus closely linked divinatory claims with diabolic forces. Although people had a genuine, natural interest in understanding what lay before them, especially during traumatic periods

---

3. See Valerie Irene Jane Flint, "The Transmission of Astrology in the Early Middle Ages," *Viator* 21 (1990): 1–27; and Flint, *The Rise of Magic in Early Medieval Europe* (Princeton, NJ: Princeton University Press, 1991). For more on the influence of divination and magic in the history of the West, see Thorndike, *HMES*; Bernard McGinn, *Apocalypticism in the Western Tradition* (Brookfield, VT: Variorum, 1994); McGinn, *Visions of the End: Apocalyptic Traditions in the Middle Ages* (New York: Columbia University Press, 1979); and Jeffrey Burton Russell and Douglas W. Lumsden, *A History of Medieval Christianity: Prophecy and Order* (New York: P. Lang, 2000).

4. Robert Lerner, "Historical Introduction" to Johannis de Rupescissa, *Liber Secretorum Eventuum: Edition critique, traduction et introduction historique*, ed. Robert Lerner and Christine Morerod-Fattebert (Fribourg, Switzerland: Éditions Universitaires Fribourg Suisse, 1994), 13–85, here 26 (hereafter referred to as *LSE*). See also Ian P. Wei, "Predicting the Future to Judge the Present: Paris Theologians and Attitudes to the Future," in *Medieval Futures: Attitudes to the Future in the Middle Ages*, ed. J. A. Burrow and Ian P. Wei (Woodbridge, Suffolk: Boydell Press, 2000), 19–36.

of crisis, the desire to peer into the future bordered on vanity, which imperiled one's soul. Moreover, demons stood ready to ensnare those humans who dabbled in the occult arts.

In addition to distinguishing between the prophetic and occult modes of revelation, educated people established basic distinctions between the disciplines of astrology and astronomy, both of which were linked to revelatory knowledge. Astronomy, as a science that required mathematical training, occupied an honored place as one of the seven liberal arts that comprised the medieval curriculum. Astrology, on the other hand, was more problematic in that it ventured beyond the firmer ground of empirical analysis. Nevertheless, the line dividing astrology from astronomy was far more blurred than it is today. In the seventh century the foremost Iberian intellectual authority, Isidore of Seville, maintained in his *Etymologiae* that there existed a partial overlap between the disciplines. Whereas *astronomia* applied to the study of the movements of the heavens and the stars, *astrologia* had a dual identity. One part was *naturalis* and concerned itself with the same principles as *astronomia*. The other part was *superstitiosa*, practiced by *mathematici* who cast nativity horoscopes and engaged in the thorny practice of predicting people's characters by the stars.[5]

Astrology could be linked with other forms of acceptable prophesying to provide legitimacy to a vision, yet it is fair to say that throughout the Middle Ages astrology was largely viewed as an illegitimate art, driven and encouraged by malevolent, supernatural entities.[6] The stage was set as early as the fifth century by Augustine, bishop of Hippo, whose influential book *De Civitate Dei Contra Paganos* (The City of God against the Pagans) linked divination and fortune-telling with demonic magic. In his reckoning, human magicians functioned merely as conduits for demons' actions; the demons served as the principal agents who taught people magical arts

---

5. See book 3 of the *Etymologiae, De Mathematica*, subsection paragraphs 24–41, titled *De Astronomia*. Isidore of Seville, *The Etymologies of Isidore of Seville*, trans. and ed. Stephen A. Barney, W. J. Lewis, J. A. Beach, and Oliver Berghof (Cambridge: Cambridge University Press, 2006), 99–107; Veenstra, *Magic and Divination*, 154–55.

6. David J. Viera, foreword to Lucas, *Astrology and Numerology*, xi. See also Stephen C. McCluskey, *Astronomies and Cultures in Early Medieval Europe* (Cambridge: Cambridge University Press, 1998); and Flint, *Rise of Magic*.

or enacted the magicians' will.[7] Augustine was operating within a framework that was already opposed to magical thought. Ever since the Roman emperor Theodosius (d. 395) had offered official sanction and protection to Christianity in the fourth century, the Church was linked to the apparatus of the state. Once that happened, all suspected magical practices, including divination, became capital offenses.[8]

It is essential, therefore, to grasp the fundamental disjunct that plagued the perception of the divinatory arts throughout the Middle Ages. On the one hand, divination of future events was legitimate insofar as prophecy was seen as divine revelation. On the other hand, divination achieved through magical or occult means was illicit, even dangerous. In the remainder of this chapter, I trace these fundamental distinctions as drawn by medieval authorities. I first turn my attention to three premier theological authorities, the aforementioned Augustine of Hippo, the thirteenth-century Dominican philosopher and theologian Thomas Aquinas, and his contemporary William of Auvergne. I discuss their particular issues with, and condemnations of, astrology and the occult. I address Aquinas's position in particular detail because he, more than any other ecclesiastical authority, clarified the medieval distinctions among various forms of occult divination.

After my analysis of William of Auvergne, I turn my attention to the matter of prophecy. I return to the early Middle Ages and Iberia with a brief discussion of Beatus of Liébana, one of the most important medieval writers on apocalyptic matters. Beatus's work was of particular importance in the history of medieval prophecy, as many subsequent claims to future knowledge were understood and created within an apocalyptic framework. I then turn to a renowned figure in the history of prophecy and apocalyptic expectations, the twelfth-century Calabrian abbot Joachim of Fiore. Finally, I end this chapter by analyzing the lesser known, yet important, late medieval apocalyptic visionary John of Rupescissa and a member of the royal family of the Crown of Aragon, Pere l'Infant, both of whom were influenced profoundly by Joachim's writings.

Let us first turn to the stars, as their role in divination and the magical arts occupied an uneasily reconciled space in the medieval worldview.

---

7. Kieckhefer, *Magic in the Middle Ages*, 10.
8. Ibid., 41.

Augustine established the authoritative opinion regarding the influence of the stars in book 5 of *The City of God*, which would have a profound effect upon people's understanding throughout the Middle Ages. Augustine begins his fifth book with a discourse on the nature of fate, where he writes, "When men hear this word [fate] as it is used in ordinary speech, they understand it to mean nothing other than the force exerted by the position of the stars when anyone is born or conceived." Yet, Augustine continues, when individuals believe that the stars have significant influence on what happens to a person throughout the course of his or her life, then that belief must be universally ignored, as ascribing such power and agency to the stars would constitute a direct affront to the power and divinity of God, "Who is Lord of both stars and men."[9]

Augustine then continues to disparage people's devotion to the stars as masters of their fate by citing the example of twins who, although born on the same day and in the same locale, nevertheless frequently have different destinies.[10] He refers to the story of Nigidius, an ancient astrologer who used a potter's wheel to demonstrate graphically this very issue. Spinning the wheel as fast as he could, Nigidius applied two spots of black ink in rapid succession to the whirling disk. Although it appeared that the marks were in the same place, when the wheel stopped its motions, there was a significant distance separating the two marks. Nigidius's analogy was that because of the rapidity of the heavens' movements, even if one twin were born immediately after his or her sibling, the vastness of heaven would determine their markedly different fates. For Augustine, "this argument is more fragile than the pots made by the spinning of that wheel," and he cites as his proof the case of the biblical twins Jacob and Esau (193). After discussing their marked differences in physical appearance, personal character, and ultimate fates, Augustine questions the motives of astrologers:

> If, then, even these things depend upon the minute intervals of time which elapse between the birth of twins and are not attributed to the constellations at large, why do the astrologers mention things of the same kind when

9. Augustine, *The City of God against the Pagans*, ed. and trans. R. W. Dyson (Cambridge: Cambridge University Press, 1998), 187. See also Flint, *Rise of Magic*, 92–101, for other early medieval authors' condemnations on astrology.

10. Augustine, *City of God*, 188–90.

examining the constellations of others? If, on the other hand, they mention these things because they are related not to incomprehensibly small moments of time, but to periods of time which can be observed and recorded, what is the point of the story of the potter's wheel? Is it to throw men who have hearts of clay into a spin, so that the astrologers shall not be convicted by them of talking nonsense? (192)

Augustine concedes some agency and power to the sidereal bodies of the sun, moon, and stars, as they have influence over the changing seasons of the year and the growth of some plants and sea creatures. Yet to grant these bodies power over humans' destinies would be fundamentally wrong (195). Ultimately for Augustine, the sum total of the "false and noxious opinions" (197) and "laughable" (196) observations of astrologers, are naught but a "vain science" (192).

Augustine did not remain silent about apocalyptic matters, either. In his opinion, the Antichrist, who did not appear in the text of John's Revelation but who was closely linked with the trauma of the End Times, was more an internalized, rather than literal, figure. For Augustine, the Antichrist appears in each individual who asserts the divinity of Christ, yet who, through his or her actions, demonstrates the exact opposite of what they say, thus ultimately denying Christ as Lord.[11] Although he discusses the nature of the Antichrist and his appearance in his *Homilies on 1 John*, Augustine spends the last three books of *The City of God* dealing primarily with eschatological matters. In particular, it is in the twentieth book, over the course of thirty chapters, where Augustine unpacks the issues and events surrounding the apocalypse at length. According to Augustine, humans' attempt to understand the course of divine future events is futile. Although God's judgment is present in all affairs, human reason, by its very limitations, cannot discern it. Augustine reminds the reader that

when we arrive at that judgment of God, the time of which is . . . called the Day of Judgment . . . it will become apparent that God's judgments are entirely just: not only all the judgments that will be given then, but also all the

---

11. Bernard McGinn, *Antichrist: Two Thousand Years of the Human Fascination with Evil* (New York: Harper Collins, 1994), 77–78.

judgments given from the beginning, and all those which are to be given hereafter until that time. . . . In this matter one thing is not hidden from the faith of the godly; and that is, that what is hidden is nonetheless just.[12]

Drawing upon the writings of biblical prophets, including John the Evangelist, Peter, Paul, Isaiah, Daniel, and Malachi, Augustine traces the course of the events of the apocalypse and how they are to be understood. Augustine sums up his twentieth book, and his understanding about all things apocalyptic, by stating:

> At that [final] judgment, or near the time of that judgment, we have learned that the following things will come to pass: Elijah the Tishbite will come; the Jews will believe; Antichrist will persecute; Christ will judge; the dead will rise; the good will be separated from the wicked; the world will be destroyed and renewed. We must believe that all these things will come to pass. But how and in what order they are to do so we shall learn by experience of the events themselves when the time comes. This is something that, at the present time, the human intellect cannot manage to teach us. My own belief, however, is that they will happen in the order in which I have here stated them.[13]

While Augustine was influential in establishing the roles of the stars and their role in divination and fate, as well as why they—or any human art or science, for that matter—cannot discern the arrival of the Day of Judgment, more important to the problematic understanding and liminal space that astrology and divination occupied within a Christian framework was the work of the Dominican theologian Saint Thomas Aquinas (1225–1274). The pupil of Albertus Magnus, whose own astronomical work written in the 1260s, the *Speculum Astronomiae* (The Mirror of Astronomy), was profoundly influential upon medieval culture, in his massive *Summa Theologiae*, Aquinas expounded upon almost every aspect of Christian theology and philosophy in a dense and intellectually rigorous philosophical system.[14] He centered his system on more than five hundred

---

12. Augustine, *City of God*, 968.
13. Ibid., 1042–43.
14. For more on Albertus Magnus' work, see Scott E. Hendrix, *How Albert the Great's Speculum Astronomiae Was Interpreted and Used by Four Centuries of Readers: A Study in Late Medieval Medicine, Astronomy, and Astrology* (Lewiston, NY: Edwin Mellen Press, 2010).

quaestiones, which he divided into three parts, respectively dealing with Christian theology, ethics, and the nature of Christ.[15]

Aquinas split his second part on ethics into two halves, and it is in the second half where he addressed superstitious and irreverent behaviors and deeds, spanning *quaestiones* 92 through 100. *Quaestiones* 95 and 96, respectively concerning divinatory and superstitious practices, were especially important in establishing subsequent authorities' positions concerning divination and magic.[16] For Aquinas, using divination and occult matters to know the future was highly problematic, as the practices relied wholly on demonic agency.[17]

Aquinas begins by considering whether foretelling the future was essentially a superstitious practice and partitions this *quaestio* into eight points. In investigating whether divination constituted a sin or might be a type of superstition, he examines the various types of foretelling the future and discusses the practices of divination through the help of demons, stars, dreams, auguries, and lots.[18] From the outset, Aquinas establishes that only God can know what is present and what is in the future and that if a person claims to foresee the future, unless God grants divine revelation to that person, then he or she "clearly usurps that which is for God alone." Divination outside of divine revelation, therefore, is inherently suspect and constitutes a sin.[19]

Furthermore, in his second point Aquinas considers that *all* forms of divination outside of God involve a compact with demonic agents to some degree and that, based on its modus operandi, "clearly . . . divination is a form of superstition."[20] But the ways in which people sought hidden answers about the future were myriad, and Aquinas provides a dense list of the many types of divination via demonic agency. For Aquinas, there are

15. Thomas Aquinas, *Summa Theologiae*, trans. Blackfriars, 61 vols. (London: Eyer and Spottiswoode, 1964-).

16. Michael D. Bailey, *Magic and Superstition in Europe: A Concise History from Antiquity to the Present* (Lanham, MD: Rowman and Littlefield, 2007); and Bailey, "The Disenchantment of Magic: Spells, Charms, and Superstition in Early European Witchcraft Literature," *American Historical Review* 111 (2006): 383–404. See also Dieter Harmening, *Superstitio: Überlieferung- und theoriegeschichtliche Untersuchungen zur kirchlich-theologischen Aberglaubensliteratur des Mittelalters* (Berlin: E. Schmidt, 1979).

17. Aquinas, *Summa Theologiae*, 2a2ae, 95.3.

18. Ibid., 95.1.

19. Ibid.: "manifeste usurpat sibi quod Dei est . . . Hoc autem constat esse peccatum."

20. Ibid., 95.2.

three main categories of divination: necromancy, which openly invokes demonic forces; augury, which predicts the future based on the movements
and positions of another living being; and sorcery, which focuses on people's actions in their attempts to discover the occult. Drawing upon Isidore
of Seville's taxonomy in the *Etymologiae*, Aquinas goes into significant detail in describing them. Demons could manifest the future via illusions
that duped humans' sight and hearing, or they might use dreams. They
could use the utterances of the dead, which Aquinas linked with necromancy, whereas divination from soothsayers sought answers to the future
via the voices of the living. Images, figures, and signs that appear on a terrestrial, aquatic, ethereal, or pyrrhic substance and that chart the course
of the future were, respectively, geomancy, hydromancy, aeromancy, and
pyromancy.[21]

Foretelling the future, however, could be practiced in two ways without expressly invoking demons. The first was through the observation of
phenomena. To Aquinas, those who do this "from the consideration of the
position and movement of stars" are astrologers, and those who cast natal
horoscopes through regarding these sidereal phenomena, genethliacs.[22]
Genethlialogy, also known as nativities, was the science of an astrologer
predicting the future of a person based on his or her natal horoscope, the
degree of the zodiac that arose over the horizon at the exact hour and
minute of birth, and it was a contentious and ambivalent practice within
Christian understanding. It was also one of four parts of the predictive
branch of the science of astrology.[23] It could, and did, put its practitioners
squarely in the sights of secular and ecclesiastical authorities alike, especially if they casted controversial horoscopes of both contemporary and
historic individuals.[24]

---

21. Ibid., 95.3. See also Isidore, *Etymologies*, 181–83.

22. Aquinas, *Summa Theologiae*, 95.3: "Et si quidem aliquis conetur futura praenoscere
ex consideratione situs et motus siderum, hoc pertinet ad astrologos; qui et geneatici dicuntur,
propter natalium considerations dierum."

23. Smoller, *History, Prophecy, and the Stars*, 17. The other three included general predictions,
which regarded the stars' effects on society and in relation to various natural events that would affect a society wholesale; elections, in which astrologers would select days that would be most propitious for one activity or another; and interrogations, when the stars would be used to answer a
question posed to an astrologer.

24. See, for instance, H. Darrel Rutkin, "Astrological Conditioning of Same-Sexual Relations in Girolamo Cardano's Theoretical Treatises and Celebrity Genitures," in *The Sciences of*

For Aquinas, relying upon Isidore, other divinatory processes that focus on observed phenomena include augury, by inspecting the flights and calls of birds; by heeding the words that a person might utter differently from their original intent; and by observing corporeal phenomena such as chiromancy or scapulomancy, respectively reading palms or shoulder blades. The second class of divination in which individuals perform actions without expressly invoking demons, yet nonetheless search for something occult, constitutes sorcery (*sortium*). This includes casting lots, a practice with which the term *sortium* is frequently linked, but also comprises geomancy, reading the meaning from shapes that molten lead takes when it is poured into cold water; investigating one's choice of certain papers or straws from a proffered group; casting dice and tallying their score; and observing what word first catches the eye of a person when he or she opens a book.[25]

Having listed the various types of divinatory activities, Aquinas states in his fourth *quaestio* that there are two principal reasons why calling upon the assistance of demonic powers is wrong. First, it is forbidden to forge such a compact, which is the origin of divinatory practices. Secondly, the result of the practice is wrong, as demons intend to lure humans into damnation by giving them true replies, therefore earning the person's trust.[26] For Aquinas, there could be nothing, "no temporal use," gained whatsoever by researching the occult, as the accompanying spiritual harm was too great a risk to run.[27]

Where do the stars fit within this scheme? In the fifth article, Aquinas deals with this topic at great length, which is crucial for understanding the problematic and uneasily reconciled place of astrology within medieval culture. As usual, Aquinas begins his article with positions that reflect some people's support of divination via astrology. He states that determining the future via an examination of their causes is a licit action, just as when a doctor predicts death in a patient through his diagnosis of a disease. Then, citing Aristotle's *Metaphysics*, Aquinas continues that "human knowledge begins from experimental origin" and concedes that individuals

---

Homosexuality in Early Modern Europe, ed. Kenneth Borris and George Rousseau (New York: Routledge, 2008), 183–99.

25. Aquinas, *Summa Theologiae*, 95.3.

26. Ibid.

27. Ibid., 95.4: "nulla ultitas temporalis."

have discovered future events from regarding the stars.[28] He readdresses his earlier statement about the illicit nature of divination because of its dependency on humans' entering into a compact with the diabolic. However, he argues that the stars are exempt from this compact and that by reading them, one may understand "the disposition of the creations of God."[29] Aquinas then cites a passage from Saint Augustine's *Confessions* in which Augustine himself admitted that he did not hesitate in consulting those astrologers who were considered mathematicians. They required neither sacrifice nor prayer to spirits and were therefore not damnable.[30]

Nonetheless, Aquinas responds that demonic entities are aware of people's "false or vain" attempts to divine future events. They therefore enter into people's quest for understanding the future so that their interference "may entwine the souls of men in vanity and falsehood."[31] Although demons themselves do not dabble with the stars, it is still a vain and false deed for people to attempt to learn any future events from the stars, as the stars themselves cannot directly do this.[32] Aquinas ultimately declares, "We cannot say that the dispositions and movements of the celestial bodies may be the effect of future events."[33] Instead, they are subject to a higher cause of divine providence. While the cosmos can affect the body, Aquinas relies on Aristotle in arguing that human beings still have their faculties of will and reason, which ultimately cannot be directly affected by the heavenly bodies. In the end, Aquinas argues that if one attempts to know the course of one's future, "he proceeds from a false and vain opinion and in this way the work of a demon enmeshes itself."[34]

---

28. Ibid., 95.5.
29. Ibid.: "Sed hoc non fit in divinatione quae fit per astra, sed solum consideratur dispositio creaturarum Dei."
30. Ibid.: "Sed contra est quod Augustinus dicit, Illos planetarios quos mathematicos vocant, consulere non desistebam; quod quasi nullum esset eis sacrificium, et nullae preces ad aliquem spiritum ob divinationem dirigentur. Quod tamen Christiana et vera pietas expellit et damnat." The passage is from *Confessions* III, 4.
31. Aquinas, *Summa Theologiae*, 95.5.
32. Ibid.: "Vana autem aut falsa opinione utitur si quis ex consideratione stellarum futura velit praecognoscere quae per ea praecognosci non possunt."
33. Ibid.: "Non autem potest dici quod dispositiones caelestium corporum et motus sint effectus futurorum eventuum."
34. Ibid.: "Si quis ergo consideratione astrorum utatur ad praecognoscendos futuros casuales vel fortuitos eventus, aut etiam ad cognoscendum per certitudinem futura opera hominum, procedet hoc ex falsa et vana opinione. Et sic operatio daemonis se immiscet."

Aquinas discusses why astrologers are sometimes accurate in their pronouncements. The first reason is "because many men follow their bodily passions," and they are thus influenced by heavenly forces via their corporeal senses. Those governed by reason are few; in fact, Aquinas declares public events to contribute frequently to the success of astrological prognostications, as the masses are governed by their passions, "and therefore astrologers foretell true things among many things, particularly in communal events, which depend on the multitude." Concerning the influence of demonic powers in helping astrologers predict future events successfully, Aquinas relies upon Augustine's early fifth-century work *De Genesi ad litteram* (The Literal Meaning of Genesis). Augustine argues that when some mathematicians/astrologers predict the truth, they rely upon "a most hidden instinct" that lays deep in the recesses of a person's mind. This, says Augustine, is the product of demons who know certain things concerning temporal affairs. The demons plant this information within people's minds, and therefore Christians should be wary of astrologers who accurately depict the future, lest their souls become entangled in the snares of a demonic plot.[35] Thus, Aquinas ends his *quaestio* on divination and the stars.

In the final three articles of his 95th *quaestio*, Aquinas investigates the lawfulness of divination via dreams, auguries and omens, and casting lots and once again warns against potentially entering, willingly or unwillingly, into a compact with demonic agents when attempting to divine the future. In his much shorter 96th *quaestio*, Aquinas investigates the various forms of superstition pertaining to magical practices and beliefs. In the first article, Aquinas firmly declares, "the notorious art is illicit and inefficacious."[36] The knowledge that magicians seek is unnatural, as the practitioner expects that knowledge to come from powers outside his or her control, and the demonic is able to imperil easily the souls of those who would dabble with magic. Aquinas focuses on the nature of acquiring knowledge throughout this first article and ultimately renders a verdict that "to acquire knowledge is good,"

---

35. Ibid.
36. Ibid., 96.1: "Dicendum quod ars notoria et illicita est, et inefficax."

but not through magical arts, and especially not about future events, as that leads to forging a demonic pact.[37]

In the second article, Aquinas focuses on magical practices that might effect corporeal changes. If people use such things to produce natural effects, Aquinas considers them legitimate, but should they produce unnatural and inexplicable marvels, then they were done so via a diabolic compact.[38] Using ciphers and sigils was especially problematic, as they "clearly do not have efficacy by nature," and it would be superstitious and wrong to use them to effect bodily change.[39] Those who rely on the stars in this process, who craft sigils that seek to harness and draw down the power of the stars to effect change on the earth below, produce these deeds by the work of demons, as the inscription of sigils and characters is essentially unnatural.[40] While astrological images differ from necromantic images, as the latter rely upon explicit invocations to demons, astrological images nonetheless imply a tacit pact with the demonic.[41] For the third article, in which Aquinas regards the rectitude of fortune-telling, he admits, citing Augustine's *De Doctrina Christiana* (On Christian Doctrine), that people have given credence to superstitious behavior in various attempts to ward off future evils instead of paying attention to present damages. He lists such superstitious apprehensions that might arise should a stone, dog, or child were to come between a person and his friend while walking together; if one were to kick another's door as he or she walked by it; or if one were to return home immediately should they stumble while beginning a journey. The problem for Aquinas lies in how people perceive the origins of these deeds.[42] These superstitions arise from a terrible combination of "human vanity in cooperation with demonic malice, which strive to entangle the souls of men in vanities of this kind,"[43] and are therefore unlawful. They function as the remnants of idolatrous practices and people's perceptions of certain days as

---

37. Ibid.

38. Ibid., 96.2.

39. Ibid.

40. Ibid. See chapter 3, where I discuss *Picatrix*, a work that relies on this process of crafting sigils to harness the stars' and planets' power.

41. Aquinas, *Summa Theologiae*, 96.2.

42. Ibid., 96.3.

43. Ibid.: "ex vanitate humana, cooperante daemonum militia, qui nituntur animos hominum huiusmodi vanitatibus implicare."

being more propitious than others, as in the belief concerning the so-called Egyptian Days, which foretold ill events,[44] "pertains to divination that is done via the stars . . . [and is] without reason and art."[45]

The final article with which Aquinas concerns himself is whether or not bearing inscribed amulets around one's neck is illicit, especially when healing a sick person or invoking the protection of a saint. Aquinas warns that people must always be cautious when dealing with incantations and inscribed words of power, as they can easily pull a person into congress with the demonic. There are two points about which one should be careful. The first concerns the words themselves. If there is even a hint that demonic powers are invoked, "clearly it is superstitious and illicit." Moreover, if one does not understand the words that are inscribed or uttered, one must be especially careful, for those words might conceal terrible and unlawful ideas. The second area that requires care focuses on images other than crosses that might be inscribed on the object. If the inscribed words or images are not unlawful, then the wearing of an amulet is not illicit.[46]

If Augustine and Aquinas established the problematic role of the stars and the occult within the Christian worldview, a more nuanced position concerning these matters came from the Parisian theologian William of Auvergne (1180–1249), who laid the basis for the systematic condemnation of astrology and magic by later theologians and exegetes. He is also known for his very damning depiction of the "criminal magician" as a figure meriting condemnation.[47] Intriguingly, Auvergne admits that his position on magic and astrology comes from firsthand experience with the disciplines.

William of Auvergne articulates his positions on these matters most clearly in his *De legibus* and his massive sexpartite work, *De universo*. Chapters 24 through 26 of *De legibus* attest to the widespread availability of magical and occult writings in Paris for William and his twelfth-century contemporaries to consult.[48] In chapter 24, which concerns people's desire to study "foolish things with curiosity," resulting in "the darkening and

---

44. Kieckhefer, *Magic in the Middle Ages*, 86–88.

45. Aquinas, *Summa Theologiae*, 96.3.

46. Ibid., 96.4.

47. Peters, *Magician, the Witch, and the Law*, 89–90.

48. Ibid.; and Guilielmi Alverni, *Opera Omnia*, 2 vols. (Paris: Apud Andream Pralard, 1674).

corruption of human nature . . . the root of idolatry . . . and the prostitution of the most noble human mind," William discusses idolatry and magic at length.[49] Using deeply sexual metaphors to link *curisoitas* with idolatry, labeling it as "namely the prostitution of curiosity, which truly debauches the human intellect indiscriminately," William considers *curisoitas* most vain and polluting.[50] Those who give credence and honor to the heavenly bodies of the sun and moon, or hold them as having great sway and authority over others, bear within themselves a "sacrilegious opinion and offend the majesty of God in the highest."[51] William is distressed with how rapidly people deride the height of divinity by ascribing that power to idols, the stars, and demons in their attempts to divine the future or effect magical operations.[52] Divination was especially problematic and led one to demonic congress, as it sought to reveal hidden wisdom and understand divine intelligence.[53]

Chapter 25 sees William of Auvergne "destroying the cult of the stars and heavenly bodies with many arguments," by depicting it as yet another idolatrous practice.[54] For William, although the sidereal writings of such sages as Plato, Aristotle, and the Muslim astronomer Avicenna were authoritative, those who nevertheless used astrology in an attempt to predict the future were wrong to do so, and their use of the stars in that manner was manifestly false.[55] Finally, in chapter 26, William of Auvergne segues to a discussion of various magical practices as further examples of idolatry,

---

49. Guilielmi Alverni, *De Legibus, Opera Omnia*, 2 vols. (Paris: Apud Andream Pralard, 1674), 1:67–84.

50. Ibid. See chapter 2 for more on *curiositas*. There is a long tradition surrounding visual and literary representation of *vana curiositas* in the Middle Ages and early modern era. See, among others, Richard K. Emmerson, "'Coveitise to Konne,' 'Goddes Privetee,' and Will's Ambiguous Visionary Experience in *Piers Plowman*," in *Suche Werkis to Weche: Essays on Piers Plowman in Honor of David C. Fowler*, ed. Míceál Vaughan (East Lansing, MI: Colleagues Press, 1993), 89–121; and Katherine Tachau, "God's Compass and *Vana Curiositas:* Scientific Study in the Old French *Bible Moralisée*," *Art Bulletin* 80 (1998): 7–33.

51. Alverni, *De Legibus*, 1:68.

52. Ibid.: "Quam cito enim altitudo divinitatis apparere potuit in idolis, vel stellis, vel Daemonibus quocunque signo, videlicet sive praedictione futurorum, sive quocunque opere magico, aut aliqua quacunque ludificatione, statim inclinati sunt homines ad adorandum."

53. Ibid., 1:69–70.

54. Ibid., 1:77: "Multis argumentis destruit cultum stellarum & corporum coelestium."

55. Ibid., 1:78: "Manifestum igitur est, vel astronomiam mendacem esse in parte illa, vel nihil habere verae divinitatis deos huiusmodi."

and these deeds include gazing into rings, mirrors, and stones in an attempt to ascertain hidden knowledge.[56]

Augustine, Thomas Aquinas, and William of Auvergne all provided essential foundational critiques of divination through occult practices. It is important, however, to distinguish this type of future insight from prophecy. During a time of grave crisis, information about the future was highly prized. Like divinatory magic, prophecy offered hidden wisdom to those who could perceive it. Yet the origins of this knowledge about future trauma were considerably different, as prophecy was understood fundamentally as divine revelation. Throughout the early Middle Ages, the Iberian Peninsula was a fertile arena for apocalyptic expectations and prophecies.

The case of the late eighth-century apocalyptic monk Beatus of Liébana shows the continuation of late antique ideas surrounding the Apocalypse and the tribulations of the Antichrist, as well as their contextualization within a period of profound political, social, and religious change in Iberia. Although in his *Commentary on the Apocalypse* Beatus was undeniably reliant upon a Tyconian-Augustinian tradition in understanding the figure of the Antichrist as an internalized, metaphorical figure, he nevertheless argued that contemporary events indicated to him that the arrival of the millennium and trauma engendered by the Antichrist's arrival was imminent, taking place within fourteen years.[57] Two contemporary developments pointed to this: the proliferation of the heretical teachings of Elipandus, the bishop of Toledo who advocated Adoptionism, which argued that Christ was solely a man adopted by God, and the arrival in Iberia of the new monotheistic and Abrahamic faith of Islam in 711, resulting in the subsequent collapse of Visigothic rule. Beatus resided in the northwestern part of the peninsula, in Asturias, whereas Elipandus dwelled in conquered Toledo. For Beatus, Elipandus was a heretical bishop living in the city that was the traditional seat of the Visigothic Church, yet which was now in a region to be under the dominion of a faith believed by some medieval Christians as "the last and worse of all heresies. . . . It was [thus] an easy move to interpret the rise of Islam as a sign of Antichrist's coming

---

56. Ibid., 1:84.
57. McGinn, *Antichrist*, 85.

and to see its founder, Muhammad, as a type of the Final Enemy."[58] This continued throughout the early Middle Ages, as seen in one account of Muhammad's life, written later in the ninth century, which applied the erroneous date of 666 for the death of Muhammad in order to link him with the apocalyptic beast referenced in Revelation 11:11, whose number was 666.[59] In Beatus's estimation, heresies abounded upon heresies, and he believed himself to be witnessing the advent of the End Times.

Twenty-six copies of Beatus's *Commentary on the Apocalypse*, produced in and for monastic houses in the Iberian Peninsula, have generated some of the most arresting visual depictions of the trauma of the Apocalypse and arrival of the Antichrist.[60] The Antichrist appears as a figure with wholly human features, for the first time, in a copy dated from the early tenth century. Instead of a monstrous and bestial figure, the Antichrist is an utterly human incarnation of supreme evil.[61] In the Beatus tradition of these illuminated apocalypses, the Antichrist functions as both a conquering sovereign and false cleric, and the horrific images are designed to provide extensive commentary on the course of the Apocalypse as described in the Johannine Revelation.[62]

Perhaps the most renowned medieval prophet who grappled with future events and contextualized them within the trauma of the impending Apocalypse was the Calabrian abbot Joachim of Fiore (1135–1202). Of seminal importance in understanding the history of prophetic and apocalyptic insight in the Middle Ages, Joachim established an exegetical technique of understanding the past, present, and future of the Church that had a profound influence on later apocalyptic visionaries.

Even if during his lifetime Joachim always eschewed the title *propheta*, he nevertheless established himself as a leading authority on scriptural

58. Ibid.

59. Rosemary Muir Wright, *Art and Antichrist in Medieval Europe* (Manchester: Manchester University Press, 1995), 36.

60. McGinn, *Antichrist*, 85. See also Richard K. Emmerson and Suzanne Lewis, "Census and Bibliography of Medieval Manuscripts Containing Apocalypse Illustrations, ca. 800–1500," *Traditio* 40 (1984): 337–79; 41 (1985): 367–409; 42 (1986): 443–72; and Wright, *Art and Antichrist*, 31–59.

61. Wright, *Art and Antichrist*, 31.

62. See also the five-volume work of John Williams, *The Illustrated Beatus: A Corpus of the Illustrations of the Commentary on the Apocalypse* (London: Harvey Miller, 1995–2005). A tenth-century illuminated manuscript, the "Beato de Valcavado," is available on CD-Rom. See Beatus

prophecy. A symbolic thinker, Joachim exhibited in his writings dual levels of meanings, operating simultaneously at the literal, or prosaic, and the dynamic levels. Each symbol that Joachim incorporated in his writings thus "finds its meaning in relation to the mind that interprets it," and he argued that the fullest meaning found in any individual symbol was in its relation to a larger symbolic context.[63] Joachim developed a dramatically symbolic and complex system for understanding the history of the Church and an unfolding of the future. In his *Liber figurarum*, written around the year 1200, Joachim read the Bible as the sole repository of knowledge to understand the *plenitudo historiae*, the fullness of history. To understand what the future Apocalypse held for the world, Joachim viewed past events through both a biblical lens and an understanding of the separate, but coequal, persons of the Trinity.[64] He based the Age of the Father, the first stage of history, on the time since the creation of the world until the reign of King Uzziah of Judah.[65] It was then that Joachim argued that the second stage of history, the Age of the Son, in which Joachim believed he and his contemporaries were living, began. Joachim believed the world was transitioning to its third and final age, the Age of the Holy Spirit, characterized by the appearance of new religious orders whose adherents would be central to understanding the future of both the Church and Christendom.[66] In Joachim's reckoning, the End Times

---

of Liébana, *Beato de Valladolid* (Valladolid: Universidad de Valladolid, 2002). My thanks go to D. Jack Norton for providing me a personal copy of this CD-Rom.

63. Bernard McGinn, *The Calabrian Abbot: Joachim of Fiore in the History of Western Thought* (New York: MacMillan, 1985), 103. The secondary literature on Joachim of Fiore is extensive. For just a sampling of the many works devoted to him, see Marjorie Reeves, *The Influence of Prophecy in the Later Middle Ages: A Study in Joachimism* (Oxford: Clarendon Press, 1969); Reeves and Beatrice Hirsch-Reich, *The Figurae of "Joachim" of Fiore* (Oxford: Clarendon Press, 1972); Reeves, *The Prophetic Sense of History in Medieval and Renaissance Europe* (Brookfield, VT: Ashgate, 1999); Harold Lee, Marjorie Reeves, and Giulio Silano, *Western Mediterranean Prophecy: The School of Joachim of Fiore and the Fourteenth-Century Breviloquium* (Toronto: Pontifical Institute of Medieval Studies, 1989); Delno C. West and Sandra Zimdars-Swartz, *Joachim of Fiore: A Study in Spiritual Perception and History* (Bloomington: Indiana University Press, 1983); Brett Whalen, "Joachim of Fiore and the Division of Christendom," *Viator* 34 (2003): 89–108; and Whalen, *Dominion of God: Christendom and Apocalypse in the Middle Ages* (Cambridge, MA: Cambridge University Press, 2009).

64. McGinn, *Calabrian Abbot*, 124–25.

65. 2 Kings 15:4–5; 2 Chr. 26:16–21.

66. Malcolm Lambert, *Medieval Heresy: Popular Movements from the Gregorian Reform to the Reformation*, 3rd ed. (Oxford: Blackwell, 2002), 195. For more on the broader connections between

were well upon their way, as evidenced by the resurgence of Islam, the bitterness of the conflict between the Holy Roman emperor and the pope, and the corruption of the Church. All these presaged "the attack of the *maximus Antichristus* of the second status represented by the dragon's seventh head."[67]

Joachim's main significance for prophets and heretics alike was that he was "a powerful preacher of coming tribulation upon the wicked, and no less potent a consoler of those in need."[68] As such, his messages were inherently controversial, as his audience might interpret Joachim's apocalyptic ideas freely. The symbolism and allegory in his concordances lent themselves to deliberate appropriation, and, consequently, creative interpretation, by many of their adherents. For instance, though Joachim himself was careful not to assign an exact date for the arrival of the Age of the Holy Spirit, he nonetheless offered certain historical signposts for people's better understanding of the future in his *Liber figurarum*, a work that referenced the great seven-headed dragon of the Apocalypse. In one pseudo-Joachite diagram, "The dragon . . . has turned into a bird of prey; the Holy Roman emperors assume a more important place on the side of evil, with both Henry I and Frederick II among the heads. . . . The text refers plainly to Frederick II and his heirs . . . as Antichrist; the great struggle of the papacy with the Hohenstaufen [dynasty] is thus seen as the prelude to the coming of the third age."[69] Joachim, and those influenced by his exegetical system, therefore read the imperial Hohenstaufen line as connected with the arrival of the Antichrist.

Not everyone was enamored of Joachim's system. Aquinas attacked Joachim's concept of the three ages of history and his method of scriptural

---

Joachim's apocalypticism and larger medieval thought, see Richard K. Emmerson and Ronald Herzman, *The Apocalyptic Imagination in Medieval Literature* (Philadelphia: University of Pennsylvania Press, 1992).

67. McGinn, *Calabrian Abbot*, 191. Reeves, *Influence of Prophecy*, 146, has stated that although Joachim always had one eye to the future, he could not describe or know exactly what this new monastic order, key to understanding the End of Days, would be: "he was a modern Moses, able to see the promised land, yet tragically unable to enter it."

68. McGinn, *Calabrian Abbot*, 236.

69. Lambert, *Medieval Heresy*, 199. See also Robert Lerner, "Frederick II, Alive, Aloft, and Allayed in Franciscan-Joachite Eschatology," in *The Use and Abuse of Eschatology*, ed., Werner Verbeke et al. (Louvain: Louvain University Press, 1988), 358–84.

interpretation through types and concordances with his trinitarian views. The Franciscan scholar Saint Bonaventure (d. 1274), who maintained an outlook on the world that was essentially apocalyptic, nevertheless rejected Joachim's position on the abolition of the Holy Gospel in the apocalyptic Third Age.[70] Still, others steadfastly clung to Joachim's apocalyptic framework and viewed the thirteenth-century appearance of the mendicant orders as the new clergy whom Joachim presaged would usher in the End Times. Moreover, there were many friars who encouraged this notion. With its rich symbolic and allegorical meanings and its emphasis on biblical exegesis, Joachim's teaching aligned with elements of Franciscan preaching, which was typically filled with symbolism and anecdote. Some Franciscans even began to identify their founder, Saint Francis (d. 1226), "with the angel of the sixth seal in the Apocalypse."[71] Franciscans who were enamored of Joachim's writings furthermore added a new twist to the abbot's conception of the past and the future. The Franciscan Order's austere and apostolic poverty, which was its premier defining characteristic, became entwined with the apocalyptic exegesis of Joachim.[72]

The adaptability of Joachim's prophetic system was crucial to the Franciscan Order's own internal struggles. At the time of Francis's death in 1226, the order swelled from an original roster of twelve members to more than ten thousand in Italy alone, drawing inspiration from Francis's

---

70. Lambert, *Medieval Heresy*, 212, 219.

71. Ibid., 198–99. Some people ascribed the gift of divinatory insight to Francis himself. In a now-lost anonymous Catalan manuscript, Francis had a vision on top of Mount Alverno, the site where he purportedly received the stigmata. In this particular pro–Spiritual Franciscan text, Francis revealed that the King of Aragon, a descendant from the Hohenstaufen emperors of Germany, would become the new Roman emperor. He would persecute the Spiritual Franciscans, who clung to the austerity of Francis's original order, and he would swear allegiance to a false pope. The persecution of the Church would endure for three years, after which a new emperor and true pope would restore it and return it to "a primitive state of purity." The Franciscan Order, moreover, would also return to its original principles. For more information on this lost source, see Pere Bohigas i Balaguer, "Profecies catalanes dels segles xiv i xv: assaig bibliogràfic," *Butlletí de la Biblioteca de Catalunya* 6, no. 9 (1920–1922): 24–49, here 35.

72. Lester K. Little, *Religious Poverty and the Profit Economy in Medieval Europe* (Ithaca, NY: Cornell University Press, 1983), examines the rise of the mendicant orders and voluntary poverty within the prosperous mercantile, urban centers of medieval Europe. See also John Moorman, *A History of the Franciscan Order from Its Origins to the Year 1517* (Oxford: Clarendon Press, 1968); and Jill Webster, *Els Menorets: The Franciscans in the Realms of Aragon from St. Francis to the Black Death* (Toronto: Pontifical Institute of Mediaeval Studies, 1993).

personal charisma and austere poverty.[73] This explosive growth brought its own challenges. During his lifetime, Francis amended the rule of his order multiple times to accommodate the growing ranks. Nevertheless, toward the end of his life, in his *Testament*, Francis once again stressed the importance of adhering to the doctrine of absolute poverty.

After Francis's death, successive leaders attempted to interpret his wishes with the practicalities and needs of the immensely popular order. By the end of the thirteenth century, however, the conflict between those Franciscans who wanted to stay true to Francis's ideas and those who faced the reality of the wider world became full blown, splitting the order in two. The first group, the Spirituals, was in the minority and demanded a more rigorous observance of Francis's concept of austere poverty. Members of the majority group were the Conventuals, who sought to relax the notion of austere individual poverty, instead advocating corporate, communal wealth.

The Spiritual Franciscans used Joachim's writings to shore up their political and theological positions. They began to portray themselves as the presaged spiritual men who indicated the advent of the Age of the Holy Spirit. One advocate for the Spirituals, Peter John Olivi (1248–1298), in his *Lectura super Apocalypsim* (Reading of the Apocalypse), adopted the Joachite concept of history, and seasoned it with a Franciscan flavor. The Spirituals believed:

> It was St Francis who was the initiator of a new age, and his rule was its gospel; full spiritual understanding would come to Francis's true disciples (i.e. the Spirituals), but only after the persecutions of the carnal Church, made up of all the evil forces in the visible Church, and especially the enemies of poverty and the advocates of pagan learning, the false doctors. A deepening

---

73. David Burr, *Olivi and Franciscan Poverty: The Origin of the Usus Pauper Controversy* (Philadelphia: University of Pennsylvania Press, 1989), 4. Burr has written much about the apocalyptic writings of Peter John Olivi, and his scholarship surrounding Olivi is stronger than Lambert's. Among Burr's many works, see especially "Olivi's Apocalyptic Timetable," *Journal of Medieval and Renaissance Studies* 11 (1981): 237–60; "Bonaventure, Olivi and Franciscan Eschatology," *Collecta Franciscana* 53 (1983): 23–40; "Apokalyptische Erwartung und die Entstehung der Usus-Pauper-Kontroverse: Zur Geschichte und Theologie des Franziskanerordens bei Petrus Johannis Olivi," *Wissenschaft und Weisheit* 47 (1984): 84–99; "Olivi, Apocalyptic Expectation, and Visionary Experience," *Traditio* 41 (1985): 273–88; and *The Spiritual Franciscans: From Protest to Persecution in the Century after Saint Francis* (University Park: Pennsylvania State University Press, 2001).

of suffering, and the falling away of many in the Church, would be followed by the joys of the new age, described in terms very like Joachim's.[74]

After Olivi's death, the blurred lines between heresy and orthodoxy, and their relation to the Spiritual Franciscans, became starker. The Spiritual Franciscans alarmed and frightened Pope John XXII to such a degree that in 1318 he declared them as both partially heretical and insane, and a papal commission condemned Olivi's writings in 1319. Additionally, John condemned Olivi posthumously as a heretic in 1326.[75]

Yet from John XXII's perspective, the damage had been done, as Olivi's message found welcoming ears among portions of the general populace, especially with the Beguins, a pejorative term applied to members of the lay populace of the regions of Languedoc and the Crown of Aragon who followed the Spirituals' message. Some of the Beguins revered Olivi to such an extent that his tomb at Narbonne became a popular pilgrimage destination.[76] More problematically, the Beguins and their supporters began to personally name the Antichrist and affix dates for the end of the world, a dangerous practice. The powerful Catalan lay mystic and papal physician Arnau de Vilanova, who wrote extensively on both occult and apocalyptic matters, argued that the end of the world would fall between the years 1366 and 1376, a declaration that outraged the theology faculty of the University of Paris in 1299 yet was embraced by the Beguins.[77] By the fourteenth century, some people perceived Franciscans, partially because of their missionary and preaching activities but also because of their affinity for

---

74. Lambert, *Medieval Heresy*, 204.

75. Marie-Thérèse d'Alverny, "Un adversaire de Saint Thomas: Petrus Iohannis Olivi," *St. Thomas Aquinas, 1274–1974. Commemorative Studies*, 2 vols. (Toronto: Pontifical Institute of Mediaeval Studies, 1974), 179–218.

76. Burr, *Spiritual Franciscans*, 91–94. Lambert, *Medieval Heresy*, 397. Although the term "Beguins" is related to the word "beguines," referring to lay religious women who often, although not always, lived free from religious vows, the two are not to be confused. See Walter Simons, *Cities of Ladies: Beguine Communities in the Medieval Low Countries, 1200–1565* (Philadelphia: University of Pennsylvania Press, 2001).

77. Clifford R. Backman, "Arnau de Villanova and the Body at the End of the World," in Bynum and Freedman, *Last Things*, 140–55. The literature on Arnau de Vilanova is extensive. For good introductions, see among others, Manuel de Montoliu, *Ramon Llull i Arnau de Vilanova* (Barcelona: Editorial Alpha, 1958); Jaume Mensa i Valls, *Arnau de Vilanova, spiritual: guia bibliogràfica* (Barcelona: Institut d'Estudis Catalans, 1994); and Juan Paniagua, *Estudios y notas sobre Arnau de Vilanova* (Madrid: CSIC, 1963).

Joachim's philosophies, as having a predilection for visions and prophecy. The Church put Beguin followers before inquisitorial commissions, and the tone of the rhetoric used on both sides of the issue became increasingly harsher. The Beguins saw themselves and their Spiritual Franciscan allies as forces that represented goodness in an apocalyptic battle against the wicked designs of a carnal Church and Antichrist pope.[78] For John XXII, the Spiritual Franciscans and the Beguins were a subversive, dangerous threat to orthodoxy, and he thus legitimized repression against those who espoused evangelical poverty.

The Joachite tradition of apocalyptic prophecy profoundly influenced later visionaries, such as John of Rupescissa, a Franciscan friar from Aquitaine. Rupescissa's own apocalyptic writings were themselves influential and in the fourteenth and fifteenth centuries were translated into various vernacular languages, including Catalan. Furthermore, Josep María Pou i Martí has shown how both Joachim's and Rupescissa's ideas were transmitted and sustained in the Crown of Aragon, as seen especially in the writings of a Catalan visionary who was a family member of the ruling house, Pere l'Infant (1305–1360). Many Catalan apocalyptic and visionary writings thus reflected Joachim of Fiore's particular partitioning of both past and future.[79] The personal histories of John of Rupescissa and Pere l'Infant, and their respective travails, illustrate well the intersection between apocalypticism and prophetic insight, especially during a time of crisis.[80]

Rupescissa's own history involved considerable trauma. In 1344 Guillaume Farinier, the provincial of the Franciscan Order in Aquitaine, deemed Rupescissa a troublemaker and suspected heretic because of his alleged support of the heretical Spiritual Franciscans and had him clapped in irons.[81] Farinier essentially waged a personal campaign to destroy

---

78. Burr, *Spiritual Franciscans*, 231–32.

79. Josep Maria Pou i Martí, *Visionarios, Beguinos y Fraticelos Catalanes (Siglos XIII–XV)* (Alicante: Instituto de Cultura "Juan Gil-Albert" Diputación-Provincial de Alicante, 1996).

80. *Fin du monde et signes des temps: visionnaires et prophètes en France méridionale (fin XIIIe– début XVe siècle)*. Cahiers de Fanjeux 27 (Toulouse: Privat, 1992).

81. John of Rupescissa is also known by his French name, Jean de Roquetaillade. Those interested in this prophet should consult the following classic works: Jeanne Bignami-Odier, *Études sur Jean de Roquetaillade* (Paris: Vrin, 1952); Bignami-Odier, "Jean de Roquetaillade (de Rupescissa)," *Histoire littéraire de La France* 41 (Paris, 1981): 75–240; André Vauchez, "Jean de Roquetaillade (†1366 ca.): Bilan de recherches et état de la question," *Eschatologie und Hussitismus: Internationales*

Rupescissa, ensuring that the visionary was incarcerated almost continuously over approximately two decades after being first arrested in December 1344. Eventually he ended up at the Franciscan convent of Figeac, fifty kilometers south of his home convent of Aurillac.

For four long years Rupescissa was shuttled between various prisons and suffered in some truly horrific conditions. In just one instance, in 1345, while held at Figeac, Rupescissa broke his leg and had to have it set a few times upon an iron device, an act that forced him to suffer, in his own words, the torments of the martyrs.[82] After such questionable physical therapy, Rupescissa continued to suffer as the wound on his broken leg attracted flies. So many maggots gathered in Rupescissa's festering injury that he could scoop them out "with both hands," although they certainly maintained his health by retarding the spread of infection.[83]

During his incarceration, Rupescissa spent his days in vigil, lamenting that he was "bound in iron in the muddy prison . . . crying and amazed why I had been cast into prison with such cruelty by Brother Guillaume Farinier . . . at the word of false and perjured witnesses."[84] As Rupescissa was crying, he reports, "suddenly, in a moment, in the twinkling of an eye, my intellect was opened and I understood . . . future events."[85] He had a vision that he would share with the world so that he, following a long-established tradition, "[should reveal] . . . the Antichrist, his people,

---

Kolloquium Prag 1.–4. September 1993 (Prague: Historiches Institut, 1993), 25–37; and Colette Beaune and André Vauchez, "Recherches sur prophétisme en occident," *Genèse de l'état moderne: Bilans et perspectives* (Paris: Editions du Centre national de la recherche scientifique, 1990), 201–06. Lerner, "Historical Introduction," 13–85; Leah DeVun, *Prophecy, Alchemy, and the End of Time: John of Rupescissa in the Late Middle Ages* (New York: Columbia University Press, 2009), 23–37; and Sylvie Barnay, "Jean de Roquetaillade: Vie, Oeuvres, et Contexte Historique," *Liber ostensor quod adesse festinant tempora*, ed. André Vauchez, Clémence Thévenaz Modestin, and Christine Morerod-Fattebert (Rome: École Française de Rome, 2005), 1–4.

82. Robert Lerner, "The Black Death and Western European Eschatological Mentalities," *American Historical Review* 86 (1981): 533–52; and Barnay, "Jean de Roquetaillade," 2. Johannis de Rupescissa, *Liber Ostensor quod adesse festinant tempora*, ed. André Vauchez, Clémence Thévenaz Modestin, and Christine Morerod-Fattebert (Rome: École Française de Rome, 2005), 517: "Bis et tertia vice fui positus in torculari ad tibiam tortam retificandum et tractus usque ad ultimos cruciatus, eo modo quo martirum antiquitus trahebantur membra usque ad extractionem fere."

83. Ibid., 86. Rupescissa, *Liber Ostensor*, 518.

84. Rupescissa, *LSE*, 137.

85. Ibid., 138: "subito in instanti, in ictu oculi apertus est intellectus meus et de futuris intellexi."

and homeland before he appeared as Antichrist."[86] Rupescissa believed that he played a significant role for his time. His endurance of his sufferings was ultimately in order to be a witness "chosen by God in order to bring to the world an important message"[87] about the tribulations that foreshadowed the imminent arrival of the Antichrist. He was to understand both the record of the past and the unfolding of the future, and thus have a present responsibility to act as an agent for helping people to resist the Antichrist.

On Friday, October 2, 1349, Rupescissa stood before Pope Clement VI and his curia in Avignon. They decided that the Franciscan would receive an inquisition into his supposed visionary activities and heretical stances and that a theological commission chaired by Guillaume Court would try Rupescissa. Wanting tangible proof of Rupescissa's visionary experiences, Court commanded him to write down his description of the revelation of the future that he had while imprisoned. On November 11, 1349, a little over a month after he stood before the curia, Rupescissa finished the final words to his *Liber Secretorum Eventuum* (The Book of Secret Events), which he presented to Court and the commission.[88]

The *Liber Secretorum Eventuum* is a massive, intensely political work comprising 161 paragraphs punctuated by 30 *intellecti*, revelations that functioned as specific signposts for Rupescissa's vision, to defend against the charges of heresy.[89] While the principal issue regarded Rupescissa's supposed sympathy to the heretical Spiritual Franciscans, another issue concerned whether Rupescissa's source of visionary insight was benign or diabolic. This was of particular importance. The popularity of apocalyptic itinerant preachers, which increased during the fourteenth and fifteenth centuries, could be dangerous if left unchecked.[90] Furthermore, if it was

---

86. Ibid., 137: "fuit michi clare datum intelligi quod ideo in tantam temptationem incideram quia futurum erat ut ego Antichristum et eius genus et terram, antequam appareret ut Antichristus."

87. Vauchez, "Jean de Roquetaillade, " 26.

88. Lerner, "Historical Introduction," 32.

89. Lerner also states that the *Liber Secretorum Eventuum* was going to be part of a tetralogy. Rupescissa was, according to Lerner, "planning to write a treatise on Antichrist and his deeds to be called *Liber conspectorum archanorum* . . . of which the *LSE* was merely the first volume," "Historical Introduction," 84.

90. Preachers' sermons were extraordinarily popular and could attract huge crowds. See Franco Mormando, *The Preacher's Demons: Bernardino of Siena and the Social Underworld of Renaissance Italy* (Chicago: University of Chicago Press, 1999).

believed that the machinations of the devil were behind a visionary's declarations, and could influence those without the reason to resist them, there could be a real danger in those words.

Rupescissa's work functioned as proof of his access to a body of privileged, divinely inspired knowledge through which he could see the course of the future and use toward a larger good. Part of this meant resisting increasing Aragonese hegemony in the Mediterranean basin. Rupescissa's condemnation of the political and economic program espoused by the rulers of the Crown of Aragon factors heavily throughout the *Liber Secretorum Eventuum*. For the patriotic Rupescissa, the beginning of the End Times occurred when "Peter, the king of Aragon, husband of Constance (the daughter of the aforementioned Manfred) . . . regained Sicily from the hand of Charles," a clear reference to the expulsion of the French forces from Sicily by combined Sicilian and Aragonese forces during the War of the Sicilian Vespers.[91]

The Aquitanian visionary was unique among late medieval visionaries by actually naming outright the Antichrist, whom he linked to the ruling dynasty of the Crown of Aragon.[92] For Rupescissa, Louis II of Sicily— "born of the seed of the deposed Emperor Frederick and of King Peter of the Aragonese; the boy-king Louis of Trinacrie, who occupies the island of Sicily," born in 1338, made king of Sicily under regency in 1342, and dead by 1355—was the Antichrist.[93]

Two major factors pointed to Louis II as Antichrist. First, for the patriotic Rupescissa, who called the French in Sicily "that most noble seed," Louis of Sicily's combined Hohenstaufen-Aragonese ancestry would be a doubtless indicator of diabolic malevolence. As Robert Lerner has remarked, "Ever since the death of the Emperor Frederick II [in 1250], eschatologically-minded Franciscans, such as Rupescissa, assumed that the great Antichrist would come from Frederick's 'seed,' and Louis met this qualification, since he was Frederick's great-great-great grandson."[94] This reckoning courses throughout the entirety of

---

91. Rupescissa, *LSE*, 139.

92. Lerner, "Historical Introduction," 54.

93. Rupescissa, *LSE*, 138: "de semine Frederici imperatoris depositi et Petri regis Aragonum orietur proximus Antichristus et quod Ludovicus puer rex Trinacrie qui tenet insulam Sicilie ipse est futurus totius seculi generalis monarcha sub quo lugebit Ecclesia sacrosancta Romana."

94. Lerner, "Historical Introduction," 54.

Rupescissa's vision. He discusses how the child-king Louis of Sicily, descended from Emperor Frederick and Louis of Bavaria, will be the eighth
king, referenced in the seventeenth chapter of the book of the Revelation,
and Rupescissa perceived the Hohenstaufens as intimately tied to the rise
of the Antichrist. His adaptation of anti-Hohenstaufen sentiment and its
connection to both the political and ecclesiastical struggles plaguing contemporary Europe directly evokes Joachim of Fiore's own powerfully anti-
Hohenstaufen prophetic framework.

In addition to the Hohenstaufens, the Aragonese were also targets of
French venom after the conclusion of the War of the Sicilian Vespers.
Begun in 1282 by Sicilians revolting against Charles of Anjou's French occupying forces, the War of the Sicilian Vespers resulted in the Aragonese
providing requested aid to the Sicilians. In defiance of the French, the Sicilians offered kingship of the island to Pere II of Aragon, who staked the
claim on the Hohenstaufen inheritance of the island through his marriage
to Constance, Frederick II's granddaughter.[95] Since therefore both Hohenstaufen and Aragonese blood flowed in the veins of Louis, Rupescissa presumed him to be the Antichrist.

The second indicator of Louis's being the Antichrist was his Latin name,
LVDOVICVS. A French name, his mother had chosen it on the advice of
a witch, according to a supernatural and apocryphal story that Rupescissa
provides toward the end of the *Liber Secretorum Eventuum.*[96] Even more
significant than issues of demonic biology or magic, Rupescissa also offers
mathematic proof of the diabolic ancestry of Louis II, hinting at a possible
mystical and kabbalistic influence upon the visionary. Adding up the numerical values of the letters in Louis's name would result in the sum 666,
the number of the Beast.[97]

Rupescissa uses biblical mathematics, rather than sidereal imagery, to
substantiate his visionary claims. Even though the stars do not appear in
the apocalyptic *Liber Secretorum Eventuum*, in the fourth section of his
autobiographical work, the *Liber Ostensor*, Rupescissa relied on sidereal

95. For more on the War of the Sicilian Vespers, see Steven Runciman, *The Sicilian Vespers: A History of the Mediterranean World in the Later Thirteenth Century* (Cambridge: Cambridge University Press, 1958); and Lawrence V. Mott, *Sea Power in the Medieval Mediterranean: The Catalan-Aragonese Fleet in the War of the Sicilian Vespers* (Gainesville: University of Florida Press, 2003).

96. Rupescissa, *LSE*, 214–16. I discuss this story further in chapter 2.

97. Apoc. 13:18; Rupescissa, *LSE*, 216. See also Emmerson, *Antichrist in the Middle Ages*, 40–41.

imagery and judicial astrology both spiritually and eschatologically. Based on the writings of learned Muslim and Jewish astronomers, Rupescissa predicted that 1345 would see a conjunction of the sun and the moon and the rise of "new future sects, horrible altercations from diverse faiths," and the Jews would see a false Messiah arrive to dupe them.[98] No astrologer himself, Rupescissa nevertheless drew upon the writings of astrological authorities to provide further reinforcement and legitimacy of his eschatology. These included historic luminaries, such as the ninth-century Arabic astronomer, Ja'far ibn Muhammad Abū Ma'shar al-Balkhī, better known in the west by his shorter name, Abū Ma'shar, or Albumasar (787–886), as well as more contemporary ones, including Levi ben Gerson and Jean de Murs, whose astrological writings circulated within the culture of the papal curia at Avignon. Yet Rupescissa himself did not appear to have any facility with sidereal matters and used astrology negligently. He picked up, yet ultimately did not comprehend, some astrological knowledge while in Avignon.[99]

Toward the end of his *Liber Secretorum Eventuum*, Rupescissa writes, "And from then I began to understand most clearly the meaning of the prophets and the writers, bound together, as much as the mystery of future events. This, therefore, I said so that the truth of the method of revealing and of understanding the mentioned secrets may be known."[100] This concept of "truth" woven within the narrative of Rupescissa's prophetic text was central for proving his innocence and therefore securing his survival. Yet it also represented the incarcerated visionary's access to knowledge that he would share with those who paid attention to his words. He thus gave his audience a powerful tool. Those who heeded his words would receive privileged knowledge, and therefore power, which they could use to prepare themselves for the advent of the Antichrist and to resist his reign, a theme prevalent in, and central to, Rupescissa's recently studied alchemical writings.[101]

---

98. Rupescissa, *Liber Ostensor*, 4.112.

99. Jean-Patrice Boudet, "Jean de Roquetaillade et l'Astrologie," in Rupescissa, *Liber Ostensor*, 954–56. Rupescissa made many astrological errors. These include, among others, his consulting erroneous astronomical tables, his misconception of the location of the great conjunction of 1365, and his misappropriation of coordinates for different events.

100. Rupescissa, *LSE*, 212.

101. For more on Rupescissa's alchemical works, see DeVun, *Prophecy, Alchemy, and the End of Time*; and DeVun, "Human Heaven: John of Rupescissa's Alchemy at the End of the World,"

After carefully scrutinizing the words of the *Liber Secretorum Eventuum*, Guillaume Court and the committee did not find Rupescissa as *haereticus* but instead deemed him *fantasticus*, an "imaginative fool."[102] Although Rupescissa escaped with his life and had to neither rescind nor abjure any errors, the commission's declaration of him as *fantasticus* was tantamount to weakening his claims to prophetic insight and his role in combating the Antichrist. Surprisingly, the cardinals never suppressed Rupescissa's writings and "passed these around so freely that his predictions were soon coursing through Europe," where their patriotic and providential tones were translated into vernacular languages and took on new significance in areas such as Bohemia and the Crown of Aragon.[103]

If Rupescissa had an ignominious personal history tied to his visionary output, the case of the Catalan royal visionary Pere l'Infant, inspired by the apocalyptic exegeses of both Joachim of Fiore and John of Rupescissa, was not markedly different.[104] Although Pere never faced incarceration, his own history as a visionary was blemished, as he had his own critics who denounced his visionary claims.

Pere was connected to the royal House of Aragon by blood. As the fourth son of King Jaume II (r. 1291–1327) of Aragon, he was the uncle of

---

in *History in the Comic Mode*, ed. Rachel Fulton and Bruce Holsinger (New York: Columbia University Press, 2007), 251–61.

102. Lerner, "Historical Introduction," 30. For the translation of *fantasticus* as "imaginative fool," see Daniel Hobbins, "The Schoolman as Public Intellectual: Jean Gerson and the Late Medieval Tract," *American Historical Review* 108, no. 5 (2003): 1308–35, here 1328.

103. Lerner, "Historical Introduction," 83. Morerod-Fattebert, in Rupescissa, *LSE*, 94–105, has demonstrated that subsequent copies of the *Liber Secretorum Eventuum* are housed in libraries in Uppsala, Paris, Bern, Milan, the Vatican, Turin, and Carpentras. Morerod-Fattebert, in Rupescissa, *LSE*, 46, has suggested that the *Liber Secretorum Eventuum* was translated into Catalan in 1449, less than a century after Rupescissa's death. For the Catalan version of the *LSE*, see Josep Perarnau i Espelt, "La traducció catalana medieval del *Liber secretorum eventuum* de Joan de Rocatalhada: edició, estudi del text i apèndixs," *Arxiu de Textos Catalans Antics* 17 (1998): 7–219. For Bohemia, see Robert E. Lerner, "Popular Justice: Rupescissa in Hussite Bohemia," *Eschatologie und Hussitismus: Internationales Kolloquium Prag 1.–4. September 1993* (Prague: Historiches Institut, 1993), 39–52.

104. For more on the history of Pere l'Infant, see Pou i Martí, *Visionarios, Beguinos y Fraticelos Catalanes*, lxiv–lxix, and 308–96; Pere Ivars Andrés, "La 'indiferencia' de Pedro IV de Aragon en el Gran Cisma de Occidente," *Archivo ibero-americano* 29 (1928): 21–97, and 161–86; Lerner, *Powers of Prophecy*, 141–52; Lee, Reeves, and Silano, *Western Mediterranean Prophecy*, 81–85; and Blumenfeld-Kosinski, *Poets, Saints, and Visionaries*, 36–38.

King Pere III, *el Ceremoniós*, and great-uncle of King Joan *el Caçador* and King Martí *l'Humà*. For decades Pere served as governor of Ribagorza and Prades and took part in the 1344 conquest of Majorca.[105] After the death of his wife, Jeanne of Foix, in 1358, Pere donned the Franciscan's habit in response to a vision he claimed to have had. Pere continued to have visions but received his greatest success, and most popular acclaim, with a controversial vision he claimed to have had in 1365. Although the trauma of the Great Western Schism had not yet begun, Pere was distraught by the translation of the papal see to Avignon. Pere claimed he had received a direct communication from God that he was to travel to Avignon and personally tell Urban V to move the papal see back to Rome. Were the pope to disobey Pere's orders, l'Infant was to announce the death of the pontiff.[106] Urban would not be the only one to suffer death; thousands more would perish because of the violence engendered by religious upheaval.[107]

Avignon received Pere cordially, and Nicolau Eymerich, upon examining Pere l'Infant's visions, deemed them unobjectionable and orthodox.[108] However, in 1379, when the Schism began, Pere entered the political fray and threw the full weight of his support behind Urban VI, a far different position from Pere III's, which was decidedly neutral. Pere l'Infant continued a visionary output that was examined by a committee of friars put together by the Aragonese king.

Yet despite Pere's close connection with the royal family, his understanding of the future of the Church and the Crown of Aragon's role within the Great Western Schism did not spare him from receiving his own fair share of criticism. Just as Rupescissa's *Liber Secretorum Eventuum* was denounced by Court and the commission as the work of a *fantasticus*, Pere's own writings engendered significant controversy and were denounced by some clerics, such as Pedro de Ribés and Tomás Alsina. For them, voting in concordance with their allegiance to Avignon, Pere l'Infant's denunciation of Clement VII as a schismatic pontiff was faulty and without merit,

---

105. Lerner, *Powers of Prophecy*, 141.

106. Lee, Reeves, and Silano, *Western Mediterranean Prophecy*, 81–82.

107. Blumenfeld-Kosinski, *Poets, Saints, and Visionaries*, 37.

108. Lee, Reeves, and Silano, *Western Mediterranean Prophecy*, 82; and Blumenfeld-Kosinski, *Poets, Saints, and Visionaries*, 38.

as the pope "truly presides over the entire Church of God."[109] Like Rupescissa, Pere viewed himself as a recipient of divine revelation, which he shared with the world at large to grant those who would heed his words a degree of agency in resisting the trials engendered by the trauma of the Great Western Schism. Still, despite the discounting of some of his prophecies, he was able to maintain some degree of political power. He eventually became vicar general of the Franciscan Order and died in 1381, on the way to Rome.[110]

Pere's reputation as a visionary, established by his 1365 success, continued throughout his life. As Rupescissa politicized his visionary insight as decidedly pro-French and anti-Aragonese, it should come as no surprise that Pere l'Infant's own prophecies had a markedly anti-French sentiment to them. Relying upon the pseudo-Joachimist work *Super Hieremiam* for his 1377 Catalan prophecy *Exposició de la visió damunt dita*, Pere argued that no savior-king or Last World Emperor, a figure popular in early medieval apocalyptic writings, would appear from the ranks of the French to right the time of crisis engendered by the Antichrist's arrival. Indeed, Pere predicted that the French kingdom would come to a most ignominious end.[111]

If Rupescissa did not understand, but still relied upon, the stars to legitimize his prophetic insight, Pere seemed to have a better grasp of the power behind astrological imagery and rhetoric. In an intensely political passage in the *Exposició*, for example, Pere l'Infant expounds upon the Cedar of Lebanon prophetic tradition using the planets as his guides. The beginning of the original prophecy reads, "The high Cedar of Lebanon will be felled. Mars will prevail over Saturn and Jupiter. Saturn will waylay Jupiter in all things."[112] In Pere's adaption of the prophecy, however, he takes considerable liberties by linking astrological imagery with contemporary political figures. In his work he identifies King Pedro *el Cruel* of Castile as a principal figure closely linked with the events of the End Times. He names Pedro as Saturn, a melancholic figure who bodes ill, one who will

---

109. Lee, Reeves, and Silano, *Western Mediterranean Prophecy*, 82.

110. Blumenfeld-Kosinski, *Poets, Saints, and Visionaries*, 36.

111. Lee, Reeves, and Silano, *Western Mediterranean Prophecy*, 83–84; and Pou i Martí, *Visionarios, Beguinos y Fraticelos Catalanes*, 370–73; and McGinn, *Antichrist*, 88–92.

112. Lener, *Powers of Prophecy*, 16.

bring Spain under his sway and conquer the Muslims of the peninsula.[113] Pere III, his nephew and the bellicose king of the Crown of Aragon, he understands as connected with Mars. He does so by playing upon the etymology of the word "Aragon," arguing that it hails from the Latin *ara agonis*, which he says refers to the sacrifices pagans used to make to honor Mars.[114] Jupiter, a benign planet, refers to the young Edward, England's Black Prince, who abandoned Pedro *el Cruel* after the 1367 victory at the Battle of Nájera. And the "bat" who would chase away Saturn, an addition to the Tripoli prophecy upon which Pere l'Infant relied, was none other than Enrique II of Castile, from the Trastámara line.[115] The planets from the Tripoli prophecy came down to earth in Pere l'Infant's reckoning and served as allegories for very real political figures.

While the foundational critiques and definitions that separated illicit divination from divine prophecy were undeniably influential on later medieval thinkers, the vast majority of people neither perceived nor received those concepts in the same way. Simply put, Augustine, Thomas Aquinas, William of Auvergne, Joachim of Fiore, John of Rupescissa, and Pere l'Infant benefited from intellectual and religious training that most people, including members of the secular elite, did not have. The rigid categories that Aquinas set out in his *Summa Theologiae*, in which he parsed the entirety of the Christian experience to the finest line, were nonetheless to be understood and elaborated upon by those with the requisite reason and linguistic training to do so.

Not surprisingly, people found it difficult to maintain fine distinctions and inevitably ended up blurring the lines that scholars worked hard to define. Writers and readers of divinatory works attempted to make sense of a complicated, often frightening world. Among these writers and readers were members of the secular elite. Some monarchs were understandably eager to know what would happen to their kingdom and their people

---

113. Ibid., 220–21; Lee, Reeves, and Silano, *Western Mediterranean Prophecy*, 83; and Pou i Martí, *Visionarios, Beguinos y Fraticelos Catalanes*, 370.

114. Pou i Martí, *Visionarios, Beguinos y Fraticelos Catalanes*, 370: "Lo Rey d Arago es entés o figurat en Mars, qui, segons los stromorians, es planeta bellicós: aytals son estats los Reys de Aragó; per co Aragó es dit ara agonis, que uol dir ara de batalla on se sacrificaua a Mars per los idólatres, qui es dit deu de batalles."

115. Lerner, *Powers of Prophecy*, 143.

during times of profound crisis and to see what future turmoil might await them. A ruler's attempt to peer into the future could, therefore, be seen as a form of good governance.[116] But this did not assuage critics, who perceived such practices as conduct unbecoming of a monarch. In their estimation, dabbling in astrology and the occult placed one in a dangerous realm from which it might not be possible to escape.

---

116. This understanding had ancient roots. See David Potter, *Prophets and Emperors: Human and Divine Authority from Augustus to Theodosius* (Cambridge, MA: Harvard University Press, 1994).

2

FOR YOUTHS AND SIMPLETONS

The Folly of Elite Astrology

In his 1420 Arabic-language autobiography, the *Tuhfat al-adīb fī al-radd ʿalà ahl al-salīb* (The Gift of the Learned One to Refute the Supporters of the Cross), known simply as the *Tuhfa*, Anselm Turmeda provides an intriguing account about his decision to convert to Islam.[1] The fifteenth-century former Franciscan states that it was his adviser, Nicolau Myrtle, who encouraged him to leave Christendom and emigrate to the Dar al-Islam to convert. Anselm's teacher suggested he do this since he was young and healthy, as "God, may he be praised, taught me the truth about . . . Islam and the greatness of his prophet . . . when I was already quite old and my body quite weak. . . . If God had directed me to this when I was your age, I would have left everything without doubt."[2] Encouraged by Myrtle,

---

1. Anselm Turmeda, *Fray Anselm Turmeda (ʿAbdallah al-Taryuman) y su polémica islamo-cristiana: edición, traducción y estudio de la Tuhfa*, ed. and trans., Míkel de Epalza (Madrid: Hiperión, 1994) (hereafter referred to as *Tuhfa*).

2. Turmeda, *Tuhfa*, 218.

Turmeda abandoned his studies at the University of Bologna, moved to the sultanate of Tunis, and became a Muslim. There he established a long and prosperous career working first as chief of customs and then as director of the Dar al-Mujtass, or the "Monopoly House," a Tunisian governmental entity that regulated the sultanate's economic monopolies of salt and soap.[3]

Although the *Tuhfa* was Turmeda's most famous work, garnering him the veneration of devout Muslims, who called him the *Zaydi-Tuhfa*, "Lord of the Tuhfa," and who made his gravesite in Tunis a celebrated pilgrimage destination well into the twentieth century, it was not his sole written work.[4] Turmeda had a significant literary output, which included a collection of aphorisms from 1396, the *Llibre de bons amonestaments*, and his 1398 literary lamentation written in honor of his natal island, Majorca, the *Cobles de la divisió del regne de Mallorques.* He also wrote satire, as evidenced in his 1417 work *La Disputa de l'Ase* (The Dispute of the Ass). Turmeda frames this particular source as a *disputa*, a type of medieval debate between two representatives from different religions in which the participants discuss the benefits of their own religion in contrast with the problems and deviations of the other faith.[5] In this piece, Turmeda has various representatives from the animal kingdom debate with the author whether it is superior to be a man or an animal. Although the author ultimately wins the debate by stating that, despite all of humanity's considerable faults, Jesus came to earth as a person, an ark's worth of animals still offer their respective positions on all aspects of existence. When arriving at the thorny subject of astrologers, magicians, charlatans, and con artists, Turmeda deliberately chose the character of the parrot to squawk, "You have mentioned the matter of astrologers and swindlers. Know that they have some enchantments and subtle tricks that they only use with the ignorant masses, women, children, and the stupid and which even remain hidden from many intelligent and learned people."[6] The message was clear. If one

---

3. Ibid., 232.

4. Agustí Calvet, *Fray Anselmo Turmeda: Heterodoxo español* (Barcelona: Casa Editorial Estudio, 1914), 80.

5. Lourdes María Alvarez, "Beastly Colloquies: Of Plagiarism and Pluralism in Two Medieval Disputations between Animals and Men," *Comparative Literature Studies* 39, no. 3 (2002): 179–200.

6. Anselm Turmeda, *La disputa de los animals contra el hombre. Traducción del original árabe de* La disputa del asno contra Fray Anselmo Turmeda, ed. and trans., Emilio Tornero Poveda

were to spend excessive time with matters of divination, astrology, and the occult, one's intelligence, wisdom, and even masculinity were called into question.

This gendered criticism of divination and the occult is significant. Even though Pierre d'Ailly dealt with occult matters in ascertaining the future of the Church, in his estimation, others' attempting to unravel and understand future events occupied an uneasily reconciled space. D'Ailly's astrological knowledge and abilities were rooted in masculine authority and reflected a university education that was entirely male in its composition and hierarchy. D'Ailly himself tended to distrust all other claims to future insight gained outside of that venue, since "he believed that the Lord had withheld any specific teaching through which their validity could be assessed."[7] Additionally, others' claims to having insight about the course of the future could be used to dupe others. In his early fifteenth-century work *De falsis prophetis*, d'Ailly expounded upon the nature of false prophets and their words and argued that those fraudulent seers "frequent the homes of foolish women and effeminate men."[8] Those individuals who held too much stock in divination and the occult could thus have their masculinity, as well as their wisdom, challenged by opponents of the occult, as is seen in Bernat Metge's depiction of King Joan in his fifteenth-century dream allegory, *Lo Somni*.[9]

(Madrid: Editorial de la Universidad Complutense, 1984), 191: "Has mencionado el asunto de los astrólogos y embaucadores. Sabed que ellos tienen unos encantamientos y astucias sutiles que sólo se usan entre el vulgo ignorante, las mujeres, los niños y los tontos y que incluso quedan ocultos a mucha gente inteligente e instruida."

7. Dyan Elliott, "Seeing Double: John Gerson, the Discernment of Spirits, and Joan of Arc," *American Historical Review* 107, no. 1 (2002): 26–54, here 30–31.

8. Pierre d'Ailly, *De falsis prophetis*, in Jean Gerson, *Opera Omnia*, ed. L. E. du Pin (Antwerp: Sumptibus Societatis, 1706), cited in D. Elliott, "Seeing Double," 31 n21: "frequentant domos muliercularum, aut virorum effeminatorum." Some medieval authors, such as the twelfth-century canon lawyer Gratian, also linked predicting the future with demonic agency and identity. Gratian, drawing upon the works of Augustine and the Carolingian scholar, Hrabanus Maurus, believed demons' subtle senses aided them in predicting the future. Dyan Elliott, *Fallen Bodies: Pollution, Sexuality, and Demonology in the Middle Ages* (Philadelphia: University of Pennsylvania Press, 1999), 132 and 245 n33.

9. For more on this, see my discussion on Metge in chapters 5 and 6. Metge foreshadows his stance on divination, the occult, and its intersection with masculinity and monarchical authority by sniffing, through the voice of the defunct Joan, himself a devotee of the occult, early in book 1: "I do not know how the premonition or divination of centuries to come attaches itself to the

In this chapter I investigate the criticism of astrology and the occult arts in elite medieval venues—in particular, the university and the royal court. Turmeda's parrot relied on a well-established rhetorical tradition in which critics of the occult arts railed against the purported credulity of simple people, arguing that they were easily duped or frightened by powerful and hidden knowledge. When this body of knowledge was applied to an environment rife with apocalyptic expectation, authorities argued that apprehension could easily turn to panic among the ignorant. The implication of such anti-occult rhetoric is that members of the intellectual, cultural, and secular elite should eschew disciplines like astrology or alchemy, lest they be perceived as juvenile, simple, or womanly, and thus undermine their own authority.

While satirically decrying astrology in his *Dispute of the Ass*, Turmeda himself was no stranger to the occult, as he used astrological imagery in an early fifteenth-century visionary poem in which he railed against the Great Western Schism that had rent Christendom asunder.[10] Turmeda wrote this brief poem, two folia long and composed as a series of rhyming couplets in the Catalan vernacular, after his conversion to Islam. His prophecy poem reflects both his interests in astrology and the current state of religious and political problems that troubled Christendom, as he directs his prophecy to a Christian audience and criticizes the indifference of leaders about rectifying the "sin of the . . . Schism."[11] The poem is also profoundly apocalyptic and chock-full of images of pervasive plague, famine, and death; Turmeda "had a clear view of a Europe devastated by religious division and endless wars, and gripped by the . . . fear of the Antichrist."[12] Throughout

minds of men, especially those of great intelligence and of superior fortitude." Bernat Metge, *The Dream of Bernat Metge*, trans. Richard Vernier (Burlington, VT: Ashgate, 2002), 13 (hereafter referred to as *The Dream*).

10. Ramón d'Alos, "Les profecies de Turmeda," *Revue Hispanique* 24 (1911): 480–96; Pere Bohigas i Balaguer, "Profecies de fra Anselm Turmeda (1406)," *Estudis Universitaris Catalans* 9 (1915–1916): 173–81; Pere Bohigas i Balaguer, "Profecies catalanes dels segles XIV i XV," *Bulletí de la Biblioteca de Catalunya* 6 (1920–1922): 38–39; 46–47; and Michael A. Ryan, "Byzantium, Islam, and the Great Western Schism," *A Companion to the Great Western Schism (1378–1417)*, ed. Jöelle Rollo-Koster and Thomas Izbicki (Leiden: Brill, 2009), 197–238.

11. Francesc Eiximenis, Art de Bé Morir. Biblioteca de Catalunya (BC), Arxiu Fotogràfic Miquel i Planes (AFMP), 22, Barcelona, 485, fol. 259v.: "pecat d[e]l cisma."

12. Lourdes María Alvarez, "Anselm Turmeda: The Visionary Humanism of a Muslim Convert and Catalan Prophet." In Classen, ed., *Meeting the Foreign in the Middle Ages*, 172–91, here 185.

the work, Turmeda boasts about his abilities to divine the future via the stars and roots his predictions within a base of authoritative astrological knowledge.[13]

Sidereal imagery played an important part within the premodern understanding of approaching traumas. Eclipses, comets, shooting stars, conjunctions of planets, and all other manners of heavenly manifestations could be, and certainly were, read as portents, frequently negative ones, of future events. Comets were especially ill omens, and their appearance in the night sky was believed to foretell impending doom, as in the reported sighting of a comet in 1315 and 1316 that foreshadowed the devastation of the Great Famine.[14] Unfavorable aspects of planets and stars, literally disasters, signified ill tidings and sparked fear and apprehension in those who perceived them as such. In one account dated August 2, 1133, an anonymous English cleric reported that the dramatic and sudden appearance of a total solar eclipse in the late afternoon so badly frightened the peasants working the land nearby that it caused many of them to immediately cease their labors, drop their tools, and flee for their lives to the neighboring fields and woods. Even though sidereal matters appealed to members of the elite and the populace alike, there was a significant separation between how they understood such events. The instance of the English peasants fleeing from the heavenly spectacle of the eclipse demonstrated this gulf between learned and popular reckonings of celestial phenomena. If not outright disdainful, the clerical author was nonetheless critical of the peasants' understanding of and response to the eclipse. For many medieval critics, astronomical and astrological ideas could be misunderstood too easily by the bulk of the populace. Because the scientific principles guiding astrology and astronomy were complex, and to understand them fully required significant levels of training and education, most people who lacked that level of education understood sidereal experiences differently. For some, the stars and their movements signified future events without the need for

---

13. BC, 485, fols. 260v. and 261v. "sera la terra / si ia no erra / la meu sciencia / sense fallenca."

14. William Chester Jordan, *The Great Famine: Northern Europe in the Early Fourteenth Century* (Princeton, NJ: Princeton University Press, 1996), 22. See also Lynn Thorndike, ed. *Latin Treatises on Comets between 1238 and 1368 A.D.* (Chicago: University of Chicago Press, 1950); and Sara J. Schechner, *Comets, Popular Culture, and the Birth of Modern Cosmology* (Princeton, NJ: Princeton University Press, 1997).

charting their courses via specialized, expensive equipment or complicated mathematical tables.

What is immediately apparent is that the English cleric positioned his learned understanding of the natural phenomenon of the eclipse and his knowledge of astronomy in stark contrast to the irrational fear of the unlettered peasants. He observed that for them the eclipse signified the Day of Judgment; for him it was a chance to demonstrate his rationality, his scientific erudition, and his application of Pliny's *Natural History* within a Christian framework.[15] Yet it was understandable why the peasants reacted as they did, as they understood that celestial phenomena would accompany the trauma of the Apocalypse. Contextualized within an apocalyptic understanding, although the End Times promised great redemption and salvation for those Christians who subscribed to its message, it would be a frightening time; the horrific events that foreshadowed Armageddon paled in comparison to the terrors unleashed on the Day of Judgment. This anticipatory fear of the Apocalypse, were it to grip the general populace, could result in almost catastrophic upheaval, as evidenced in a document from 1310. Originally proceeding from the parochial archive of Moià, this document relates that in August of that year, the sermons of a Majorcan preacher, who paraphrased the apocalyptic predictions of Arnau de Vilanova, frightened the people of Palma de Majorca so badly that they consigned their worldly possessions to a bonfire of the vanities and that there were not "enough preachers, nor friars minor, nor clergy to hear [the people's] confession. . . . The king of Majorca, knowing the fear of the people . . . requests that the bishop of Majorca, who was in Perpignan, come back to comfort the people and that . . . the preaching friar be imprisoned."[16] One needed great care, therefore, in interacting with both apocalyptic and astrological ideas, lest miscomprehension breed terror.

What of the ruling elite? Purportedly they had a greater soundness of mind and educational background to concern themselves "safely" with

15. G. Waitz, ed. "Handschriften in Englischen Bibliotheken: Beilage zu dem Bericht über die Reise nach England," *Neues Archiv der Gesellschaft für ältere deutsche Geschichtskunde zur Beföderung einer Gesammtausgabe der Quellenschriften deutscher Geschichten des Mittelalters* 4:2 (Hannover: Hahn'sche Buchhandlung, 1879), 328.

16. Martí de Barcelona, *La cultura catalana durant el regnat de Jaime II* (Barcelona: Estudios Franciscanos, 1991), 179–80. For more on Arnau's various writings, especially his apocalyptic

these matters. In the opinion of the fourteenth-century theologian Nicole Oresme (ca. 1320–1382), one's soundness of mind determined whether one were interested in magic in the first place. For Oresme, one should shun the magical arts, as there could be nothing gained for anyone to study magic, and he sought to "lay bare the falsity of this malign art, so that no person of sound mind [would] be affected by such arts in the future."[17] Powerful people might be interested in astrology, divination, and other occult arts during the later Middle Ages, in response to the crises of the times, yet there was also an increase in other people's incredulity of magicians' and seers' words. As such, the kings received their own fair share of criticism in engaging with these occult subjects. Some of the most strident criticism came from individuals who personally negotiated the courtly demimonde and witnessed the excessive importance of the occult within that elite venue. Heinrich von Langenstein (1325–1397), for instance, writing at the University of Paris, which "hates those who observe vanities to excess and has never been the source of rumors and superstitions as other universities have been," roundly criticized astrologers and their unwarranted weight in the courtly demimonde.[18] In his opinion, astrologers were granted fame only because monarchs or noble lords patronized them. It was detrimental for a king to support an astrologer, however, as Heinrich linked astrology closely with the darker arts of geomancy and necromancy.[19] In Heinrich's

---

ones, see Joaquín Carreras y Artau, "La pólemica gerundiense sobre el Antichristo entre Arnau de Villanova y los dominicos," *Anales del Instituto de Estudios Gerundenses* 5 (1950): 34–44; Raoul Manselli, "La religiosità d'Arnaldo da Villanova," *Bulletino dell'Istituto storico italiano per il medio evo e archivio Muratoriano* 63 (Rome, 1951), 13–14; Harold Lee, "*Scutamini Scripturas:* Joachimist Themes and *Figurae* in the Early Religious Writing of Arnold of Villanova," *Journal of the Warburg and Courtauld Institutes* 37 (1974): 33–56; Manfred Gerwing, *Vom Ende der Zeit: der Traktat des Arnald von Villanova über die Ankunft des Antichrist in der akademischen Auseinandersetzung zu Beginn des 14. Jahrhunderts* (Münster, Achendorff, 1996); Jaume Mensa i Valls, *Les raons d'un anunci apocalyptic: La polèmica escatològica entre Arnau de Villanova i els filòsofs i teòlegs professionals (1297–1305): anàlisi dels arguments i de les argumentacions* (Barcelona: Facultat de Teologia de Catalunya, 1998); Mensa i Valls, *Arnau de Villanova (c. 1240–1311)* (Madrid: Ediciones del Oro, 2000).

    17. Cited in Joel Kaye, "Law, Magic, and Science: Constructing a Border between Licit and Illicit Knowledge in the Writings of Nicole Oresme," *Law and the Illicit in Medieval Europe*, ed. Ruth Mazo Karras, Joel Kaye, and E. Ann Matter (Philadelphia: University of Pennsylvania Press, 2008), 225–37, here 230.

    18. Thorndike, *HMES*, 3:496; Hobbins, "Schoolman as Public Intellectual," 1326; Justin Lang, *Die Christologie bei Heinrich von Langenstein* (Freiburg: Herder, 1966).

    19. Thorndike, *HMES*, 3:494.

estimation, prophecies based on astrological utterances were nothing but superstition and foolishness.[20]

Additionally, courtly critics of the occult arts labeled their practitioners—the magicians, astrologers, and alchemists who plied their arts within the royal court—as charlatans who could too readily take advantage of a gullible king. In the twentieth *exemplo* from Don Juan Manuel's fourteenth-century literary work *El Conde Lucanor*, a vagabond *golfín* promises great riches to a king who is a devotee of alchemy and therefore judged to be "not very cautious."[21] The charlatan has great skill in producing gold from a combination of materials, including an unfamiliar substance that he calls *tabardíe*, a word of his own creation.[22] He therefore earns the trust of the naive king and ultimately robs him substantially. To add insult to injury, once the king discovers the crime and seeks to imprison the fraud, the scoundrel has already fled, leaving behind a note in which he mocks the king, explaining there is "no such thing in the world as *tabardíe*."[23] Don Juan Manuel's account is supposed to be didactic and shows that a skilled swindler can take in even a king when he shunts trusted nobles to the margins of courtly society in exchange for the splendid tricks of charlatans.

Yet some of these swindlers also engaged with what people considered legitimate magical practices. One document from 1435, a Venetian manuscript copy of the *Liber Lapidum Pretiosorum* attributed to Marbodus, is a compendium of magical writings that enumerates the magical properties of certain stones and objects. It includes legitimate magical practices and rites as well as sleights of hand that a swindler could use to con someone to earn quick money.[24] "Real" and "fake" magic alike simultaneously existed within this specific text, occupying the same physical and intellectual space. It was thus small wonder why those who purported to understand the occult arts could dupe some people, including those who occupied the highest echelons of power.

---

20. Blumenfeld-Kosinski, *Poets, Saints, and Visionaries*, 186.

21. Don Juan Manuel, *El Conde Lucanor o Libro de los enxiemplos del conde Lucanor et de Patronio*, ed. José Manuel Blecua (Madrid: Clásicos Castalia, 1969), 122–26, here 123: "un rey que non era de muy buen recado."

22. James Burke, "Juan Manuel's Tabardíe and Golfín," *Hispanic Review* 44, no. 2 (1976), 171–78.

23. Manuel, *El Conde Lucanor*, 125: "Bien creed que non a en l'mundo tabardíe."

24. Beinecke Rare Book and Manuscript Library, Yale University, Mellon Collection of Alchemy and the Occult, MS 6.

One of the earliest authors whose writings best illustrate the liminality of magic and the occult within the culture of the medieval royal court was the twelfth-century English scholar John of Salisbury (ca. 1115/20–1180). In his 1159 work, *Policraticus*, "a moral treatise for courtiers," Salisbury sought to educate others against those vices in the culture of the court that were most difficult for him to stomach.[25] Drawing from his firsthand experience in many of the courts of medieval Europe, John of Salisbury, who would end his career prestigiously as bishop of Chartres, wrote the work to serve as a pedagogical guide meant to instruct rulers, their courtiers, and their aides about adhering to certain virtues and eschewing detrimental vices within the atmosphere of the courtly demimonde. It was more than just a "mirror of princes," as it provided a foundational study for medieval political thought, one that systematically described contemporary medieval political practices, especially in relation to the occult arts, and provided a significant base upon which subsequent courtly critics built their own arguments.[26]

The *Policraticus* spans eight books. The first two focus on Salisbury's "observations . . . upon those vices to which courtiers are particularly prone,"[27] including hunting, gambling, music, and illusion working. Toward the end of the first book, he tackles the subject of magic. Chapter 10 of the first book concerns the general nature of magicians, whose tricks "disturb the minds of men," and briefly discusses Moses's victorious miracles over the mages of the pharaoh in Egypt, a particularly wicked land in Salisbury's estimation, "for indeed Egypt is the mother of these kinds of superstitions and evil deeds."[28] In chapter 11 he briefly discusses Varro's four categories of divination by the elements—namely, pyromancy, aeromancy, hydromancy, and geomancy—but admits there are far more types of magical practices than just these, and in chapter 12 he enumerates the

---

25. Peters, *Magician, the Witch, and the Law*, xvii and 46.

26. John of Salisbury, *Policraticus: Of the Frivolities of Courtiers and the Footprints of Philosophers*, ed. and trans. Cary J. Nederman (Cambridge: Cambridge University Press, 1990); and John of Salisbury, *Policraticus I–IV* (Corpus Christianorum, Continuatio Mediaevalis, CXVIII), ed. Katherine S. B. Keats-Rohan (Turnholt, Belgium: Brepols, 1993).

27. Peters, *Magician, the Witch, and the Law*, 46.

28. John of Salisbury, *Policraticus I–IV*, 56–57. See also A.-J. Festugière, *La revelation d'Hermès* Trismégiste (Paris: Les Belles Lettres, 2006) and Christopher I. Lehrich, *The Occult Mind: Magic in Theory and Practice* (Ithaca, NY: Cornell University Press, 2007), 1–17.

various types of magicians and their practices, which includes incantators, haruspices, dream interpreters, chiromantics, mathematicians, casters of lots, and augurs.[29]

After the final "potpourri" chapter of book 1, in which Salisbury discusses a variety of matters, including people's belief in the role of birds in divining the future, he segues into the second book of *Policraticus*. An extraordinarily complex book, it appears that John of Salisbury attacks both the literary tradition of magic in the West as well as contemporary, twelfth-century conceptions of the practice of magic.[30] It is in this second book where Salisbury goes into substantial detail about the magical practices of the courtly demimonde that he both witnessed and, as a youth, experienced as he attests in chapter 28.[31]

Beginning his second book by briefly discussing some powerful individuals' historical rejection of the vanities of dreams, superstitions, and prophecies, Salisbury then proceeds, in the second chapter, to point out that not all natural signs should merit condemnation as mere vanity, for "God instructs his creature by multifarious and many signs."[32] Farmers, sailors, and physicians all look to natural signs to foresee future events, but they do so solely in service of their respective professions. Continuing further, in the third chapter he relates that the sun and moon also serve as natural and accurate harbingers of catastrophic events, such as floods, and should not be immediately doubted as portents, for "Who would dare call the sun false?"[33]

In addition to divinatory omens, destructive imagery also figures heavily in the *Policraticus*; the fourth chapter concerns the signs that accompanied the destruction of Jerusalem. The narrative of the destruction of that "most famous city" continues in the subsequent chapter, with the arrival of a devastating famine, which permits Salisbury to relate, in the sixth chapter, the brief but horrific warning about a woman driven insane by hunger during the city's siege and who ate her own child. The destruction

---

29. Ibid., 57–61.

30. Peters, *Magician, the Witch, and the Law*, 47.

31. Ibid., 47.

32. John of Salisbury, *Policraticus I–IV*, 74.

33. Ibid., 76: "Solem dicere falsum quis audeat?"

of Jerusalem was profound, Salisbury writes, with casualties approaching 110,000 souls.[34]

Besides spinning apocalyptic narratives, within the second book of *Policraticus*, Salisbury addresses another problematic practice that appealed to courtiers: their interest in reading dreams as signs that hearkened to the future. In particular, he addresses the duplicities of *coniectores*, those types of magicians who "by artifice sell the interpretation of dreams," and urges people not to follow their words.[35] He cites biblical figures such as Daniel and Joseph as those proper prophets to whom God granted true information via dreams, but says that contemporary and fraudulent *coniectores* are to be avoided at all costs, as their "vanities and insane falsehoods" open up individuals to demonic depredations.[36]

From dream interpreters John of Salisbury then segues to *mathematici*, those magicians who "by the position of the stars and the situation of the firmament and the movement of the planets conjecture about those things that may come to pass."[37] For John, although the mathematic arts broadly constitute the quadrivium—the disciplines of arithmetic, music, geometry, and, of course, astronomy—there are nevertheless those who do not follow the true movements of the stars and heavens, but instead fall into imaginary fables.[38] To prevent courtiers from doing just that, Salisbury spends the entirety of chapter 19 distinguishing between the doctrines of true astronomers and reprobate astrologers. In his estimation, the astronomers practice and provide a "noble and glorious science," whereas the astrologers who engage in *mathēsis* do not draw from nature and instead only offer vain superstition.[39] Moreover, one had to be careful in dealing with astronomy in general, as it was still possible for one to fall dangerously close to perdition by granting the stars too much agency over human destiny: "In truth, *mathematici* or *planetarii*, while striving to declare broadly

---

34. Ibid., 86.
35. Ibid., 59 and 94–106.
36. Ibid., 106.
37. Ibid., 59: "qui a positione stellarum situque firmamenti et planetarum motu quae sint uentura coniciunt."
38. Ibid., 111.
39. Ibid., 112. See also Tester, *A History of Western Astrology*, 134.

the power of their profession, most destructively sink into error and throw down the lies of impiety."[40] To look for signs of the future via the stars was damning, because it bypassed the recognition and honor that was due to God. Salisbury's ultimate verdict was that the signs provided by the heavenly bodies "were given to men for edification, not to those accomplices who would long for heavenly secrets through non-existent signs."[41] He returns to this exact theme later, in chapter 26, when he considers *mathēsis*, this magical divination via the stars and the reading of signs that never existed in the first place, to be "the way of damnation" as it attempts to pierce the mysteries of God, who would make his plans visible to people if he so wished.[42] For John of Salisbury, these particular astrologers led people to their damnation, and their widespread presence and popularity in royal courts frustrated him so much that he asks: "What more is there to say? Is it not enough that this vanity [of astrology] is detested by the catholic and universal church and that it [the Church] should strike down, with legitimate punishments, those who might presume to cultivate it further?"[43]

John of Salisbury wrote well before the appearance of the devastating crises that struck fourteenth- and fifteenth-century Europe. Yet his arguments against astrology and its popularity in the royal demimonde foreshadowed those that later critics would level. As astrological writings proliferated during the later Middle Ages, ecclesiastical and secular authorities became increasingly concerned about the circulation of these writings and their receptivity by members of both the clergy and the general populace. This growing concern, however, first appeared in the thirteenth century, when Arabic occult and magical matters became increasingly popular among members of the intellectual elite.[44]

The interest in the magical arts, with the potential answers to hidden mysteries that they could provide, was a crucial ingredient of the

---

40. Ioannis Saresberiensis, *Policraticus I–IV*, 115: "Verum mathematici uel planetarii, dum professionis suae potentiam dilatare nituntur, in erroris et impietatis mendacia perniciosissime corruunt."

41. Ibid., 117: "Signa siquidem hominibus data sunt ad eruditionem, non illis qui caelestium conscii secretorum nullis indigent signis."

42. Ibid., 143–46.

43. Ibid., 146–47: "Quid plura? Nonne satis est quod hanc uanitatem catholica et uniuersalis ecclesia detestatur et eos qui eam ulterius exercere praesumpserint legitimis poenis percellit?"

44. Peters, *Magician, the Witch, and the Law*, 85–109.

intellectual renovation of the High Middle Ages. The twelfth and thirteenth centuries saw an important shift within the intellectual and cultural
history of medieval Europe. At that time there was both an increase in, and
transformation of, scientific and mathematic writings, influenced by an increasing influx of Arabic scholarship filtered through Europeans' contacts
with Jewish and Muslim scientific and occult writings in Iberia and the
Middle East. Closely linked with this was the transmission of centuries-
old Greek scientific and philosophical works, especially those attributed to
Aristotle, which Arabic scholars translated and glossed. This information
profoundly affected the intellectual environments of European universities and provided the foundation for an intellectual florescence within medieval culture.

Yet this Arabic literary, philosophical, and scientific corpus also
brought a corresponding interest among university students and faculty
in an assortment of occult practices, including astrology, alchemy, and
various magical rites, which rose more than a few authorities' eyebrows.
As previously mentioned, William of Auvergne was able to attest to the
widespread availability of such texts for students to consult, a situation
that distressed him greatly. Members of the clergy and the laity alike criticized scholars' increasing fascination with these occult texts, especially
when that interest bordered on the heretical. By 1258 Pope Alexander IV
granted inquisitors the right to hunt persons who engaged in divination
and sorcery that clearly reflected "manifest heresy."[45] The situation came
to a head in 1277, when Etienne Tempier, the bishop of Paris, condemned
outright various intellectual positions based upon the philosophies of Aristotle, Averroes, and others, as well as certain practices he deemed occult.[46]
The fascination with the occult as a way to perceive certain hidden wis-
doms, although condemned, did not end, and Arabic glosses on the works
of Aristotle turned the medieval Mediterranean basin into a cauldron of
medical, scientific, and magical development. One particular new Arabic

---

45. Ibid., 99–100. For Alexander's text and accompanying gloss, see *Sextus Decretalium Liber*
(Antwerp: Apud Philippum Nutium sub Ciconlis, 1572): Bk. V, Title II, Chpt. VIII, 633–40.

46. Etienne Gilson, *History of Christian Philosophy in the Middle Ages* (New York: Random
House, 1955), 387–409; Peters, *Magician, the Witch, and the Law*, 90–91; and J. M. M. H. Thijssen, *Censure and Heresy at the University of Paris, 1200–1400* (Philadelphia: University of Pennsylvania Press, 1998), 40–56. The text is published by Henricus Denifle and Aemilio Chatelain, eds.,
Chartularium Universitatis Parisiensis, 1 (Paris: Delalain Bros., 1889), no. 473, 543–44.

text attributed to Aristotle, which appeared in the middle of the twelfth-century, was the *Kitāb Sirr al-Asrār*. The *Book of the Secret of Secrets*, also known as the *Secretum Secretorum*, had a significant influence on establishing the liminal nature of medieval astrology and its application within the royal demimonde, as at least one prominent medieval scholar, Roger Bacon, argued on astrology's behalf, deeming it a valuable discipline for sovereigns to study.[47]

The origins of the *Secretum Secretorum* are shrouded in obscurity, but elements of Aristotelian philosophy clearly appear within it. The work itself is of Arabic origin and is a collection of wisdom attributed to Aristotle, the foremost intellectual authority in medieval understanding, which he supposedly imparted to his pupil Alexander the Great, the supreme representation of secular authority. As it was a compendium of "revealed knowledge of arcana," very few were meant to distribute and understand it.[48] The work originally hails from the tenth century, but in the eleventh and twelfth centuries, additional scientific and occult writings were added, producing a "Long Form" of the text that spanned ten books.[49]

One individual upon whom the *Secretum Secretorum* had great influence was the Franciscan scholar Roger Bacon (ca. 1220-ca. 1292). For Bacon, who developed his own edition of the work, the *Secretum Secretorum* functioned as "a key to the 'true sciences' of astrology, alchemy, and physiognomy, which work 'by art assisting nature' . . . and not by magic or old women's charms."[50] Bacon himself was a luminary within the history of astrology in the Christian West. In contrast to other thirteenth-century Christian scholars, in both the fourth book of his *Opus Maius* and his version of the *Secretum Secretorum*, Bacon took a different approach to astrology by focusing on its utility and acceptability within a Christian framework. For the Franciscan, astrology was neither a heretical discipline nor a vain pastime, but instead a useful tool that was part of the original revelation of God. Bacon, more than other medieval writers, expounded upon the

---

47. William Eamon, *Science and the Secrets of Nature: Books of Secrets in Medieval and Early Modern Culture* (Princeton, NJ: Princeton University Press, 1994), 45–53. I discuss further Arabic contributions to the occult arts in chapter 3.

48. Ibid., 48.

49. Ibid., 45. Steven J. Williams, *The Secret of Secrets: The Scholarly Career of a Pseudo-Aristotelian Text in the Latin Middle Ages* (Ann Arbor: University of Michigan Press, 2003).

50. Ibid., 47.

utility of studying astrology for members of the secular elite. In addition to being religiously orthodox, astrology could be harnessed in service to the state. Bacon believed:

> Astrology does not undermine the doctrine of the free will . . . because true astrologers do not presume to foretell future events with certainty. Instead they foretell future possibilities, which are contingent upon God's will and sufficient causes. Astrology is an essential science for princes because it enables them to prepare for events that are likely to occur. Although these events might be inevitable, foresight might mitigate their impact.[51]

For Bacon, using the stars to foretell future events could grant individuals a powerful degree of agency, as they could use the information to prepare themselves against the upcoming tribulations engendered by the certain arrival of the Antichrist. Like Rupescissa's visionary insight, used to understand better the trauma of the future Apocalypse, Bacon believed that the occult sciences could contribute toward a person's preparation. In Bacon's *Opus Maius*, the stars could pour information upon the senses "with great clarity" and reveal "arcane things of great magnitude."[52] Concerning those arcane matters, the future trauma of the Apocalypse and "the fury of the Antichrist" loomed large, and the stars factored largely with this dramatic narrative.[53] Referencing the *Cosmography* of the ancient astronomer Ethicus, Bacon believed that the stars foretold the appearance of new tribes, especially those of Gog and Magog, who, during the ordeal of the Apocalypse, would adhere to the Antichrist and venerate him as "God of Gods" before he laid waste to the world.[54]

Additionally, the stars could govern all aspects of existence. Citing the *Secretum Secretorum*, Bacon states that "the wisest philosopher Aristotle

---

51. Ibid., 49. See also Roger Bacon, *Secretum Secretorum cum glossis et notulis* (Opera hactenus inedita Rogeri Baconi, fasc. 5) (Oxford: Clarendon Press, 1920).

52. Roger Bacon, *Fratris Rogeri Bacon, ordinis minorum, opus majus ad Clementem quartum, pontificem romanum: Ex MS codice Dubliniensi, cum aliis quibusdam collato, nunc primum editit S. Jebb, M.D.* (London: William Bowyer, 1733), 111 (hereafter referred to as *Opus Majus*); and Kaye, "Law, Magic, and Science," 227.

53. Bacon, *Opus Majus*, 248.

54. Ibid., 190: "Et in cosmographia sua Ethicus astronomus dicit gentes varias debere exire circa dies antichristi, & eum vocabunt Deum Deorum, prius mundi regiones vastaturi." See also Andrew Runni Anderson, *Alexander's Gate, Gog and Magog, and the Inclosed Nations* (Cambridge, MA: Medieval Academy of America, 1932).

teaches Alexander, in the book of secrets, that he should neither eat, nor drink, nor do anything without the advice of an astronomer."[55] More importantly, in the Franciscan philosopher's opinion, the use of astrology was worthy of a Christian sovereign, as long as he did not perceive it as magic.[56] Understandably, this could be difficult for those without the requisite training and education to comprehend those fine distinctions.

For Bacon, astrology could be used in service of statecraft and religious orthodoxy, yet sidereal study nevertheless occupied and maintained a problematic and liminal space through the medieval period. Additionally, Bacon's support of the utility of astrology was in the minority, as medieval critics, drawing upon a tradition that had deep roots, tended more to condemn than to support astrology and its application within elite venues, especially the royal demimonde.

Significant documentary and literary evidence exists from medieval writers who rebuked kings and princes for their interest in divination, necromancy, and the occult.[57] Late medieval authors reviewed astrology, magic, and their popularity among members of the populace. By the late medieval period, astrology was not seen as an appealing body of knowledge that might help a person understand temporal and spiritual mysteries, but instead as something more sinister. More critics began to perceive it as a practice that imperiled people's souls, and practitioners of the occult were increasingly depicted as insidious individuals whose occult actions enchained them to demonic entities. Those diabolic forces were always eager to try to ensnare gullible people, seduced by the honeyed words and duplicitous actions of magicians, and draw them toward damnation. Within this understanding, magicians became detestable.

The infamous medieval figure who represented the untrustworthy and loathsome mage, even linked with the figure of the Antichrist in early Christian apocalypses, was Simon Magus. Found in both the biblical Acts of the Apostles 8:9–24 and the apocryphal Acts of Peter, Simon Magus was the foremost medieval example of the duplicitous magician, one who uses chicanery and ruses to make it appear that he works miracles. In the Acts of

55. Bacon, *Opus Majus*, 246: "ideo Aristoteles sapientissimus philosophus docet Alexandrum in libro secretorum, quod nec comedat, nec bibat, nec aliquid faciat sine consilio astronomi."

56. Ibid., 249.

57. Veenstra, *Magic and Divination*, 9.

Peter, because of his diabolically given wonderwork, in which people witnessed "the dead raised and some healed from various diseases," Simon Magus is able to sway the Roman populace, who "called [the apostle] Paul a sorcerer and a deceiver and [thus] all of the great multitude which had been confirmed in the faith were led astray."[58] It was not just the Roman people whom Simon Magus duped, but also members of the political elite, such as the senator Marcellus, with whom Simon stayed while in Rome. In the thirteenth-century *Aurea Legenda* of Jacobus de Voragine, Simon Magus even circulates with the degenerate Emperor Nero, who favors him highly, thus further attesting to the iniquitous character of the magician.[59]

To win back the belief of the fickle Romans, Peter travels to the city and challenges Simon Magus to engage in a competition of various supernatural deeds. Declaring that he shall manifest all of Simon Magus's "doings . . . as sorcery and magical deception,"[60] Peter consistently works miracles that best Simon Magus's trickeries. The culmination of the contest happens when Simon Magus attempts to raise a dead boy, yet uses deceit to make it seem as if the boy were alive. Peter discovers Simon Magus's fraud and exposes him as such. The Roman populace clamor for the charlatan's blood and fetch tinder to burn him alive, yet Peter admonishes them and warns, "If you continue, the boy shall not rise. We have learned not to recompense evil for evil, but we have learned to love our enemies and to pray for those who persecute us."[61] With the crowd having been stayed, Peter touches the boy's side and tells him to rise from the dead, "and the lad arose, took up his garment and sat and untied his chin."[62]

Jacobus de Voragine's *Aurea Legenda* adds a final touch to the account of the contest between the apostle and the magician. In it, Simon Magus attempts to fly by being borne aloft by demons, but as Peter prays, "I adjure

58. See J. K. Elliott, *The Apocryphal New Testament: A Collection of Apocryphal Christian Literature in an English Translation* (Oxford: Clarendon Press, 1993), 401–20, here 401; Jan N. Bremmer, ed. *The Apocryphal Acts of Peter: Magic, Miracles, and Gnosticism* (Leuven: Peeters, 1998). For more on Simon Magus himself, see Alberto Ferreiro, *Simon Magus in Patristic, Medieval and Early Modern Traditions*(Leiden, Netherlands: Brill, 2005) and for Simon Magus linked with the Antichrist, see Emmerson, *Antichrist in the Middle Ages*, 75–76.

59. Jacobus de Voragine, *The Golden Legend: Readings on the Saints*, trans. William Granger Ryan, 2 vols. (Princeton, NJ: Princeton University Press, 1993), 1:342.

60. Elliott, *Apocryphal New Testament*, 410.

61. Ibid., 420.

62. Ibid.

you, angels of Satan, you who are holding Simon up in the air, I adjure you in the name of Jesus Christ our Lord! Stop holding him up and let him fall," the demons "released him at once," and the magician falls to his doom, "as he crashed to the ground [and] his skull was fractured."[63] The flight of the ruined magician provided an enduring image for later medieval critics of magic, who used it to expose the supposed furtiveness and wickedness of sorcerers. In one extract from the thirteenth-century *Chronicle* of Ralph, abbot of the Cistercian monastery of Coggeshall from 1207 to 1218, the monk discusses an account of a young girl suspected of being a Publican heretic. Contained in the part of the *Chronicle* that spans the years 1176 to 1180, Ralph reports that authorities brought the adolescent before the archbishop of Rheims and his episcopal court to face charges of heresy. Before the assembled ecclesiastics, she took out a ball of thread from her blouse, threw it out the window, yelled "Catch! . . . and was lifted from the earth before everyone's eyes and followed the ball [of thread] out the window in rapid flight, sustained, we believe, by the ministry of the evil spirits who once caught Simon Magus up into the air."[64]

The story of Simon Magus conjures the trope of the magician as fraud, and labeling one's enemy a "Simon Magus," as Benedict XIII's critics had called him for his obstinate refusal to abdicate the papal throne during the crisis of the Great Western Schism, was damning indeed.[65] Besides perceiving him as a modern-day Simon Magus, Benedict XIII's enemies also considered him a demoniac and heretic. In 1409, using the damning rhetoric designed to delegitimize the pontiff and his supporters, the cardinals at the Council of Pisa called him, along with the Geronese Franciscan Francesc Eiximenis, devil worshippers because of their reputed affinity for works of

---

63. De Voragine, *Golden Legend*, 1:344. See also Kieckhefer, *Magic in the Middle Ages*, 34. Valerie Flint discusses alternate accounts in which Simon Magus survives the fall and merely breaks his leg. Ashamed, he later commits suicide. Flint, *The Rise of Magic in Early Medieval Europe*, 121 and 343.

64. Walter L. Wakefield and Austin P. Evans, eds. and trans. *Heresies of the High Middle Ages* (New York: Columbia University Press, 1991), 253. See also Christine M. Neufeld, "Hermeneutical Perversions: Ralph of Coggeshall's 'Witch of Rheims,'" *Philological Quarterly* 85, no. 1/2 (2006), 1–23.

65. Delaruelle, *L'Eglise au temps du Grand Schisme*, 1:95. See also Thomas Prügl, "Der häertische Papst und seine Immunität im Mittelalter," *Münchener theologische Zeitschrift* 47, no. 3 (1996), 197–215.

astrology and alchemy.[66] Yet Eiximenis himself wrote extensively against magical matters, rebuking them unequivocally in his work *Cercapou*.[67] In it, Eiximenis defines the various categories of divination and categorically rejects every one of them:

> divination is done via lots, via magical arts or the constellations of the stars, sun, moon, or other planets or heavenly signs, believing that according to them, one must use free will or has to do good or ill, and similar things; in dreams and necromantic practices, invocations, pacts, or answers from demons, pertaining to hands, facial signs, or other corporeal signals; in divinations that are made by verses from the Psalter or Gospels or other Scriptures. And of using or giving other divinations that are made by people, which are deeds administered by the devil, in diverse manners, such as through elements, circles, *rotulae*, or sacrificial permissions that they make to the devil.[68]

The enduring image of miscreant mages like Simon Magus cast doubt on all late medieval claims to divinatory insight. To set himself apart from such wicked individuals, in his *Liber Secretorum Eventuum* Rupescissa explicitly links the birth of the Antichrist, Louis II, with the sinful magic practiced by a Sicilian sorceress. She fancies herself as having access to secret knowledge in this anecdote, which Rupescissa "learned by the true narration by one worthy priest who was present on . . . Sicily at the time when these events occurred."[69] In Rupescissa's estimation, the witch does not offer knowledge, but instead pure evil:

66. León Esteban Mateo, *Cultura y prehumanismo en la curia pontificia del Papa Luna, 1394–1423* (Valencia: Universitat de Valencia, 2002), 197.

67. For more on *Cercapou*, see Francesc Eiximenis, *Cercapou*, ed. Guiseppe E. Sansone, 2 vols. (Barcelona: Editorial Barcino, 1957–1958); and Guiseppe E. Sansone, "Un nuovo manoscritto di Francesc Eiximenis e la questione del Cercapou," *Filología Romanza* 3, no. 9 (1956): 11–29.

68. Cited in Mateo, *Cultura y prehumanismo*, 198: "en adivinació que 's fa per sorts; en art magica o costellacions de esteles, sol, luna, o altres planets o senyales del cel, creent que segons aquells l'om, de necessitat, use de franch arbitre o haje a fer be o mal, e semblants coses; en sompnis en nigromantichs, invocacions, pactes o respostes de dimoni, esguardaments de mans, philosomia o altres senyals del cors; en adivinacions que's fan per versos del Saltiri o dels Evangelis o altres Escriptures. E de usar o darse en adivinacions altres que's fan per persones qui sont fetes ministres dels diables, en diverses maneres, axí per via de alaments com per cercles, rotols, permissions de sacrificis qui fan al diable."

69. Rupescissa, *LSE*, 216.

Peter, king of Sicily, had many sons by his own queen and wife [Constance], but none had been able to come to maturity. . . . It happened so that the queen, wife of the aforesaid king Peter, became pregnant with a son. . . . One day she became sad and, speaking with her ladies concerning the death of her sons, [said,] "What will I do, since I am pregnant and all my sons die?" One from among her women said to her, "Lady, do not be sad, since in a certain place on this island of Sicily there is a woman who will give you advice so that your sons may live."

The queen, by her womanly character, was very soon joyful, and summoned that woman, who literally was a famous witch, to [come] quickly to her. And the queen exposed her heart to her and asked her whether this sorceress were able to give her advice so that the offspring that she conceived and was carrying in her womb could live, so that her kingdom might not remain without a male heir. The sorceress responded to her, "I firmly promise you, queen, that no child that you carry in your womb may live unless you make him to be called Louis at baptism. And no son of yours will live unless you consent to my words, that the son whom you carry will be called Louis."

The queen suggested to King Peter of Sicily, her husband, that their future son should be called Louis so that he might live; and by importunity, the queen procured from the king what she wished and the newborn son was called Louis. And a little after Peter, King of Sicily, the aforementioned father of Louis, died, the boy Louis obtained the kingdom of Sicily, who holds the island of Sicily until this day.[70]

Immediately following this story, Rupescissa offers the arithmetical proof of Louis's diabolic ancestry, as discussed earlier, in which he adds the numerical values of each letter in Louis's name to arrive at the figure 666. Rupescissa declares Louis as the Antichrist and then concludes his work with a traditional, orthodox invocation to the Trinity, the Virgin Mary, Saint Francis, the apostles Peter and Paul, the saints, and the glory and praise of the Roman Church.[71] Rupescissa's invocation of orthodox principles therefore reinforces his claim to the divine, rather than diabolic, source of his revelation.

One unique rhetorical strategy that courtly critics used to denigrate the occult arts focused on their personal experiences with those disciplines. As

---

70. Ibid., 214–16.
71. Ibid., 217–18.

both the thirteenth-century Oxford scholar Robert Grosseteste and the fourteenth-century Philippe de Mézièrs admitted, so too did William of Auvergne write that he had engaged in an adolescent dalliance with astrology, a pastime he had now outgrown. In William of Auvergne's estimation, like other idolatrous practices, divination was puerile and thus not fit for mature minds.[72] This rhetorical strategy, in which the mature author deliberately puts away the childish things from his youth, attempted to relegate astrology to the margins of intellectual pursuits and cast suspicion on both the intelligence and maturity of those who would adhere to it. A discipline he now rejected as an adult, William of Auvergne denounced his past interest in astrology as simple *curiositas.*

Curiositas occupied a particularly challenging space in Christian theology, because those who wrote against it argued that some people could be tempted to use excessive inquisitiveness to attempt to peer into God's incomprehensible plans. In calling *curiositas* the "lust of knowing unnecessary things," William of Auvergne echoes exactly the position that Augustine of Hippo established in his fourth-century *Confessions.*[73] In the *Confessions*, Augustine considered *curiositas*, along with lust of the flesh and ambition for worldly gain and honors, as a form of concupiscence that was the genesis of all sin. For Augustine, excessive curiosity constituted "lust of the eyes," the organs used to seek out and acquire knowledge, and to know things just for the sake of knowing was a most grievous sin, as it led to pride and one's eventual downfall.[74]

If earlier medieval authors established the problematic space of the stars and magic within the culture of the royal court and called for the punishment of those who held too much stock in such matters, later medieval authors criticized astrology in terms that many people today might find more familiar. Between 1361 and 1365 the philosopher Nicole Oresme (d. 1382), counselor to the French king Charles V (d. 1380), composed the first critique of astrology in the French vernacular, the *Livre de divinacions*, in which he condemned astrologers for deceiving the gullible. And in his 1389 work *Le Songe du Vieil Pelerin*, the chancellor of Cyprus, Philippe de Mézièrs (d. 1405), attested to a dalliance with astrology, to which he succumbed

---

72. Guilielmi Alverni, *De Legibus*, 1:75.
73. Peters, *Magician, the Witch, and the Law*, 90: "libido sciendi non necessaria."
74. Eamon, *Science and the Secrets*, 60.

due to both the foolishness of youth as well as the bad influence of certain wicked Spaniards.[75]

Nicole Oresme railed against the widespread interest in using astrology to divine future events, a practice then *en vogue* in France among members of both the elite and the general populace.[76] In his *Livre de Divinacions*, Oresme took a stance on astrology and divination that was "authorised, orthodox, [and] traditional."[77] The ability to peer into the future, according to Oresme, was awkward, especially in relation to traditional notions of authority, for divinatory insight ran counter to the divinely planned and authoritative order of the universe.[78]

An additional criticism that Oresme leveled against astrology, one that dovetailed with notions of sound secular authority, was that it was unseemly for a king or lord to divine the future or to hold too much stock in astrologers, especially at the expense of his older, more experienced councilors.[79] First, it manifested poor governance: "especially [in] the case that the rulers of this world, who are ordained to govern and preserve their subject people by good counsel, prudence and practice, should not give their minds to belief in divinations."[80] Second, monarchs' undue interest in divination could cost them their lives as well as their kingdoms. Oresme included examples of monarchs from antiquity who were overly interested in astrology, such as Thales of Miletus and Mithridates, as well as lords from more recent history, including Ferrand, the Count of Flanders, and, in an Iberian example, "In our own day we have seen James of Majorca, who was too much given to divinations, and used astrology to choose the

---

75. Philippe de Mézièrs, *Le Songe du Vieil Pelerin*, ed. George William Coopland. 2 vols. (Cambridge: Cambridge University Press, 1969) :II:105, vol. 1:518: "Dont il avint . . . que l'escripvain de cestui Songe demoura un temps avec lesdiz Espaigneulx, et participa avecques eulx comme jeune et fol en dicte science, par telle maniere que le dit escripvain x ans ou xii après qu'il se fu party desdiz Espaigneulx a sa volente ne pouoit pas bien extirper de son cuer les dessus signes el l'effet d'iceulx contre Dieu." Cited also in Veenstra, *Magic and Divination*, 140, n12.

76. Nicole Oresme, *Nicole Oresme and the Astrologers: A Study of His Livre de Divinacions*, trans. George William Coopland (Cambridge, MA: Harvard University Press, 1952), 50.

77. Ibid., 41.

78. Ibid., 28–29.

79. Carey, *Courting Disaster*, 93.

80. Oresme, *Nicole Oresme*, 84: "Or est il ainsi par especial que les prisidens de ce siecle sont ordenez a gouverner et a garder le peuple subset par bon conseil et par bonne prudente et pratique, nom pas a soy occuper no croire a telx divinemens."

hour at which to set out from Avignon on the expedition that cost him his life and his kingdom."[81]

The James about whom Oresme referred was Jaume III of Majorca, Turmeda's former island home, known for its production of astrological and astronomical texts, and it appears that Oresme confused some of the historical issues surrounding Jaume III's death. King Pere III, for whom the recovery and reincorporation of Majorca into the Crown of Aragon was a paramount concern, took advantage of a tangled system of vassalic obligations in order to pursue his designs. King Philip IV of France had pressed upon the lordship of Montpellier, which was part of the kingdom of Majorca. Jaume III, son of Jaume II, was technically the vassal of the count-king of the Crown of Aragon, according to the terms of the 1295 Treaty of Anagni. Jaume III, however, delayed in declaring his vassalage, and King Pere summoned Jaume to his court. This was an almost impossible demand, considering Jaume's need to defend the city of Montpellier against the forces of Philip IV. As a result, Jaume failed to appear before Pere, who declared the king of Majorca to be a contumacious vassal and whose fiefs he confiscated in 1343.

To stave off insurrection, Pere sailed to Majorca and promised the citizens of the island that he would guard their privileges and would call a general legislative *cort* every five years. Pere's troops also captured Perpignan, the capital of Roussillon, and proclaimed a perpetual union of Majorca, Roussillon, and the Crown of Aragon in 1344. Jaume III, a fugitive, ended up selling his rights to Montpellier to the kingdom of France in 1348. Queen Joanna I of Naples provided the renegade vassal with a fleet, but Jaume was defeated and killed on Majorca at the battle of Llucmajor, on August 25, 1349. For Oresme, it was small wonder why Jaume lost both

---

81. Ibid., 72: "Nous avons veu en nostre temps que Jaques, roy de Mallogres, qui estoit trop enclin a tieulx divinemens et eslut heure par astrologie de partir d'Avignon quant il ala ou il perdi la vie et le royaume." For more information, see Joseph F. O'Callaghan, *A History of Medieval Spain* (Ithaca, NY: Cornell University Press, 1975), 415; and Mary Hillgarth and Jocelyn N. Hillgarth, trans. and eds., *Pere III of Catalonia*, 2 vols. (Toronto: Pontifical Institute of Mediaeval Studies, 1980), 1:24–28. For a later example on the belief of interest in divination contributing to downfall, see Estrella Ruiz-Gálvez Priego, "'Fállase por profecía': les prophètes, les prophéties et la projection sociale: Le *Rimado o Cancionero* de Pedro Marcuello et la prophétisme de la fin du XVe siècle," in *La Prophétie comme arme de guerre des pouvoirs, XVe–XVIIe siècles*, ed. Augustin Redondo (Paris: Presses de la Sorbonne Nouvelle, 2000), 75–95.

his kingdom and his life. He was a monarch who was too enamored with astrological matters and, therefore, no sound sovereign, allowing himself to be bullied by Philip and destroyed by Pere.

In light of the ambiguity engendered by the crises of the later Middle Ages, it is understandable why some people might turn to the stars for solace. Not everyone did, of course, and there were certainly those who lived through these crises with nary a worry about the future. However, others hoped the stars and the occult might offer tantalizing glimpses of information about the future. This controversial practice was, within Christian understanding, the domain of the occult and thus fundamentally linked with the diabolic. The archetypical figure of the magician, Simon Magus, who could produce magical wonders only with the aid of demons, confirms this understanding. Those who were overly beholden to astrology and other occult arts were following in the footsteps of the disgraceful mage and, as some feared, were ripe for the plucking by demonic hosts.

The medieval criticism of the occult, in general, and of astrology, in particular, had well-established foundations, as seen in the writings of Augustine of Hippo, Thomas Aquinas, and William of Auvergne. In their estimation, engaging in astrology was suspect and could easily put one in contact with occult and diabolic forces. Despite Roger Bacon's support of astrology as a discipline worthy of kings, other medieval critics, such as John of Salisbury and Nicole Oresme, adapted the theological criticisms of astrology and the occult and applied them to the demimonde of the medieval royal court. They were not the sole medieval critics of courtly astrology, but they were important figures whose condemnation of the sidereal and magical arts refined the earlier positions of other authoritative figures and laid the basis for subsequent medieval and early modern authors' criticisms. These critics of astrology both explicitly and implicitly warned sovereigns from seeking information from the stars, lest they risk losing their reason, intellect, wealth, masculinity, realms, and even their lives. Furthermore, if these kings were exposing themselves, wittingly or unwittingly, to demonic forces who actively sought to defraud humans, they could very well lose their souls.

Despite these authors' criticisms of these allegedly diabolic subjects, in which they denigrated astrology and other magical arts by portraying them as disciplines that appealed to those of a less sophisticated, more immature mind, these occult subjects and principles were nevertheless quite complex and required significant training and education to understand them. This would be expected for those members of the clerical underworld who had the requisite level of education to write about and engage with these difficult subjects. One had to be able to access, read, and, most crucially, comprehend these texts in order to most effectively use the information hidden within them. For the medieval student of magic and the occult, the region of Europe that had some of the greatest texts available for consultation and investigation, in terms of both quantity and quality, lay south of the Pyrenees Mountains, in the land where Gerbert d'Aurillac studied science and the stars.

3

THE IBERIAN PENINSULA

Land of Astral Magic

Eustache was a wicked monk. He was a lout, a wastrel, a scoundrel, and therefore no paragon of Christian virtue. Thus was he portrayed in the thirteenth-century anonymous French poem *Li Romans de Witasse le Moine*, or *Eustache the Monk*.[1] Among his other less-than-fine qualities, however, was that he also dabbled in the magical arts. He did so only after having acquired them in the Iberian city of Toledo, home to Arabic, Jewish, and Christian scholars and translators. It was there where he learned "a thousand conjurations, a thousand *sortilegia*, a thousand vaticinations."[2]

---

1. Denis Joseph Conlon, ed. *"Li Romans de Witasse le Moine." Roman du trezième siècle.* Édité d'après le manuscrit, fonds français 1553, de la Bibliothèque nationale, Paris (Chapel Hill: University of North Carolina Press, 1972). See also Stephen Knight and Thomas H. Ohlgren, eds., *Robin Hood and Other Outlaw Tales* (Kalamazoo, MI: Medieval Institute Publications, 1997). My thanks go to Tom Ohlgren for this reference.

2. Conlon, *Li Romans de Witasse le Moine*, 39: "Il aprist mil conjuremens, Mil caraus, mil espiremens."

The historical Eustache, a northern French priest who lived from around 1170 to 1217, became, not unlike Charlemagne or Ruy Díaz de Bivar, better known as "the Cid," a figure in which myth, legend, and fantasy coalesced around a kernel of historical truth.[3] Even though Eustache's magical abilities are briefly described in comparison with tales of his other skills and exploits, his acquisition of those skills from Iberia nonetheless well illustrates a larger medieval perception of the Iberian Peninsula and the theme of this current chapter: that to other medieval Europeans, Spain was a shadowy land of magic. A supposedly nefarious region no good Christian should visit, lest they be tempted in acquiring secret knowledge aided by demonic agency, the Iberian Peninsula represented, in some medieval writers' understanding, a domain of occult and dark knowledge. The presence there of Jewish and Muslim communities, whose knowledge, culture, languages, and religious practices seemed to some Christians alien, at best, and abhorrent, at worst, contributed to this understanding of Iberia.

Contemporary medieval writers themselves believed Iberians to have a predisposed facility with astrology and for divining the future, which was contextualized within an apocalyptic framework. Dominican and Franciscan preachers, who foretold the advent of the Antichrist and the Apocalypse, were popular in Iberia and, in the case of Saint Vincent Ferrer, even circulated among members of elite social circles. One popular Parisian proverb from the thirteenth century, for example, deemed the Spanish as being the best preachers.[4] Yet another reason why some medieval people may have perceived Spain as a land of prognosticators might be a theory ascribed to the ancient astronomer Claudius Ptolemaeus.

Better known as Ptolemy, his second-century *Almagest*, in which he described the movements of the planets through a rigorous and mathematically complex system of uniform circular motions, was a work of seminal importance for the study of astronomy and astrology.[5] In his *Tetrabiblos*, sometimes referred by its Latin name, *Quadripartitum*, Ptolemy

---

3. Introductions to the study of "the Cid" include R. A. Fletcher, *The Quest for El Cid* (New York: Oxford University Press, 1989); and the classic, yet nevertheless highly problematic, Ramón Menéndez Pidal, *La España del Cid* (Madrid: Editorial Plutarco, 1929).

4. Georges Adrien Crapelet, *Proverbes et Dictons populaires, avec les dits du mercier et de marchands, et les Crieries de Paris, au XIIIe et XIV siècles* (Paris: Impr. de Crapelet, 1831), 82. "Li meillor prégator sont en Espaingne." My thanks go to Michael Sizer for this reference.

5. Smoller, *History, Prophecy, and the Stars*, 13.

systematized various ancient astrological theories that incorporated Babylonian, Egyptian, and Indian knowledge.[6] Because of his sidereal works,
medieval scholars considered Ptolemy one of the foremost ancient authorities in astronomy and astrology and used his authoritative writings to
legitimize their own contemporary views of astrology and astronomy.[7] Nicole Oresme used Ptolemy's geography from the *Tetrabiblos*, for instance,
to shame those members of the French court who dabbled with judicial
astrology:

> Again, according to Ptolemy in the *Quadripartitum*, those who live towards
> the south are more apt for the knowledge of astrology than those who live
> towards the north, and to this Haly adds that those who live towards the
> east are similarly more fitted for it than those who live further west. And
> this is true, and more especially so in the case of judicial astrology. And, ac-
> cording to the opinion expressed by Ptolemy in his *Centiloquium* and also
> according to human reason, those men can profit little in astrology who are
> not inclined thereto by human nature; hence it follows that Frenchmen, and
> still more Englishmen and those further away yet, who live near the con-
> fines of the habitable north or of the west, can commonly have little profit
> from judicial astrology.[8]

For Oresme, the northern French elite should eschew astral matters
entirely. Those "southerners" and "easterners," the individuals of the Mediterranean, were more inclined toward astronomy, astrology, and divination because they were better at those disciplines than their contemporaries
who lived north and west of the Mediterranean. Even though the sunny
sky and temperate climate of the Iberian Peninsula, which lay south of the
cloudy regions of France and England, might lend themselves to astronomical observations, it made sense why Iberia, broadly, and the Crown
of Aragon, specifically, might occupy a space within the medieval mind as
leaning toward astrology and astronomy. The proliferation of late medieval
and early modern astrological and astronomical sources of Catalan provenance has generated a resurgent interest among modern scholars. The

---

6. Ptolemy, *Tetrabiblos*, trans. F. E. Robbins (Cambridge, MA: Harvard University Press,
1940; rev. ed. 2001), 139–45.

7. Smoller, *History, Prophecy, and the Stars*, 15–16.

8. Oresme, *Nicole Oresme*, 86.

Crown of Aragon and the island of Majorca provide important arenas for studying the history of sidereal matters, and until recently scholars had not tapped the well of astrological manuscripts of Iberian origin.[9] Moreover, it was during the reign of Pere III that some of the greatest developments in Catalan astronomy and astrology occurred.[10]

The Iberian Peninsula and its linkages with the occult have been studied largely from a literary perspective.[11] The intellectual output of the substantial and historic Jewish and Muslim communities in the Iberian Peninsula, some of the most cosmopolitan and erudite in all of medieval Europe, particularly fixed the peninsula in many medieval Europeans' minds as a land of magic. A significant product from these communities was their translations and glosses of scientific, astrological, and astronomical writings of all stripes, as Jewish and Muslim scholars wrote upon a host of scientific, philosophical, and occult matters. This corpus of material granted these communities no small amount of intellectual sophistication over contemporary medieval European Christians. Those Jewish and Muslim scholars who lived in the Iberian Peninsula and found themselves residing and working in intellectual centers like Córdoba, Granada, Sevilla, Toledo, Salamanca, Valencia, Barcelona, and, especially for Jews, Gerona, constituted some of the most vibrant intellectual communities in all of medieval Europe.

Astrology was crucial to this intellectual florescence, especially for developments in medical and scientific knowledge.[12] The influence of Islamic science—in particular, upon the improvement of both science and magic in the medieval Christian West and the Iberian Peninsula—cannot

---

9. Lucas, *Astrology and Numerology*, 28–30. For an introduction to medieval Iberian astrology and astronomy, see José María Millás Vallicrosa, *Assaig d'història de les idees físiques i matèmatiques a la Catalunya medieval* (Barcelona: Institució Patxot, 1931); Millás Vallicrosa, *Estudios sobre historia de la ciencia española* (Barcelona: Consejo Superior de Investigaciones Científicas, 1949); and Millás Vallicrosa, *Nuevos estudios sobre historia de la ciencia española* (Barcelona: Consejo Superior de Investigaciones Científicas, 1960).

10. Lucas, *Astrology and Numerology*, 20.

11. See, for instance, Samuel M. Waxman, *Chapters on Magic in Spanish Literature*, PhD dissertation, Harvard University, 1912; Jennifer M. Corry, *Perceptions of Magic in Medieval Spanish Literature* (Bethlehem, PA: Lehigh University Press, 2005); and François Tobienne Jr., *The Position of Magic in Selected Medieval Spanish Texts* (Cambridge: Cambridge Scholars Publishing, 2008).

12. Anna Maria Garbarino, *Donne e medicina nel medioevo: la scuola medica salernitana* (Empoli, Italy: Ibiskos Editrice di Antonietta Risolo, 2005), 20.

be understated.[13] Arabic names of stars, including Aldebaran, Altair, Betelgeuse, and Deneb, in addition to the preponderance of Arabic vocabulary used for sidereal matters ("alidade," "almanac," "azimuth," "nadir," and "zenith," among others), attest to the enduring influence of this Arabic contribution. Furthermore, the Islamic refinement of the astrolabe, a tool known since antiquity, contributed significantly to this intellectual growth.

The astrolabe is a sophisticated measuring device. It consists of a "mother," a circular disk of brass or copper, which has both a graduated circle and an alidade, a sighting strip, on one side. The alidade is fastened directly to the mother and has sighting holes on either end. This device permits great exactitude, close to one degree, in measuring the height of the sun or a star in the sky. The precision provided by this instrument could thus permit medieval astronomers "to measure certain celestial phenomena and express them with numerical precision rather than in vague, qualitative terms. As a consequence, astronomy once more became linked with mathematics."[14]

The astrolabe could also be used for terrestrial engineering, to measure accurately the heights of buildings or towers, and was a necessary tool for maritime navigation. Some believed, however, that the astrolabe could be used in service of the occult. In the *Compilatio Prima* of the *Quinque compilationes antiquae*, there is a letter from Pope Alexander III to the Patriarch of Grado. In the letter a cleric known only as *V* sought to recover stolen Church goods. Somewhat suspiciously, he decided to travel "with several infamous people to a private place" in order to divine the location of these purloined goods with the aid of an astrolabe. Although he did not seek to call up a demon, since juvenile "zeal and simplicity had driven him to do this," he nevertheless engaged in a most impious act and was forced to undergo penance from Alexander.[15] Youthful foolishness in dabbling with the occult, however, could lead others to considerably worse ends, as in one exemplum from the thirteenth-century Cistercian monk Caesarius

---

13. Julio Samsó, *Islamic Astronomy and Medieval Spain* (Brookfield, VT: Variorum, 1994); and Samsó, *Astronomy and Astrology in al-Andalus and the Maghrib* (Burlington, VT: Ashgate, 2007).

14. Olaf Pederson, "Astronomy," in *Science in the Middle Ages*, ed. David C. Lindberg (Chicago: University of Chicago Press, 1978), 303–37, here 309.

15. Peters, *Magician, the Witch, and the Law*, 99.

of Heisterbach. In that anecdote, a lackluster student heeds the devil's advice to engage with magic in order to do well in his studies and accepts a diabolic talisman. Although he improves considerably in his work, he nevertheless feels remorse and ultimately confesses to a priest while he lay dying. Although the priest tells the dying student to discard the talisman, "he dies and his soul is transported into a horrible valley, where spirits with long, pointed fingernails toss him about like a ball and cruelly wound him. God takes pity on him and orders the demons to cease their torture."[16] The student's soul returns to the dead student, who comes back to life, and he is so terrorized by his experiences in the afterlife that he becomes a member of the Cistercian order and, ultimately, the abbot of Morimond.

Despite its potentially occult uses, the importance and contribution of the astrolabe to the development of astronomy and astrology in the medieval West demonstrates the level of intellectual sophistication of Arabic scholarly communities in the Middle Ages. This refinement was a testament to the plurality of cultures within the Mediterranean basin. The intellectual exchanges that took place among these peoples who lived along its coasts and sailed its waters helped contribute to the reckoning of the Mediterranean, and Mediterranean peoples in particular, of having a predilection for divination, especially astral-themed fortune-telling.[17] Additionally, the Iberian Peninsula was the genesis of, and conduit for, important Arabic science and was a popular destination for those who wished to study that subject, influencing well-known scholars such as Daniel of Morley, Adelard of Bath, Roger of Hereford, and Gerard of Cremona, as well as lesser-known ones, like Robert of Chester, Alfred of Sarashel, John of Seville, Plato of Tivoli, Marc of Toledo, and Stephen of Antioch.[18]

One relatively understudied source that sheds light on the intellectual sophistication of the Iberian Muslim communities comes from the

---

16. Cited in Jacques LeGoff, *The Birth of Purgatory*, trans. Arthur Goldhammer (Chicago: University of Chicago Press, 1984), 301.

17. Marie-Thérèse d'Alverny, "La survivance de la magie antique," *Miscellanea Medievalia, I: Antike und Orient im Mittelalter*, ed. Paul Wilpert (Berlin: De Gruyter, 1962), 154–78. David M. Gitlitz, *Secrecy and Deceit: The Religion of the Crypto-Jews* (Albuquerque: University of New Mexico Press, 2002), 184, explicitly links Mediterranean Jews with an affinity for astrology and suggests that the linkage endured well into early modernity.

18. Ṣāʿid al-Andalusī, *Science in the Medieval World: Book of the Categories of Nations*, ed. and trans. Sema'an I. Salem and Alok Kumar (Austin: University of Texas Press, 1991), xxv.

1068 work the *Kitāb Ṭabaqāt al-ʿUmam*, or *The Book of the Categories of Nations*, from the historian and natural philosopher from Almería, Ṣāʾid al-Andalusī (1029–1070). The son of a prestigious judge, Ṣāʾid al-Andalusī moved to the old Visigothic capital of Toledo, known by its Arabic name, Ṭulayṭitilah, when he was around seventeen years old. He most likely moved there for his studies, but little is known about his early years (xi). In the *Kitāb Ṭabaqāt al-ʿUmam*, he divides the known world into two broad groups: those nations that cultivated the sciences and those that did not. Those nations that belong to the former group, and who have "given rise to the art of knowledge . . . [and] have focused their attention to achieve the purity of soul that governs the human race and straightens its nature," include the Indians, Persians, Chaldeans, Greeks, Romans, Egyptians, Arabs, and Hebrews (6, 9). After dismissing those nations that did not cultivate scientific knowledge, whom, with the exception of the Turks and the Chinese, he states, instead "resemble animals more than human beings," (7) Ṣāʾid al-Andalusī discusses the specific offerings that each scientifically minded nation contributed to the body of human knowledge. As might be expected, his chapter on the Muslims of al-Andalus is the lengthiest, and he lists dozens of historic and contemporary Andalusian scholars and scientists. Astrologers were particularly important, as "in al-Andalus, the practice of astrology has met some acceptance, both in the past and the present; there were some well-known astrologers in every period, including our own" (77). One of the most significant contemporary astrologers with whom he corresponded was ʿAbd Allah ibn Khalaf al-ʿIstijī, whom Ṣāʾid al-Andalusī lauds as the foremost astrologer in the history of al-Andalus, as "I do not know anyone . . . past or present, who has known all the secrets and marvels of this science as well as he does" (78).

Even though Ṣāʾid al-Andalusī held astrology and astrologers in high esteem, there were other Jewish and Muslim philosophers and scholars who were highly critical of astrology and of people's fascination with those disciplines. One of those critics was the premier medieval rabbinical authority Moses Maimonides (1135–1204), who hailed from the intellectual center of Córdoba, where he was thoroughly steeped in contemporary, groundbreaking scientific and philosophical writings. In his most important work, *The Guide of the Perplexed*, in which "every word . . . is chosen with exceeding care," Maimonides deals with the scientific nature of astronomy at length.[19] Drawing heavily upon Aristotle's astronomical writings, Maimonides focuses chapters 21 through 24 of his second part of the *Guide* to cast doubt on those who supported the eternality of the world.[20] Yet Maimonides's position on astrology, especially judicial astrology, was another matter entirely.

Judicial astrology was especially controversial for Jewish, Muslim, and Christian critics alike, who argued that adherents to the practice believed the stars determine all that happens in a person's life. Two aphorisms attributed to Ptolemy—"The wise person will dominate the stars" (*Sapiens dominabitur astris*) and "The stars incline, they do not compel" (*Inclinant astra non necessitant*)—sought to dissuade those individuals who held too much stock in the effect that the stars reportedly had upon a person's life.[21] In response to requests for clarification on the subject from his colleagues, Maimonides wrote that judicial astrology constituted nothing but foolishness and folly.[22] In contrast to the rigorous scientific underpinnings of astronomy, astrological points were "far from being scientific; they are stupidity," and Maimonides proclaims no sage would ever "busy himself with this matter or write on it."[23] He also argued that the practice of judicial astrology rejects the dual roots of faith as established by Moses and denies both human freedom and agency, on the one hand, and chance

---

19. Leo Strauss, "How to Begin to Study *The Guide of the Perplexed*," in Moses Maimonides, *The Guide of the Perplexed*, trans. Shlomo Pines, 2 vols. (Chicago: University of Chicago Press, 1963), 1:xi–lvi, here xv.

20. For more on Maimonides and his position vis-à-vis astronomy, see Menachem Kellner, "On the Status of the Astronomy and Physics in Maimonides' Mishneh Torah and Guide of the Perplexed: A Chapter in the History of Science," *British Journal for the History of Science* 24, no. 4 (1991): 453–63, here 455–56.

21. Moriz Sondheim, "Shakespeare and the Astrology of His Time," *Journal of the Warburg Institute* 2, no. 3 (1939): 243–59, here 245; and Theodore Otto Wedel, *The Mediaeval Attitude toward Astrology, Particularly in England* (Hamden, CT: Archon Books, 1968), 135–36.

22. Menachem Kellner, *Maimonides on the "Decline of Generations" and the Nature of Rabbinic Authority* (Albany, NY: SUNY Press, 1996), 114 n25. Kellner cites Moses Maimonides, "Letter on Astrology," trans. Ralph Lerner, in Ralph Lerner and Muhsin Mahdi, eds. *Medieval Political Philosophy* (Ithaca, NY: Cornell University Press, 1972), 227–36; Y. Tzvi Langermann, "Maimonides' Repudiation of Astrology," *Maimonidean Studies* 2 (1991): 123–58; Jacob I. Dienstag, "Maimonides' Letter on Astrology to the Rabbis of Southern France," *Kiryat Sefer* 61 (1987): 147–58; and H. Kreisel, "Maimonides' Approach to Astrology," *Proceedings of the Eleventh World Congress of Jewish Studies, Division C*, 2 vols. (Jerusalem: World Union of Jewish Studies, 1994), 2:25–32.

23. Kellner, *Maimonides on the "Decline*," 62.

and predetermination, on the other.[24] Maimonides recognizes that some scholars would nonetheless search the sacred and authoritative texts of the Talmud and Midrashoth for information, "and find sayings of some individuals sages . . . whose words appear to maintain that at the moment of a man's birth, the stars will cause such and such to happen to him," but he warns:

> Do not regard this as a difficulty. . . . It is not proper to abandon matters of reason that have already been verified by the proofs, shake loose of them, and depend upon the words of a single one of the sages from whom possibly the matter was hidden. Or there may be an allusion in those words; or they may have been said with a view to the times and business before him. . . . A man should never cast his reason behind him, for the eyes are set in front, not in back.[25]

Despite the criticisms of astrology by individuals such as Maimonides, the stars, and the promise of privileged and hidden knowledge that they contained, nonetheless drew Jews and Muslims alike. As such, scurrilous astrologer-charlatans might readily dupe those who consulted the stars, as seen in *The Book of Tahkemoni* by Judah al-Harīzī (1170–1235). In a rhyming prose work that the Jewish author based on the structure of the Arabic work *Maqamat*, the narrator, Heman the Ezrahite, relates the adventures of the wandering scholar Hever the Kenite.[26] In the twenty-second chapter of the *Tahkemoni*, in which Jewish collective fate and astrology are discussed at length, Heman stumbles upon a disconsolate Hever and asks him what misfortunes have befallen him. Hever explains to his associate that he, along with his fellow Jews, "ill-fated and star-led,"[27] came upon an Arab astrologer in a city, a person who spoke "of stars and fate, one who unrobed the future before it came, revealing mysteries that bore no name" (199). In this account the astrologer is clearly painted as an unscrupulous

---

24. Ibid., 63.

25. Ibid.

26. Judah al-Harīzī, *The Book of Tahkemoni*, ed. and trans. David S. Segal (Portland, OR: Littman Library of Jewish Civilization, 2001), also published in "Jewish Listeners and an Arab Astrologer," in Olivia Remie Constable, ed. *Medieval Iberia: Readings from Christian, Muslim, and Jewish Sources* (Philadelphia: University of Pennsylvania Press, 1997), 198–202.

27. Judah al-Harīzī, *Book of Tahkemoni*, in Constable, *Medieval Iberia*, 200.

individual, a provocateur whose abilities are simultaneously elaborate and suspect, yet the astrologer's renown was such that there was nonetheless "a large melee, a swirling tide, men pushing in from every side," (199) who crowded to hear his words.

The Muslim astrologer relied heavily on the stars to legitimate his divinatory pronouncements. Hever related that the seer held a complex astronomical instrument made of copper, most likely an astrolabe, with which he traced the sun's heavenly circuits and thus "learn[ed] the secret laws of sun and moon, the heaven's highroads, the five planets' thoroughfares and byroads" (199). The astrologer told the assembled crowd that his skills in all things sidereal were unparalleled and that he knew intimately the characteristics of all the planets: "Saturn's ills I know, know Jupiter and all the good his to bestow, and warrior Mars of the blood-red glow. I hold the sun in his might, Venus with her delight, Mercury, wise and bright, and the moon of silvered light" (199). Not only did he hold the planets in his sway, but by dominating the allegorical signs of the zodiac, the old sage also made them spill their secrets:

> If Fortune be a throne, I be its legs; if a tent, its pegs. I snap my fingers, the Ram turns lamb; I yoke the Bull and bid him pull; Pollox and Castor call me master; I am the lancer who skewers Cancer; I lift my brows and Leo meows; Virgo, sweet maid, is by me unmade; my mind's fierce flail o'erturns the Scale; the tramp of my feet sounds Scorpio's retreat; I shoot—the Archer makes swift departure; I cut the throat of the bleating Goat; frown, and Aquarius drown; I carve the fish on a serving dish (199).

Hever relates that the seer's skills in divination were such that he was able to "probe the stars' secrets and judge them rightly . . . [and] tell each man where fate will call him and what shall befall him from his first-drawn breath until his death," (199–200) an ability that contributed to his renown and popularity. Hever and his companions decided to test the Muslim astrologer's claims by indirectly questioning him about when the restoration of Israel would occur and what aftermath the Jewish people would face. After the astrologer told Hever and his friends to imprint their handprints on the sand, he began a complex ritual in which he "drew on the sand myriad dots and signs and crisscrossed many lines. Once done [with] these intricate designs he made many a calculation, lifting an astrolabe before his face and fixing the sun in its station; then, with lines for borders and partition, he fixed the ascending planet in its exact position until each star nearly fell from its berth to bow before him to the earth."[28] He then sat silently for a long while.

Even though the ritual involved in predicting the Jews' fate was intricate, there is a note of skepticism in Hever's relation of the events that followed. Although Hever and his friends asked about the Jews' fate obliquely, it was easy for someone to understand what they were getting at; the sidereal ritual of the astrologer, although used to provide an additional level of legitimacy to the seer's utterances, also seemed to function as an elaborate mask for providing an answer already known. Regardless if this ritual were a ruse, the astrologer whipped the city's populace into an anti-Semitic frenzy and called Hever and his associates "accursed . . . Sons of death."[29] The assembled crowd fell upon the Jews en masse and thoroughly abused them before dragging them in front of the magistrate and calling for their punishment. The official was merciful and made a show of imprisoning the Jews for a night, but, upon sunrise, he let them go on their way.[30]

Muslims were also critical of those who believed the planets to have inordinate sway over individual destinies. The tenth-century Iberian scholar Aḥmad ibn Muḥammad ʿAbd Rabbih (d. 940) was best known for his medical and pharmacological writings, as his most famous work was *al-Dukkān* (The Pharmacy Shop). Over the course of seventeen chapters, ʿAbd Rabbih discusses the methods of concocting various potions, unguents, salves, syrups, and powders.[31] Yet he also wrote poetry and used his verse to cut his rivals. Against a certain Abū ʿUbayda al-Laythī, who appears to have had isolated himself from his intellectual peers, ʿAbd Rabbih questions his very

---

28. Ibid., 201. According to the description in the story, it appears the astrologer may have been engaging in a geomantic ritual. For more on this, see Emilie Savage-Smith and Marion B. Smith, "Islamic Geomancy and a Thirteenth-Century Divinatory Device: Another Look," *Magic and Divination in Early Islam*, ed. Emilie Savage-Smith (Aldershot, UK: Ashgate, 2004), 211–76. Astral Magic was not solely the dominion of Islam. See Dov Schwartz, *Studies on Astral Magic in Medieval Jewish Thought*, trans. David Louvish and Batya Stein (Leiden: Brill, 2005).

29. Ibid., 201.

30. Ibid., 201–2.

31. Sami Hamarneh, "Development of Arabic Medical Therapy in the Tenth Century," *Journal of the History of Medicine and Allied Sciences* 27, no. 1 (1972): 65–79, here 76.

intelligence and uses the images of the stars and planets to sting: "You refused but to be different from us; the opinion of those who segregate themselves is never on target. Thus, first, the Qiblah is changeable, but you refused to accept anything in its place. You believe that Mars or Venus controls our destiny, or even Mercury or Jupiter or Saturn. You say that all the creatures are in a sphere that surrounds them and dictates their fate."[32]

There was an established tradition that linked sidereal imagery with magic, divination, and the occult; constellations of astral imagery and rhetoric dot the pages of many a medieval hermetic and occult text. Take the case of the *Liber Antimaquis*, a collection of astrological and magical aphorisms that are drawn from an Arabic corpus of hermetic literature and are supposed to be Aristotle's instructions to his most illustrious pupil, Alexander the Great, in which the philosopher reveals all the secrets of the sage Hermes.[33] In this work, in which, within Western reckoning, the premier intellectual authority distributes knowledge to the supreme secular authority, the stars are undeniably important. The influence of the stars and planets upon the world, which is divided into twelve parts, feature significantly in the fifteenth-century copy of the *Liber Antimaquis*. Throughout the course of the entire work, "Aristotle" repeatedly expounds upon the various effects a certain planet or star would have as it entered the house or exaltation of another heavenly body. They might have beneficial effects on a populace, as when the sun enters the house of Saturn, producing abundance and concord between a people and their sovereign.[34] Alternatively, they could be detrimental, as when Venus enters the exaltation of Mars, generating war, discord, storms, plague, poverty, and drought.[35]

---

32. Cited in Salem and Kumar, *Science in the Medieval World*, 60.

33. Aristotle/Hermes, *Liber Antimaqvis*, ed., Charles Burnett, in *Hermetis Trismegisti: Astrologica et Divinatoria*, ed. Gerrit Bos, Charles Burnett, Thérèse Charmasson, Paul Kunitzch, Fabrizio Lelli, Paolo Lucenti (Corpus Christianorum, Continuatio Mediaeualis, CXLIV C) (Turnhout, Belgium: Brepols, 2001), 179–221, here 179. Almost all of the sources published in this particular volume contain some degree of sidereal writing.

34. Aristotle/Hermes, *Liber Antimaquis*, 200: "Si Sol intrat domum Saturni, mittit illuc spiritum suum fortunatum; ita clima illud erit habundans et populus concordabit cum rege suo."

35. Ibid., 201: "Et quando [Venus] intrat exaltacionem eius [Mars], mittet inter populum illum guerram et discordias, tormenta, pestilencias, paupertatem et malum."

One figure in particular, King Alfonso X, *el Sabio*, or "the Wise," of Castile-León (r. 1252–1284), whose sobriquet attests to his love of learning and scholarship, is crucial for the history of astrology, astronomy, and the occult in medieval Iberia. He was a devotee of the sidereal arts, yet he nevertheless sought to restrict access to those subjects, as seen in his massive thirteenth-century compilation of legal code, the *Siete Partidas*. The compilation of the *Siete Partidas* was begun during the reign of Alfonso X, but they were not formally adopted as Castilian law until the reign of Alfonso XI in 1348.[36] Even though the *Siete Partidas* was mostly composed of seven sections of law—including canon law, public law concerning government and administration, property rights, domestic relations, maritime law, inheritance law, and criminal law—it also addressed the theology and philosophy behind legal explanations. Significant for legal, philosophical, and canonical thought in the Iberian Peninsula, they were also influential for the early modern Spanish empire in the Americas, where they held sway in the Iberian colonies of Louisiana, Texas, and California.

Although the *Siete Partidas* are from Castile and the laws would not have applied to the late medieval Crown of Aragon, there is nonetheless a section germane to the issues surrounding magic and divination. In the seventh section of the *Siete Partidas*, which concerned criminal law, the twenty-third title referenced the legal issues "Concerning Diviners, Fortune-Tellers, Soothsayers, Wizards, and Buffoons."[37] This topic was no mere afterthought within medieval Castilian law. Those jurists and lawyers who compiled the *Siete Partidas* found it of sufficient import that they linked this section with criminal law, the transgressions of which were most detrimental to the integrity of a society. Echoing Aquinas, the legal compilers conceded that "men naturally desire to ascertain coming events," but the danger was that in doing so, "they attempt this by numerous methods, they are guilty of sin and induce many others to do wrong" (5:1431) Legal experts argued that these individuals "[were] very injurious to a country," and the jurists divided this title into three laws.

---

36. See Constable, *Medieval Iberia*, 255; and Samuel Parsons Scott, trans., and Robert Ignatius Burns, ed., *Las Siete Partidas*, 5 vols. (Philadelphia: University of Pennsylvania Press, 2001) (hereafter referred to as *LSP*).

37. *LSP*, 5:1431.

The first law concerned what constituted divination and the multiple rituals and practices that comprised divinatory acts. The jurists defined divination in a straightforward manner, as it "means the same thing as assuming the power of God in order to find out things which are to come," of which there were two types. The first type of divination was accomplished "by the aid of astronomy, which is one of the seven liberal arts," but this type of divination was not illicit if the person who engaged in it was authoritative. That is, only "those who are masters and understand it thoroughly" were able to engage in this type of divinatory activity, because "the conclusions and estimates derived from this art are ascertained by the natural course of the planets and other stars, and are taken from the books of Ptolemy and other learned men, who diligently cultivated the science" (5:1431). The second type of divination, however, was far more dangerous, because it flouted authority and provided access to hidden knowledge for those who were untrained. This was divination that bordered on ritual magic, the type

> practiced by fortune-tellers, soothsayers, and magicians, who investigate omens caused by the flights of birds, by sneezing, and by words called proverbs; or by those who cast lots, or gaze in water, or in crystal, or in a mirror, or in the blade of a sword, or in any other bright object; or who make images of the metal, or any other substance whatsoever; or practice divination on the head of a dead man, or that of an animal, or in the palm of a child, or that of a virgin. (5:1431)

This type of divination was so dangerous to the health of a kingdom, the jurists argued, that the "wicked and deceitful persons" who practiced these acts were forbidden from living within the dominions of Castile (5:1431).

The second law within this title focused on other forms of ritual magic. The jurists labeled "the strange art of calling up evil spirits" as *necromantia*, an injurious practice that sowed much fear and confusion within a society "because those who believe in them and ask for information on this subject suffer many accidents through fear caused by their going about at night looking for things of this kind in strange places, so that some of them die or become insane, or lose their minds" (5:1431). Medieval Castilian lawyers also argued that practices including the creating of wax figures and the administration of herbal tinctures for amorous enchantment were just as dangerous in summoning spirits, because "it sometimes happens that such beverages cause the death of those who take them, and they contract very serious diseases with which they are afflicted for life" (5:1431–1432). Because all of these three practices could potentially end a person's life, the jurists bundled them together.

The third law concerned those who prosecuted "the above-mentioned imposters and swindlers and what penalty they deserve." The law permitted that "anyone of the people" could prosecute prophets and necromancers, and the penalties were severe. Those convicted of these crimes, by witness or by confession, received the death penalty, and those who hid suspected sorcerers in their houses were banished from the kingdom for life. The intention of the practitioner, however, was an important factor. If people practiced enchantments for the good of society, which included exorcising demons from possessed individuals, removing spells that prevented husbands and wives from copulating, or averting natural disasters such as hail and locusts, they were not to be punished. On the contrary, the jurists "decree[d] that [they] shall be rewarded for it" (5:1432). While divining future events was an understandable transgression spurred by natural human curiosity, it was nonetheless dangerous and could have grave consequences.

Despite Alfonso promulgating laws that prohibited people from dabbling with the occult, the king nevertheless took a pronounced interest in the sidereal arts. And the medieval source that best exemplifies the medieval notion that particularly linked "exotic" Arabic astral magic with the Iberian Peninsula would be the Arabic *Ghāyat Al-Hakīm*, known in the West as *Picatrix*. Even though hailing from the Kingdom of Castile, and composed well before Pere and Joan would wear their crowns in Barcelona, *Picatrix* intimately connected the Iberian Peninsula with astrology and the occult arts more than any other medieval sidereal-themed work. Like King Pere and King Joan of the fourteenth-century Crown of Aragon, King Alfonso was a sovereign who actively patronized intellectual and cultural programs, especially those dealing with astral matters, yet Alfonso has been considered by some historians as a lackluster administrator because of his interest in those subjects, a monarch who "pondered the heavens but lost the earth."[38] Alfonso had his scholars translate the work

---

38. Robert Ignatius Burns, "*Stupor Mundi:* Alfonso X of Castile, the Learned," *Emperor of Culture: Alfonso X the Learned of Castile and His Thirteenth-Century Renaissance* (Philadelphia: University of Pennsylvania Press, 1990), 1–13, here 4. The quote comes from the seventeenth-century Jesuit historian Juan de Mariana.

from the original Arabic source, ascribed to the pseudo-Abū al-Qāsim Maslama ibn Ahmad al-Majrītī, into the Castilian vernacular between 1256 and 1258.[39] His encouragement of the translation of the *Ghāyat Al-Hakīm* has provided modern scholars with an invaluable resource to analyze the theory and practice of medieval Arabic astral magic.[40]

Picatrix deals with astral magic, but approaches it largely in a dualist manner. That is, as would be expected, *Picatrix* portrays the spiritual world as superior to the carnal world. The spiritual made its abode in the sidereal heavens, where it was in its purest form, and *Picatrix* was a ladder for those individuals who would wish to harness that spirit to affect the world below, thus connecting the material and spiritual worlds through the actions and words of the operator.[41]

More troubling to some authorities, *Picatrix* was also regarded as a text that bordered on dark magic, as it could be read through a necromantic lens. This was because both astral magic and necromancy relied on the ritual of suffumigation, in which the smoke of magical herbs envelops an image or representative object of an intended recipient for a particular magical process, and rules for suffumigation appear throughout the entire work. Regarding necromancy itself, *Picatrix* occupied an ambivalent space.

---

39. For more on the Castilian translation of this work, see David Pingree, "Between the *Ghāya* and *Picatrix* I: The Spanish Version," *Journal of the Warburg and Courtauld Institutes* 44 (1981): 27–56. For studies on the culture of Alfonso X's court, see Evelyn S. Procter, "The Scientific Works of the Court of Alfonso X of Castile: The King and His Collaborators," *Modern Language Review* 40, no. 1 (1945): 12–29; Procter, *Alfonso X of Castile, Patron of Literature and Learning* (Oxford: Clarendon Press, 1951); and the collection of essays edited by Robert I. Burns, *Emperor of Culture.* For more on depiction of Alfonso X as an unwise king, see Burns, "*Stupor Mundi,*" 4–5.

40. *Picatrix: The Latin Version of the* Ghāyat Al-Hakīm, ed. David Pingree (London: Warburg Institute, 1986), is the sine qua non for all studies on this fascinating source and for studying the intersection of the stars and magic. Although Pingree's is the premier critical edition of the various Latin manuscripts of this work, his work was predated by other scholars. See, for instance, the Arabic version by Hellmut Ritter, *Ghayat al-hakim wa-ahaqq al-natijatayn bi-aitaqdim: Das Ziel des Weisen* (Studien der Bibliothek Warburg 12) (Berlin: B. G. Teubner, 1933); and Ritter, with Martin Plessner, the German translation, *Picatrix: das Ziel des Weisen, von Pseudo-Magriti* (Studies of the Warburg Institute 27) (London: Warburg Institute, 1962); and the Spanish translation by Marcelino Villegas, *Picatrix: el fin del sabio y el mejor de los dos medios para avanzar* (Madrid: Editorial Nacional, 1982). Recently a French translation of the work has appeared by Béatrice Bakhouche, Frédéric Fauquier, and Brigitte Pérez-Jean, *Picatrix: un traité de magie médiéval* (Turnhout, Belgium: Brepols, 2003).

41. Kieckhefer, *Magic in the Middle Ages*, 133.

It is a text that frequently refers to itself as necromantic, possibly as a result of errors in translation from the original Arabic to Castilian, but necromancy was no mere extension of astral magic.[42] In the second chapter of the first book of *Picatrix*, which concerns the definition of necromancy and its properties, the text defines the practice of necromancy as "everything that man labors upon and from which understanding and spirit follow, from that work, through all parts and for wondrous deeds which work, on which account understanding might follow by reflecting upon or admiring it. . . . and generally we say 'necromancy' for all things hidden from understanding and which the greater part of men do not get how they may be or from what causes they may come."[43] Necromancy exists in two parts, one theoretical and the other practical. The theoretical aspect of necromancy focused on "the knowledge of the movements of the fixed stars, because from these, celestial figures and heavenly forms are composed; and how their rays project into the moving planets; and how to know heavenly figures when they intend to make that which they want," whereas the practice of necromancy entailed "the composition of three natures with the virtue of the infusion of the fixed stars; and what the sages call virtue, they do not know of what kind it might be nor how the aforesaid virtue might be attached."[44]

Picatrix is a dense, substantial text that spans four books. The translator's prologue dedicates the work to King Alfonso, who commissioned the translation, and refers to the monarch as "most illustrious king of Hispania and all of Al-Andalus by the grace of God." The prologue continues that the magical text, "compiled from twenty books," was completed in 1256, according to the Western calendar, but in the year 1568 since Alexander the Great's reign, 1295 in the "year of Caesar," and in the Arabic year 655.[45] A compendium of the shared secrets of sages and philosophers, *Picatrix* is a powerful tool of occult knowledge, but one that should be used only "for good and toward the service of God."[46]

The first book of *Picatrix* concerns the sky, the heavenly bodies that dwell within it, and their various effects on images that reflected them

42. Ibid., 166.
43. *Picatrix: The Latin Version*, 5.
44. Ibid., 6.
45. Ibid., 1. See also Pingree, "Between the *Ghāya* and *Picatrix*," 27.
46. *Picatrix: The Latin Version*, 2: "ad bonum et ad Dei servicium operetur."

upon the world below, bridging the terrestrial and celestial worlds. It addresses the general nature of knowledge and argues that the daily increase of knowledge and contemplation of the divine is a "high and noble light," and that studying "is to serve God."[47] By studying, one learns more about the materials that compose the sky and the quality of the celestial spheres themselves. This was crucial to know for the practitioner of astral magic, as the planets' respective characters had a direct influence upon the efficacy of any astral magic conducted in their name. Saturn was cold and dry, whereas Jupiter was hot and moist. Mars had a dry and hot quality to it, and Venus was a little warm but very humid. Mercury had a dry, weak heat, and the moon, understood as a planet in its own right in the Ptolemaic system, was cold and dry.[48]

The first book of *Picatrix* also teaches the basics of the propositions and compositions of the sky and the fundamentals of making images used in performing astral magic. Astral magic could effect beneficial ends—such as producing concord between two people, establishing an enduring love, repelling scorpions, and being a good subject to one's lord and having said lord recognize you as such—as well as harmful ones, including destroying an enemy or laying waste to a city.[49] It discusses the nature of the human body and how it functioned as a world unto itself, a microcosm that directly reflected, and was affected by, the heavenly macrocosmic harmonies.[50]

Book 2 of *Picatrix* delves much deeper into the qualities and natures of the celestial bodies as brought forth in the first book. One can acquire the knowledge of the stars and astral magic solely by consulting the traditional authorities on all sidereal matters; the anonymous author himself refers to his prior study of the *Centiloquium*, attributed to Ptolemy, to understand one of the chief tenets of astral magic: that all the planets and their movements have a direct effect upon everything in the world below.[51]

---

47. Ibid., 4: "lux nobilis et alta . . . Nam studere servire Deo est."
48. Ibid., 8.
49. Ibid., 14–25.
50. Ibid., 25–28. For more on this linkage between the macrocosmic and the microcosmic, see Charles Clark, "The Zodiac Man in Medieval Medical Astrology," *Journal of the Rocky Mountain Medieval and Renaissance Association* 3 (1982): 13–38; and Michael A. Ryan, "Sidereal Remedies: Healing and the Stars in Newberry Library Ayer 746," *AVISTA Forum Journal: Medieval Science, Technology, and Art* 17, no. 1/2 (2007): 8–20.
51. *Picatrix: The Latin Version*, 32.

The author addresses the secrets of the various constellations of the sky and the qualities of the planets, the sun, the moon, and the effects of their interaction with each other, as well. He warns the potential practitioner to be intimately familiar with the principles laid out in this book, especially if he wished to apply the knowledge to the controversial practice of judicial astrology, the secrets of which were powerful but also contributed to the scrutiny and prohibition of the discipline by authorities.[52]

The qualities of the celestial spheres that housed the eight planets and the ninth sphere of fixed stars that revolved around the planets, based on principles stemming from Greek philosophy, focus on the spheres' vitally important circular shape. These represented the perfect form and suggested "inward-looking strength combined with maximal power to influence other beings."[53] The author argues that knowledge of astrology is the root of all magical knowledge as demonstrated by the sidereal and occult writings of the Greeks, Indians, and Chaldeans.[54] The second book also focuses on technically complex procedures that would lay the foundation for all subsequent discussion within *Picatrix* about casting the dozens of diverse spells contained in the tome. *Picatrix* discusses the qualities of frigidness, heat, humidity, and aridity, and how they affect the six orders of all things in nature, and teaches the magician how to inscribe various sigils based on their respective zodiacal signs.[55]

Book 3 of *Picatrix* further links the macrocosmic and microcosmic worlds. The book focuses on the properties and colors of the planets and the specific powers that each planet has for various tasks, as reflected in terrestrial flora, fauna, and minerals. The principle of sympathetic or imitative magic, encapsulated in the phrase *sicut hic, ita illic*, argues that like flows to like. That is, the parts of the plant, animal, or mineral that

---

52. Ibid., 44–45.

53. Ibid., 45. Richard Kieckhefer, *Forbidden Rites: A Necromancer's Manual of the Fifteenth Century* (University Park: Pennsylvania State University Press, 1997), 176.

54. *Picatrix: The Latin Version*, 46: "astrologie sciencia pro radice tocius magice sciencie reputatur."

55. Ibid., 62–74. These six orders were the single and complex combinations of the four qualities; the four elements of earth, air, fire, and water; the four seasons of the year; the four humors of the human body; and the qualities of the parts of plants. For more on magical sigils, see Fred Gettings, *Dictionary of Occult, Hermetic, and Alchemical Sigils* (London: Routledge and Kegan Paul, 1981).

are closely allied with their respective astrological bodies will most effectively receive and respond to the powers of said planet.[56] Saturn is good
for the study of law and profound sciences; Jupiter can help one interpret
dreams. Mars, not surprisingly, helps with the establishment of defensive
structures and for waging war, whereas Venus helps in creating song and
music.[57]

In outlining the planets' important qualities and what professions might
best benefit from them, one of the most relevant parts for occult matters
concerns the planet Mercury. In *Picatrix* Mercury is regarded as the heavenly body that best governs mental acuity, having favorable aspects for
mathematics, wisdom, grammar, philosophy, foreign languages, and the
occult arts, including "astronomy with its judgments, geomancy, the *ars
notoria*, and augury of birds."[58] This connection of Mercury with occult
and rational disciplines is a theme that carries throughout the entirety of
Picatrix. Those individuals who depend on their minds for their livelihood,
including mathematicians, astrologers, scribes, and poets, are encouraged
to petition Mercury for success in all their endeavors, as the planet con-
tributes to sound reason, eloquence and memory, and the knowledge of
all things visible and invisible.[59] Hence, the magician should petition the
planet for "knowledgeable and wise things in interpretation, astrology,
and divination."[60]

The fourth and final book of *Picatrix* delves further into the properties
of the celestial spirits themselves and how working with them always must
be done via images and suffumigations. It contains various astrological authorities' aphorisms regarding astral magic.[61] Forty-five of these are attributed to Babylonian mages, twelve come from the *Centiloquium*, attributed

---

56. Kieckhefer, *Forbidden Rites*, 70–71.

57. *Picatrix: The Latin Version*, 91–93.

58. Ibid., 94. This was a particularly ancient reckoning of Mercury, one that had been expounded upon by Vettius Valens in the second century C.E. and which subsequent authorities, including Pseudo-Manetho in the fourth century and the early fifth-century Hephaestio of Thebes,
continued. See Paul Magdalino and Maria Mavroudi, Introduction to *The Occult Sciences in Byzantium*, eds. Paul Magdalino and Maria Mavroudi (Geneva: La Pomme d'or, 2006), 11–37, here
26–27.

59. *Picatrix: The Latin Version*, 113, 116, 202.

60. Ibid., 133: "petant sciencias et sapiencias in redditibus, arismetrica, astrologia et divi-
nacionibus."

61. Ibid., 173.

to Ptolemy, and other gems of wisdom hail from Greek authorities such as Plato, Hippocrates, and Aristotle.[62] This final book also offers an intriguing bit on the history of the transmission of magical knowledge, as it discusses the contents of some necromantic spells and rites "found in *De agricultura Caldea*, which Abū Bakr Ibn Wahshīya translated from Chaldean into Arabic."[63] Having been discovered within a book on agriculture, it is therefore not surprising that the necromantic and magical rituals contained in this book of *Picatrix* center on plants. There are a great number of spells contained within this chapter, ranging the gamut from spells that heal, to those that kill fleas, to those that repel hail.[64] The book also addresses the properties of other magical substances, such as stones, minerals, and even the bones of a hoopoe, an "extraordinarily crested" bird believed to be especially important for magical and necromantic rituals. Some medieval writers also perceived it to engage in repellent habits such as collecting human dung and eating excrement.[65]

Although a dense tome full of esoteric and alien material, *Picatrix* is nonetheless a fascinating glimpse into one of the most important understandings of medieval magic and its connection to the stars and planets. More than any other text, this collection of Arabic astral magic, translated into Castilian at the behest of Alfonso X of Castile, linked the Iberian Peninsula with magic and necromancy. It was also a text that had a profound influence on both the medieval Arabic and Latin literary traditions. In the Arabic *Qissat Salāmān wa-Absāl* (The Tale of Salāmān and Absāl), which traces the "desperate and tragic love of a youth for his wet-nurse," there is a direct linkage to the many procedures and rituals as referenced in *Picatrix*. The story, ascribed to one Hunayn Ibn Ishāq, was inserted in a

---

62. Ibid., 190–98.

63. Ibid., 205: "De his que ex arte nigromancie inventa sunt in libro De agricultura Caldea, quem Abubaer Abenvaxie de lingua Caldeorum transtulit in Arabicum." Ibn Washiya was a noted authority on botany and the potions and poisons that could be made from plants. See Martin Levey, "Medieval Arabic Toxicology: The Book of Poisons of ibn Wahshiya and Its Relation to Early Indian and Greek Texts," *Transactions of the American Philosophical Society*, New. Ser. 56, no. 7 (1966), 1–130; and George O. S. Darby, "Ibn Wahshīya in Medieval Spanish Literature," *Isis* 33, no. 4 (1941): 433–38.

64. *Picatrix: The Latin Version*, 205–18.

65. Ibid., 218–22. For more on the hoopoe, see Kieckhefer, *Magic in the Middle Ages*, 6 n4; and Alexandra Cuffel, *Gendering Disgust in Medieval Religious Polemic* (Notre Dame, IN: University of Notre Dame Press, 2007), 235.

work of Avicenna, the intellectual authority who connected *Picatrix* with other Arabic Hermetic writings.[66] In this particular anecdote, a magician engages in rituals and rites found and similar to those described in *Picatrix*: he burns resins and prepares suffumigations; his ritual is performed at a time that is most astrologically propitious, when the rays of the specific celestial body being invoked by the magician are able to be most effective; and he prepares an elaborately inscribed talisman, pierced with seven holes, referencing the seven climates into which the world is divided.[67] Thus is *Picatrix* echoed in this contemporary text.

Within some medieval people's conceptions, the stars, magic, and the occult were intertwined inextricably. While I have not discussed every single medieval author who wrote either in support of or against divination, magic, and the occult, as the task would be beyond the constraints of this work, in the first half of this book I have nonetheless staked the intellectual terrain that constructed this reckoning by investigating the positions of some of the more important and authoritative writers. The exact boundaries that separated these disciplines were problematic, nebulous, uneasily reconciled, frequently even blurred, yet the connection nonetheless existed.

Yet I must now reorient the analysis along a different axis. What happened when powerful people, bucking centuries-long proscriptions against magic, divination, and astrology, were interested in these problematic and borderline dangerous and heretical concepts? How did the kings of the Crown of Aragon reconcile their access to bodies of knowledge with their ideas of what constituted their secular authority? To what degree did the kings' position as monarchs protect them from these dangerous pastimes? How did the sovereigns' contemporaries react to their interests and criticize them? Was the Crown of Aragon essentially a "kingdom of stargazers?" These are the questions that I answer in the second half of this book.

---

66. N. Peter Joosse, "An Example of Medieval Arabic Pseudo-Hermetism: The Tale of Salāmān and Absāl," *Journal of Semitic Studies* 38, no. 2 (1993): 279–93.
67. Ibid., 281.

Part II

A Kingdom of Stargazers

4

KINGS AND THEIR HEAVENS

The Ceremonious and the Negligent

In the first half of this book, I investigated the place occupied by astrology and divination within late medieval culture. These disciplines touched upon a number of aspects of medieval life and connected with notions of power and authority, the nature of revelation and intelligence, and the juncture between scientific inquiry and magical practice. In the second half of this book, I discuss the extent to which the interest in prophecy and the occult intersected with the construction of kingship, specifically in the Crown of Aragon. The two fourteenth-century kings I focus on for this chapter are Pere *el Ceremoniós*, the Ceremonious (r. 1336–1387), and Joan *el Caçador*, the Hunter (r. 1387–1396). The starkly divergent characters and regnal styles of these two late medieval count-kings, and their approaches to astrology and the occult, highlight the liminal and shifting status of these disciplines, as well as their intersection with notions about these kings' construction of regnal strength. Both Pere and Joan were interested in astrology, divination, and magic. Yet because Pere was a strong king, whereas Joan was weak, Pere was able to indulge in sidereal and occult proclivities with relative impunity, but Joan was subject to intense scrutiny and criticism for engaging with the same pastimes.

As Pere was a patron of culture and the arts within the royal court, he was also a powerful sovereign who manifested his strength through traditional means, especially the waging of war. Joan, on the other hand, had a different approach to ruling his kingdom. He was an avid sportsman, and the hunt was his favorite pastime, even at the expense of the quotidian administration of his realms. In addition to hunting and the occult, Joan enjoyed trendy fashion, troubadour music, and Provençal literature. Joan's intellectual interests also earned him the lesser-known, and much less flattering, sobriquet of *el Descurat*, "the Negligent."

Even though both Pere and Joan frequently directed their gaze heavenward to better ascertain the future of their domains, in terms of the practical duty of ruling their kingdoms, the two monarchs had very different approaches.[1] These were the premier distinctions that separated the kings and explained why they received different degrees of criticism over their problematic interests. The first, and major, difference was the lengths of their respective reigns. In the history of the kings of the Crown of Aragon, Pere had the second longest reign, which spanned fifty-one years, from 1336 until 1387. Because of his long tenure as king, Pere had many opportunities to enforce his monarchical powers over purportedly rebellious regional lords, to increase the physical territory of the realms that he governed, and to function as a champion of his rights as sovereign of the Crown of Aragon. Compare that with the brief reign of Joan, which lasted only nine years, from 1387 until 1396, cut short because of a tragic hunting accident. Joan had less time to engage in such practices that his father put into motion, but he also appeared to be less able than his father in enforcing those rights.

Additionally, both Pere and Joan governed over a kingdom that faced several significant crises. Like the rest of Europe during the fourteenth century, the Crown of Aragon did not escape unscathed from the many

---

1. For general studies on the history of the Crown of Aragon, see the following works: H. J. Chaytor, *A History of Aragon and Catalonia* (New York: AMS Press, 1969); J. N. Hillgarth, *The Spanish Kingdoms, 1250–1516*. 2 vols. (Oxford: Clarendon Press, 1976–1978); Rafael Tasis i Marca, *Pere el Cerimoniós i els seus fills* (Barcelona: Editorial Teide, 1957); and Thomas N. Bisson, *The Medieval Crown of Aragon: A Short History* (Oxford: Clarendon Press, 1986).

disasters plaguing the continent. The major urban centers of the kingdom, especially Barcelona and Valencia, suffered grave demographic
losses during the arrival and aftermath of the Black Death, which appeared on the eastern shores of the Iberian Peninsula in March 1348, thus
hitting the Crown of Aragon before other Iberian kingdoms. In addition,
the Crown of Aragon suffered from an economic crisis during the fourteenth century that pitted merchants and wealthy citizens against artisans
and artists—the "Busca" and "Biga" conflict—which at times erupted
into outright urban violence.[2] One of the worst outbreaks of violence
within the kingdom occurred in 1391 when a massive pogrom against
Jews in urban centers in the Crown of Aragon took place, a cataclysm
from which the historic Jewish community in Barcelona never recov-
ered completely. Multiple disturbances thus struck the Iberian kingdom
in relatively rapid succession, creating a climate that was conducive for
some people, including secular authorities such as Pere and Joan, to determine what the future held in store. Stronger medieval kings, such as
Pere, were able to dabble with the problematic subjects of astrology and
the occult with far less fear of censure than those who were perceived
to be weaker in mind or kingly mien, such as Joan. The way they, and
others, perceived their application of royal authority demonstrates the
importance of studying the shifting spaces that astrology and the occult
occupied in the locus of the royal court of the late medieval Crown of
Aragon.

One of the most powerful sources that sheds light on the construction of late medieval kingship and authority in the fourteenth-century
Crown of Aragon is Pere III's own chronicle.[3] Regarded by historians
as one of the "four great Catalan chronicles" of the thirteenth and fourteenth centuries—which includes the *Llibre dels feits*, written by King
Jaume I; Bernat Desclot's *Crònica*, which traces the history of the kingdom from the twelfth-century union of Aragon and Catalonia through the
events of the Sicilian Vespers; and the highly patriotic *Crònica* of Ramón

2. Claude Carrère, *Barcelone, centre économique à l'époque des difficultés, 1380–1462*, 2 vols. (Paris: Mouton, 1967).

3. Pere *el Cerimoniós*, *Chronicle*, trans. and eds. Mary Hillgarth and Jocelyn N. Hillgarth, 2 vols. (Toronto: Pontifical Institute of Mediaeval Studies, 1980).

Muntaner—Pere III's autobiographic chronicle functions as a medieval public relations statement, as it were, in which the sovereign outlines his many deeds in great, and self-promoting, detail.[4]

Spanning six chapters and chronologically covering the years 1319 until 1369, the *Crònica* of Pere lauds the king's military deeds and portrays him as a strong, militant sovereign, one concerned with the "glory of his royal House and the expansion of his 'patrimony.'"[5] Yet the *Crònica* is an incomplete narrative of the deeds of King Pere, as it only focuses on thirty years of his reign. The years from 1369 until his death, almost twenty years later, are not recorded in the *Crònica*, but the documents conserved in the Crown of Aragon's state archive help substantiate the record as depicted in the *Crònica*.[6]

Pere had an uneasy childhood. His mother, Teresa of Entença, the Countess of Urgell, died five days before Alfons, her husband and Pere's father, became king of the Crown of Aragon. Alfons's second wife and Pere's stepmother, Leonor of Castile, sought to pave the way for her own children to gain semi-autonomous regions within Pere's royal domains. It was an apprehensive situation for the young Pere, compounded further by his suspicions that Leonor was trying to poison him.[7] The personal character of the king, especially in the realm of Catalan politics, was no small matter. The integrity of the Crown of Aragon, a kingdom that comprised a confederation of states, was perilous, as the division between the existing states of the realm could be profound. This is seen clearly in the 1347–1348 revolt of the *Uniones*, led by Pere's own brothers and which had the support of many of the lords of Aragon, as well as some of the principal cities of the kingdom, most especially Valencia (1:11). Thus, both the king's personal character and the construction of his regnal authority were of singular importance in maintaining the integrity of this confederation, which

---

4. Jaume I, *Crònica, o Llibre dels feits*, ed. Ferran Soldevila (Barcelona: Edicions 62, 1982); Bernat Desclot, *Crònica*, ed. Miquel Coll i Allentorn (Barcelona: Barcino, 1949–1951); and Ramón Muntaner, *Crònica*, ed. J. F. Vidal Jové (Madrid: Alianzo Editorial, 1970). See also J. C. Russell, "Chroniclers of Medieval Spain," *Hispanic Review* 6, no. 3 (1938): 218–35; Ferran Soldevila, *Les quatre grans cròniques* (Barcelona: Selecta, 1971); and Josep Miquel Sobré, *L'èpica de la realitat: l'escriptura de Ramón Muntaner i Bernat Desclot* (Barcelona: Curial Edicions Catalanes, 1978).

5. J. N. Hillgarth, Introduction to Pere el Cerimoniós, *Chronicle*, 1:4.

6. Mary Hillgarth and J. N. Hillgarth, Preface to Pere el Cerimoniós, *Chronicle*, xii–xiii.

7. J. N. Hillgarth, Introduction, 1:4.

could readily fracture. A king who was perceived as weaker, who might prefer to hunt, wear trendy fashion, or chart the stars' courses instead of govern those dominions, was detrimental indeed.

One immediately recognizable way to demonstrate medieval monarchical authority was through the waging of successful military campaigns. For Pere, military endeavors were a permanent fact. It is not surprising to see military might appearing as an important theme within the narrative of the *Crònica* as Pere faced rebellious nobles in Aragon, squared off against one of his principal cities, fought against Sardinian rebels, and eventually engaged in a bitter war with Castile (1356–1366). Yet perhaps another reason why military deeds factor heavily within the narrative of the *Crònica* is that Pere's own military was comparatively weak. Despite his military bravado, the reality was that Pere had a much weaker army at his disposal than his peers. J. N. Hillgarth has assumed a population base for the Crown of Aragon during Pere's reign as approximately one million inhabitants, compared with five million for the rival state of Castile and fifteen million for the kingdom of France. Having fewer people to draw from meant, in the case of armed conflict, Pere would take to the field with a substantially weaker army. Moreover, in the case of defeat, the consequences could be more devastating. Additionally, Pere's naval forces were just as weak as his ground forces by the 1350s. A decade earlier, Catalan fleets conquered the island of Sicily and repulsed invading French forces. By the 1350s, however, Pere needed to supplement his fleet with Venetian galleys purchased abroad (1:13).

The most significant military endeavor that appears in the narrative of the *Crònica* appears in the third, and longest, chapter. It focuses on Pere's acquisition of the island of Majorca, the deed Nicole Oresme referred to in his dismissal of kings' interest in astrology. This conquest of the island of Majorca, in response to the perceived slight from Jaume, Pere's brother and sovereign of the island, fits within the providential tone of the *Crònica*. At many points throughout the chronicle, Pere portrays his actions as guided by God. This, of course, is through his role as a king who, in both his own and in his people's estimation, functioned as "a direct instrument of divine intervention in history" (1:76). Indeed, at points in the chronicle, Pere proclaims himself directly inspired by God in the choice of his decisions. In one instance, having been encouraged by one of his advisers, Bernat de Cabrera, to abandon military hostages by declaring them lost in battle,

Pere initially agreed to the plan, but later changed his mind, declaring, "By the inspiration of God and through counsel We found that leaving the hostages would be a great wrong" (2:418).

The depiction of Pere's moral rectitude is another theme that courses throughout his chronicle. Before his military conflict with the contumacious Jaume, king of Majorca, Pere assembled a force of approximately twelve hundred knights and four thousand pack mules in his retinue. While camping at the site of Jonquera, Pere received a letter from the king of Majorca, delivered by his representative, the Augustinian friar Antoni Nicolau. In the letter the king of Majorca cryptically requests King Pere to "give the friar a secret audience; there is a reason for this" (1:297). Pere drew aside Antoni Nicolau, who spoke to the king about the matter of the ownership of Majorca and whether it was to belong to either Jaume or Pere. Jaume was willing to have a cardinal of Pere's choosing decide the matter. For Pere, this was an inexcusable suggestion, and "without having a discussion with the princes or any one else We at once replied to him [Antoni Nicolau] that We marvelled greatly that the friar, who was such a learned man, should bring Us such credentials and, besides, that the former king should send Us such a message; it appeared he took Us for a child" (1:298). Pere was depicted in the *Crònica* as being aghast at the prospect that "a stranger" should decide the case of Majorca, which Pere believed rightly belonged to him. Moreover, for Pere, the imminent conquest of Majorca was no fault but Jaume's own, for

> We had no covetousness for anything that was his, that We were content with the kingdom God had given Us and that We had bestowed many honors on him, not such as a lord should do to a vassal, but more as to a companion, for We had done him such great honor than We could do no more to the King of France, and he, not content with this, denied Us Our fief and for that reason We had to proceed and take Majorca. . . . We were his judge and his lord in the crime that he had committed and no one else was this (1:298).

Besides his deeds in arms, his increase of lands that comprised the royal demesne, and his use of providential rhetoric in fashioning this program, another way Pere manifested his authority was through his patronage of the arts and sciences. It was during Pere's reign when Catalan astronomy reached its greatest height. Not unlike Alfonso X of Castile, whose courtly culture he actively emulated, or his own son, Joan, Pere was especially supportive of the sidereal disciplines, and he patronized astrologers early in his reign.[8] In March 1349, for instance, Pere requested an astrolabe for personal use, and some years later he wrote to a certain "Master Alfonso," requesting that he translate a book of figures and astronomy from the Castilian Juan Gil de Castiello into Catalan.[9]

Furthermore, Pere encouraged those close to the royal household, such as his own royal physician, Bartomeu de Tresbéns, to study the stars. He also encouraged his other administrators to help the members of his royal household with all their sundry, sidereal-related tasks. In 1360 Pere wrote his lieutenant and justice of Aragon, Johan Lopez de Sesse, ordering him to provide ironworkers from Zaragoza to Bartomeu de Tresbéns for an unnamed project, perhaps related to his astrological work, upon which the physician had been laboring.[10]

Bartomeu was an accomplished astrologer, and his most famous written work was his important treatise on astrology that he wrote in the Catalan vernacular, the *Tractat d'Astrologia*. His astronomical writings were of such quality that in 1371 the young prince Joan requested that Tresbéns send him copies of all of his astrological and medical writings for his own edification.[11] Evidently, in Bartomeu de Tresbéns's sidereal works, the future destinies of the king, the young prince, and the Crown of Aragon itself were intertwined. Three years later, in 1374, Joan wrote to his father regarding some predictions that the physician Tresbéns made in his various astrological writings. He told his father that it was important for them

8. J. N. Hillgarth, *Spanish Kingdoms*, 1:350; José María Millás Vallicrosa, ed. *Las tablas astronómicas del rey Don Pedro el Ceremonioso* (Madrid: Consejo Superior de Investigaciones Científicas, 1962); Millás Vallicrosa, *Nuevos estudios sobre historia*, 279–85. Additionally, Pere supported the works of the Jewish alchemist Magister Menahem. See Raphael Patai, *The Jewish Alchemists* (Princeton, NJ: Princeton University Press, 1994), 235.

9. Antonio Rubió i Lluch, *Documents per l'història de la cultura catalana medieval.* 2nd ed., 2 vols. (Barcelona: Institut d'Estudis Catalans, 2000), 1:155–56 and 164–65.

10. Ibid., 2:131–32.

11. Archivo de la Corona de Aragon, Cancellería Real, Registro (hereafter referred to as ACA, CR, R.) 1739, f. 44; and Rubió i Lluch, *Documents*, 1:250. See also Bartomeu de Tresbéns, *Tractat d'Astrologia*, ed. Juan Vernet Ginés and David Romano (Barcelona: Biblioteca catalana d'obres antigues, 1957).

to meet, since "Your and my faithful physician, Bartomeu de Tresbéns, has told me some words, about which he had spoken with you in Barcelona, touching upon you and me and all your domains and which he found about through the science of astrology."[12] Joan wished to discuss these matters with his father and ensure that what Tresbéns told him agreed with what he predicted to his father.

The royal physician was not the sole intellectual whom Pere encouraged. The king also patronized Dalmau Sesplanes, another renowned astronomer, whose sophisticated astronomical tables and almanac further attest to the high levels of astrology and astronomy in the court of King Pere.[13] The king supported this particular astronomer for quite a while. On October 24, 1359, King Pere wrote his head archivist and told him to permit Dalmau Sesplanes, who was working on his own astronomical work, free reign to consult all the astronomical books housed in the archive, excepting those two Arabic astral works attributed to the eleventh-century Toledan scholar Abenragel.[14] That same day, the king wrote Sesplanes as well, commanding him and another astrologer, Pere Gilbert, to provide him, "without delay," all the information contained within their joint astrological work.[15] Over the course of the next twenty years, King Pere repeatedly requested the products of Sesplanes's knowledge. As late as 1381, Pere requested from the astrologer "a great and solemn work of astrology," which might have been the astrologer's planned magnum opus.[16]

Sesplanes's skill in astrology and astronomy were distinguished. His knowledge about sidereal matters was such that in 1376 King Pere excused him from requisite military service for three years in exchange for his work on the stars.[17] There were other points where Pere was interested in the fate of this particular astrologer. In a more troubling instance, in 1362 Pere wrote the *veguer* of Barcelona on behalf of Bernat Gilbert, the brother of the recently deceased astrologer Pere Gilbert.

---

12. Rubió i Lluch, *Documents*, 2:175.

13. Lynn Thorndike, "Introduction and Canon by Dalmatius to Tables of Barcelona for the Years 1361–1433," *Isis* 26, no. 2 (1937): 310–20.

14. Rubió i Lluch, *Documents*, 1:190. Rubió i Lluch suggested that one of the unnamed works might have been *De judiciis seu fatis stellarum*, "one of the most cited books in medieval libraries."

15. Ibid., 1:191.

16. Ibid., 1:298–99.

17. ACA, CR, R. 1095, f. 47v.

Dalmau Sesplanes was suspected of having been involved in the death of Pere Gilbert, and the sovereign wanted to be kept abreast of this situation, commanding that he be notified immediately if Dalmau were found guilty.[18]

Sesplanes wrote upon a host of astrological and astronomical subjects. In 1379 Prince Joan received a *llibret*, a small book, from Sesplanes concerning solar and lunar eclipses. Like Bartomeu de Tresbéns, it appears that Dalmau Sesplanes used astrology to predict propitious dates for important future events. The same year he received the *llibret*, King Pere wrote the astrologer, requesting from him a list of the days in February, March, or April 1380 that would be most auspicious for a royal wedding for his son.[19]

Commissioned astrological works and the equipment used in creating them were expensive. In 1362 King Pere contacted Berenguer de Reelat and commanded him to pay Sesplanes some fifty florins from one hundred that was owed him already.[20] Yet one of the most spectacular works, in terms of scope, cost, and scale, was the construction of a celestial sphere that the king commissioned from the astronomer in 1362. This particular armillary sphere, constructed using great quantities of gold, precious stones, and expensive pigments, cost hundreds of Barcelonan solidi, much of which came from Sesplanes's own pocket.[21]

As mentioned above, Pere emulated the intellectual atmosphere of the court of the Castilian king Alfonso X. Indeed, drawing upon the Alfonsine astronomical tables the Castilian king commissioned, Pere had his own astronomers produce one of the most important Catalan astronomical works, a new canon of astronomical tables named in honor of the sovereign, the *Canones super tabulis ilustrissimi Regis Petri tertii nomine Regum rex Aragonum*. Pere had his astrologers advance the tables beyond the Alfonsine tables by making newer calculations of the heavens and translating their findings into Hebrew, Latin, and Catalan. Pere's astronomical tables concern the physical and mathematical movements of the heavens and instruct

18. Rubió i Lluch, *Documents*, 2:142–43.
19. ACA, CR, R. 1746, f. 50.
20. Rubió i Lluch, *Documents*, 1:199.
21. Ibid., 2:139–142.

the potential astronomer to figure, among other examples, modes of ascension and declension of heavenly bodies, ascertain their conjunctions in the sky, and how to read solar and lunar eclipses.[22]

As is evident, the monarchs of the House of Aragon were very much involved with sidereal matters. More significantly, astrology and astronomy were disciplines passed on to the children of the royal household as Pere encouraged his children in their astrological pursuits. In 1376 King Pere sent his daughter a small device that told the time by sounding the hours and which also had a miniature astrolabe on it, charting the movements of the stars and displaying the signs of the zodiac.[23] Having a father predisposed toward astrological matters, it is no wonder that the young prince Joan would have been similarly inclined. As mentioned above, in September 1373 Joan requested copies of books on astrology and medicine from Bartomeu de Tresbéns.[24] The prince also wrote to Yusuf Avernarduc, a Muslim doctor, requesting that he find him an astrolabe and books of astronomy in 1378; to the governor of Majorca in 1381 requesting some astrological treatises that Jews from the island had written; and that same year commanded the vice governor of Majorca not to permit the Jewish astronomer Vidal Afrahim to leave the island until he finished composing the astrological works that had been commissioned from him.[25]

If Joan shared the same interest in the stars as his father, he nonetheless had a markedly different method of rule. Compared with his father, Joan was no strong sovereign. Despite his weaker administrative style, by dint of his position as king, Joan was still able to tap in to great reservoirs of power and authority. His status as a monarch granted him enough inherent power to deflect at least initial criticism of his spending too much time at hunting, music, and astrology. However, his perceived frivolities did garner significant criticism from people who were close to him and had firsthand familiarity with his rule.

Not unlike his father, aspects of Joan's childhood appear to have affected his tenure as king. One facet of Joan's childhood history, his poor health,

22. Millás Vallicrosa, *Nuevos estudios sobre historia*, 283–84.
23. Rubió i Lluch, *Documents* 1:284, 265–66.
24. Ibid., 1:264, 250.
25. Ibid., 1:274, 295; 1:287–88, 312; and 1:293, 319.

affected his regnal style significantly, as the adult Joan was hypochon-
driacal. As a prince, Joan was shuttled between various physicians, and
his family paid handsomely for his physicians' services.[26] The fourteenth
century, moreover, was marked by endemic outbreaks of plague; after its
initial outbreak in 1349, subsequent eruptions of plague in the kingdom
appeared for generations.[27] Repeatedly, the historical record indicates that
Joan was greatly concerned about the various outbursts of the disease in
his realms.[28] When the plague became perilously close to the royal person,
Joan took action. In 1395 King Joan, Queen Yolande, and their retinue fled
from Catalonia to Majorca to avoid an outbreak of plague.[29]

If military endeavors were one way through which a medieval sovereign could demonstrate his authority, this lesson was not lost upon Joan.
However, unlike his father, Joan was not able to actively wrest lands from
purportedly contumacious vassals and add to the royal patrimony. On the
contrary, one of the more significant crises that both Pere and Joan faced
was the distinct possibility of losing their domains. The island of Sardinia,
whose leaders and people chafed under Aragonese dominion, engaged in
a violent insurrection against the Catalan-Aragonese forces. The leaders of
the rebellion, the self-styled, messianic-named Judges of Arborea, cast the
struggle of the Sardinians in decidedly apocalyptic terms. Indeed, during
Joan's principate, Sardinia was on the verge of being lost completely.[30] As
such, the rebellion was hard-fought and costly for both Sardinia and the
Crown of Aragon.

The dream allegory of the French author Honoré Bovet (ca. 1345/50–
ca. 1410), the *Somnium super materia scismatis* (Dream on the Matter of the
Schism), which he dedicated to the French king Charles VI, sheds more

26. Daniel Girona i Llogastera, *Itinerari de l'infant en Joan, primogènit del rei En Pere III, 1350–
1387* (Valencia: Impremta de "Fill de F. Vives Mora," 1923), 19, 30, 36, 37, 38, 71, 108, 323.

27. Jean-Noël Biraben, *Les hommes et la peste en France et dans les pays européens et mediterranéens*, 2 vols. (Paris: Mouton, 1975–1976).

28. Daniel Girona i Llogastera, *Itinerari del rei En Joan I* (Barcelona: Extret de la Revista
D'Estudis Universitaris Catalans, 1931), 16, 17, 40, 241–42, 249–50.

29. I am profoundly indebted to Donald Kagay for providing me a copy of his unpublished
article "Poetry in the Dock: The Court Culture of Joan I on Trial (1396–1397)" (paper presented
at the 36th International Congress on Medieval Studies, Western Michigan University, Kalamazoo, MI, May 5, 2001). See also Metge, *The Dream*, xviii.

30. Girona i Llogastera, *Itinerari de l'Enfant en Joan*, 353.

light on the situation concerning Sardinia and the Crown of Aragon. In the 1394 work Bovet takes himself, a dreaming sleeper, on a journey in which he visits the various princes of contemporary medieval Christendom.[31] Bovet was able to draw upon firsthand knowledge for his dream vision, because he circulated within late medieval elite diplomatic and intellectual circles.

After studying law in Montpellier and becoming a member of the Benedictine Order, by 1371 Bovet was prior at the prestigious monastery at Selonnet, a position that permitted him to negotiate the political and diplomatic worlds of fourteenth-century Europe. Most of Bovet's political transactions had centered on the local Angevin court until 1386, when he was drawn into the French royal demimonde. Drawing upon prophecies that circulated at the time, in which it was predicted that a person of royal lineage would end the Great Western Schism and usher in an age of peace, Bovet identified Charles VI as the possible incarnation of this fulfilled prophecy, a position that is reflected in his *Apparicion Maistre Jehan de Meun*.[32] Bovet further earned King Charles's favor with his *L'arbre des Batailles* and, as a result, was sent to represent the royal court on both domestic and foreign missions alike. Included among the latter was his diplomatic stint in the Crown of Aragon, where he stayed for several months between 1387 and 1392. Duke Louis II of Anjou may have sent Bovet to the Aragonese court to help arrange the marriage between Joan and Yolande de Bar, niece of Charles VI.[33] He thus had

31. For more on Honoré Bovet, see Michael Hanly and Hélène Millet, "Les Batailles d'Honorat Bovet: Essai de biographie," *Romania* 114 (1996), 135–81; Gilbert Ouy, "Honoré Bovet (appelé à tort Bonet), prieur de Selonnet," *Romania* 85 (1959): 255–59; and Ivor Arnold, "Introduction," *L'Apparicion Maistre Jehan de Meun et le Somnium Super materia scismatis d'Honoré Bonet* (Paris: Société d'Édition: Les Belles Lettres, 1926), i–xi. See also Michael Hanly, ed. and trans., *Medieval Muslims, Christians, and Jews in Dialogue: The Apparicion Maistre Jehan de Meun of Honorat Bovet: A Critical Edition with English Translation* (Tempe: Arizona Center for Medieval and Renaissance Studies, 2005).

32. This was not restricted to the French sources. The Majorcan convert Anselm Turmeda also prophesizes that a specifically Catalan royal figure would appear to end the turmoil afflicting Christendom, in *P[ro]fecies q[ue] frare encelm turmeda feu el añy mccccv: En tunis de barberia/ço es de algunes cosses esdeuenidores (1405)*. Biblioteca de Catalunya (BC), MS 485, 261r.

33. Hanly, *Medieval Muslims*, 7 n15 and 13. See also Noël Valois, "Un ouvrage inédit d'Honoré Bonet, Prieur de Salon," *Annuaire-Bulletin de la Société de l'Histoire de France* 27 (1890): 193–228.

immediate knowledge of Joan's regnal style and intellectual interests, which functioned as a double-edged sword for the sovereign in Bovet's dream allegory. In the *Somnium* Bovet depicts the count-king of the Crown of Aragon as being more concerned with his own diplomatic affairs than with helping the Church negotiate the trauma of the Great Western Schism.

At the opening of the *Somnium*, Bovet is resting on a *grabatum*, an uncomfortable bed, reflecting on the nature of the Schism, when the allegorical Church, Ecclesia, "both a victim and the embodiment of moral failure," comes to him weeping and distraught because of the fracturing of Christendom.[34] Upon seeing Ecclesia's emotional state, Bovet also becomes distraught and commits his energies to rally the princes of Christendom to help rectify the situation. With Bovet having pledged himself as her champion, Ecclesia then disappears. Even though Bovet wants to forget the vision, he nevertheless follows through on his promise to Ecclesia, traveling to the bridge of Blind Ignorance and meeting the guards War and Opinion. The allegorical figure of Sweet Speech comes to guide the dreamer past the guards into a palace that lay beyond the bridge, in which he will meet with the various territorial princes of Christendom and "reliv[es] . . . a number of his real previous journeys and diplomatic missions in the framework of a vision."[35]

The dreaming Bovet visits twelve princes in all, whose domains cover the length and breadth of Christendom.[36] Among them is Joan *el Caçador*. Before meeting with Joan, Bovet is distraught because of the other kings' inability to help him and, by extension, Ecclesia. Upon beholding Joan, however, Bovet is cheered, exalts the monarch, and relates his vision yet again. After he finishes, Bovet excitedly tells the king, "And behold, lord King, why I came, and I rejoice in finding you, not doubting certainly

---

34. Blumenfeld-Kosinski, *Poets, Saints, and Visionaries*, 141.

35. Ibid., 142.

36. Ibid., 142 n21. These sovereigns include Charles III, king of Navarre; João I, king of Portugal; King Robert III of Scotland; Joan *el Caçador*, count-king of the Crown of Aragon; King Enrique III of Castile; King Jacques I of Cyprus; Sigismund, king of Hungary, with whom Bovet has the longest dialogue in the *Somnium;* Louis II, Count of Anjou and king of Jerusalem and Sicily; King Richard II of England, with whom Bovet also has a substantial visit; Jean of Valois, the Duke of Berry; Philippe II *le Hardi*, the Duke of Burgundy; and, finally, King Charles VI of France.

that you hold the aforesaid lady [Ecclesia] in great reverence and honor."[37] Joan listens to the diplomat who formerly visited his court and explains to Bovet that he is unable to help, as he was currently fighting for his domains. He explains to the sleeping prior that he was embroiled in a costly and significant war against the Judges of Arborea on Sardinia. As a result, he has lost many Catalan soldiers. Moreover, his younger brother, Martí, faced insurrection on Sicily.[38] Joan also refers to the poor state of finances of the kingdom, of which Bovet was aware, saying, "You frequented our palace and lived with my subjects for many months not so long ago."[39] He therefore must excuse himself from rectifying the Great Western Schism. In the allegory Bovet is undaunted and passionately presses King Joan to consider the sorry state of the Church and come to Ecclesia's aid, but Joan ultimately tells him, "Dearest, you argue too much with me. And because we struggle more with our own discomforts, and we see the weight and burdens by which now the Holy Church is pressed, we dare not begin what you demand and therefore we pray you leave us in peace."[40]

In light of his problems abroad and at home, it is small wonder why Joan appeared to be more interested in his pastimes. As a devotee of hunting, music, fashion, astrology, and the occult, he was tapped into, and actively contributed toward, a cultural network of which his other contemporary secular contemporaries were a part. One way Joan contributed to this network was through sharing his interest in sidereal matters with his social and political peers. For example, Jean, Duke of Berry, became Joan's brother-in-law after Joan's marriage to Yolande de Bar. The two nobles freely lent each other books on astrology and astronomy.[41] Additionally,

---

37. Bovet, quoted in Arnold, *L'Apparicion*, 73: "Et ecce, domine Rex, quare veni, et vos gaudeo reperisse, pro certo non dubitans quod vos prefatam dominam habeatis in magnis reverentia et honore."

38. Ibid., 73.

39. Ibid.: "dudum per multos menses nostrum palacium frequentasti, et cum regnicolis habitasti."

40. Ibid.: "Carissime, nimis contra me arguis. Sed quia magis propria certamus incomoda, et videmus pondus et onera quibus nunc premitur Sancta Ecclesia, non sumus ausi ingredi que desposcis; et ideo rogamus, nos in pace relinquas."

41. Alejandro García Avilés, "Two Astromagical Manuscripts of Alfonso X," *Journal of the Warburg and Courtauld Institutes* 59 (1996): 14–23, here 20. See also Rafael Olivar Bertrand, *Bodas reales entre Francia y la Corona de Aragón: política matrimonial de los príncipes de Aragón y Cataluña, con respecto a Francia, en el siglo XIV* (Barcelona: Editorial Alberto Martín, 1947); and García Avilés, "Two Astromagical Manuscripts," 20 n39.

they shared their specialists in the stars, as evidenced by correspondence from 1388 in which Joan requested that the renowned Parisian astrologer Guillem Lunell be permitted to travel from France to Aragon.[42] Joan was already familiar with the quality of Lunell's work, having paid the astrologer some thirty gold Aragonese florins almost four years earlier, in 1384.[43]

As mentioned above, these works were costly. Some years later, as king, Joan requested from his treasurer the funds to pay another of his astrologers, one "Master" Ramar, the promised quantity of forty Aragonese florins.[44] Astrologers occupied powerful positions in King Joan's court and were close to the king. In 1389 King Joan wrote his vassals in the Crown of Aragon, declaring the Jewish astrologer Cresques de Vivers to be "[my] familiar and my astrologer" and demanding that his vassals give him all due respect as such.[45]

However, Joan sometimes also dabbled in activities that were far more problematic than astrology, as in September 1386, when he requested to consult a book of geomancy, a complex divinatory practice that involved discerning patterns of the future through figures that appeared when a clump of dirt was thrown or when random lines were drawn.[46] Some medieval writers decried this art as an occult science that drew its power from diabolic forces.[47] In addition, in the summer of 1390 King Joan wrote the governor of Roussillon to requisition all of the books on necromancy that the priest Blas de Corbera had in his possession.[48] Queen Yolande also shared many of her husband's interests in less than orthodox practices. During a bout with a grave illness in 1387, Yolande requested to consult a magical book written by the bishop of Lérida and Tortosa, Jaume Cigó, and thus titled *Cigonina*, to help her ward off the effects of witchcraft.[49]

---

42. García Avilés, "Two Astromagical Manuscripts," 21. The letter has also been referenced in Rubió i Lluch, *Documents*, 1:354.

43. Rubió i Lluch, *Documents*, 2:278.

44. Ibid., 2:333–34.

45. ACA, CR, R. 1896, f. 46–46v.: "familiarem et strologum meum."

46. Rubió i Lluch, *Documents*, 1:344.

47. Veenstra, *Magic and Divination*, 239.

48. ACA, CR, R. 1959, f. 59v.

49. Rubió i Lluch, *Documents*, 1:378. For more on *Cigonina*, see Félix Torres Amat, *Memorias para ayudar a formar un diccionario critico de los escritores catalanes* (Barcelona: Impr. de J. Verdaguer, 1836), 179; and José Coroleu, *Documents historichs catalans del sigle XIV* (Barcelona: Impr. la Renaixensa, 1889), 127.

To my knowledge, there is nothing in the historical record that indicates that the inquisitor general of the Crown of Aragon, Nicolau Eymerich, was aware of Yolande's wanting to investigate a book of magic. However, the queen's request for this book likely would not have sat well with him, as Eymerich took a dim view on magic and those who would patronize it. In part two of his 1376 work the *Directorium inquisitorum* Eymerich wrote about magic at length. Specifically, he focused on the issue of heretical magic in *quaestiones* 42 and 43, which respectively addressed divination via lot-casting and demonic invocations.[50] For Eymerich, there were two types of magicians and diviners. The first type included those individuals who judged the future condition of people from natural effects. These included chiromancers, who determined a person's future by regarding the lines that stretched across a person's palm. The more problematic magicians and diviners, however, were those who

are contracted to heretics, as are those who show the honor of *latria* [venerating God] or *dulia* [venerating holy individuals and saints] to the demons, who rebaptize children and do other similar things. And they do these things in order to foresee the future or penetrate to the innermost secrets of the heart. These people are guilty of manifest heresy. And such magicians and diviners do not evade the judgment of the Inquisitor, but are punished according to the laws pertaining to heretics.[51]

In requesting *Cigonina*, Queen Yolande did not appear to be engaging in either the practice of *latria* or *dulia*, yet she skirted dangerously close to precarious practices, and Joan and Yolande patronized the occult arts that rankled Eymerich so.

While the monarchs of the Crown of Aragon sometimes dabbled in affairs that were somewhat less than orthodox, they also sought to control access to the occult, especially when they perceived that the interest bordered on the diabolic. Popular anti-Semitism, which manifested itself to destructive effect during the 1391 pogroms within the Crown of Aragon, smeared Jews as being in league with the demonic, as seen in the slur of blood libel, in which Jews were believed to convene in

---

50. Peters, *Magician, the Witch, and the Law*, 196.
51. Ibid., 197.

secret to conduct nefarious rituals, including various occult practices, host whippings, and the slaughter of Christian children.[52] Even though the king attempted to protect Jewish communities in his domain, secular authorities sometimes targeted those communities in search of suspected occult practices. For instance, in 1380 King Pere ordered that proceedings begin against a Valencian Jew, Salamies Naci, accused of invoking demons, and in 1381 the king investigated other Jewish and Muslim men and women reported to have invoked demons.[53] Joan was involved in this type of hunt as well. During Joan's principate, he requested that the bishop of Valencia investigate the matter of Christians rumored to be summoning demons in the home of a Jew.[54] Yet Jewish astronomers occupied positions of great power and influence in Joan's court, as evidenced in the case of the official astrologer to King Joan, the aforementioned Cresques de Vivers.[55]

When Joan ascended to the throne as king, his interest in the occult did not abate. In fact, King Joan confiscated magical items, books, and artifacts from some individuals. In 1387 he requisitioned the occult books of Ponc de Jovals, as well as all of his astronomical instruments.[56] Additionally, in 1391 King Joan demanded a goat's horn inscribed with arcane symbols found in the possession of Miguel Perez de Guardia.[57] Even though it was tempting to access the powerful and esoteric secrets of the occult, such access needed strict control, because not everyone was permitted to interact with that body of knowledge.

The memory of Pere and Joan's devotion to astrology echoed generations after their death. One of the most significant, and understudied, sources that specifically recollects King Pere's interest in astrology comes

52. For Jewish-Christian violence in the Crown of Aragon, see David Nirenberg, *Communities of Violence: Persecution of Minorities in the Middle Ages* (Princeton, NJ: Princeton University Press, 1996). For the blood libel in Europe, see, among others, R. Po-chia Hsia, *The Myth of Murder: Jews and Magic in Reformation Germany* (New Haven, CT: Yale University Press, 1988) and Miri Rubin, *Gentile Tales: The Narrative Assault on Late Medieval Jews* (New Haven, CT: Yale University Press, 1999).
53. Rubió i Lluch, *Documents*, 2:232; ACA, CR, R. 1375, f. 193v.
54. ACA, CR, R. 1662, f. 35.
55. ACA, CR, R. 1896, f. 45. For more on Cresques de Vivers, see also ACA, CR, R. 1697, f. 106.
56. Rubió i Lluch, *Documents*, 1:349–50.
57. Ibid., 2:325–26.

from the manuscript of Pere Miquel Carbonell's (1434–1517) *Dança de Mort e de aquelles persones qui mal llur grat ab aquella ballen e dançen* (The Dance of Death and of Those People Who Unwillingly Dance with It). Housed in the archive of the Crown of Aragon under the "Miscellaneous Manuscripts" section of the royal chancellery, Carbonell's *Dança de Mort* has been published previously.[58] It is a translation of a traditional French *Danse Macabre* that levels medieval society, having emperor, pope, king, bishop, and the rest of medieval society take their turn at the dance with Death. Carbonell appended a section to his translation, however, in which he had various contemporary members of the royal archive, bureaucracy, and court of Fernando *el Católico* dance with the allegorical figure of Death.[59]

After the various bureaucrats take turns dancing with Death, an addendum to the text provides a tantalizing glimpse concerning the constructed memory regarding the long-dead King Pere. Beginning on folio 200 of the manuscript, this is a copy of a "letter" supposedly written by King Pere to his son, Joan, in November 1369, chastising him for marrying against his father's wishes.[60] This refers to the conflict between Pere and Joan over the prince's decision to marry Yolande de Bar, and in a series of rhyming couplets attributed to the king, Pere lays out the potential consequences of his actions. He warns Joan that he could end up in hell or, at the very least, lose his great inheritance by denying his father's wishes.[61] In discussing the defunct King Pere, the anonymous scribe who recorded these couplets

58. Pere Miquel Carbonell, *Dança de Mort e de aquelles persones qui mal llur grat ab aquella ballen e dançen*, ACA, CR, MS Misc. 26, ff. 140–62v. See also *Colección de documentos inéditos del Archivo de la Corona de Aragon*. Barcelona: J. E. Montfort, 1847–1910. Carbonell's work has also been published in Joël Saugnieux, *Les Danses Macabres de France et d'Espagne et leurs prolongements littéraires* (Lyon: Emmanuel Vitte, 1972): 213–25.

59. Florence Whyte, *The Dance of Death in Spain and Catalonia* (New York: Arno Press, 1977), 30, has deemed Carbonell to be an uncreative author, as a result. A more recent and comprehensive study of the genre of the *Danse Macabre* in medieval and early modern Europe, with a special focus on Iberia, is that of Víctor Infantes, *Las Danzas de la Muerte: Génesis y desarrollo de un género medieval (siglos XIII–XVII)* (Salamanca, Spain: Ediciones Universidad de Salamanca, 1997).

60. ACA, CR, MS Misc. 26, ff. 200–201v. The piece begins and is dated on f. 200: "Record com en lo libre o Registre cubert de pergami Secretari del Rey en Pere de aquest nom Terç Rey de Arago: trobareu en lo Segon quiuern de dit Libre vna Lettra/que Lo dit Rey fae a son primogenit don Ioan reprenent aquell de hauer fet matrimoni contra sa voluntat e consell." I further discuss Pere's displeasure with Joan's decision to marry Yolande in chapter 5.

61. ACA, CR, MS Misc. 26, f. 200v.: "En infern ab lo demoni . . . Quen perdes tan gran heretat."

granted him an additional level of intellectual legitimacy by calling him "a great troubadour and a learned man in astrology and other liberal arts, well-read, and a good writer."[62] Although the focus is on Pere's literary skills, it is nonetheless telling that the sole liberal art that the scribe referenced was that of astrology.

Although Pere and Joan were father and son, they were two very different kings. All medieval sovereigns had great reservoirs of power at their disposal, but that power was not unlimited. The recognition and enforcement of monarchical rights, and the application of monarchical authority, was a constant struggle for medieval kings. Unlike his father, Pere, Joan, a much weaker king, was unable to tap into that reservoir of monarchical power and use it to the same degree of success. Even though Pere had inherently controversial intellectual interests, his own levels of power and authority prevented others from making too significant a criticism. When Joan ascended to the throne as the new king, he continued his problematic practices and pastimes from his principate and spent a large amount of royal resources upon them. This, in addition to his lackluster administrative style and indifference in resolving the crisis of the Great Western Schism, made him the perfect target for censure.

By the end of the fifteenth century, King Pere's interest in astrology and the occult in his lifetime had gained him posthumous fame as a renowned astrologer in his own right. This astral interest he passed on to his son. Unlike his father, however, who faced rebellion, extended the royal domains, and fought against Castile, King Joan was neither as strong nor as effective. His undue interest in the occult and astrology could thus not be easily reconciled or ignored by some of his critics. People reacted to these monarchs' interests in the subject of astrology and divination in direct response to the level of authority each respective king demonstrated. Joan's interest in such matters at the expense of governing his kingdom soundly engendered significant controversy during the king's lifetime, and his contemporaries criticized his undue interest in occult and sidereal matters. It is to those criticisms that we must now turn.

---

62. ACA, CR, MS Misc. 26, f. 200: "en lo peu dela qual ha sobre aquesta materia vnes cobles compostes per lo dit Rey lo qual era gran trobador e home docte en Astrologia/e en altres arts. Liberals /e molt Litterat/e bon Scriptore."

5

TO CONDEMN A KING

The Inquisitor and the Notary

The ghost of King Joan decided to pay Bernat Metge a visit. After falling into a restless sleep, one that a feverish or starving person might have,
the distraught scribe saw the shade of the dead king standing before him,
"accompanied by two very tall men. One was young, very handsome, and
in his hands he held a rota; the other was very old, with a long beard and
no eyes, and he held a staff in his hand. And all around these two there
were many falcons, goshawks, and dogs of all kind, crying and howling
most hideously."[1] Thus opens Metge's magnum opus, titled *Lo Somni*, or
The Dream. Metge's work, composed soon after King Joan died, is a dream
allegory, a popular genre of medieval literature that frequently functioned

---

1. Metge, *The Dream*, 3. Bernat Metge, *Lo Somni*, ed. and trans. Lola Badia (Barcelona: Quaderns Crema, 1999), 53: "E acompanyaven-lo dos hòmens de gran estatura, la u dels quals era jove,
fort bell e tenia una rota entre les mans; e l'altre era molt vell, ab llonga barba e sens ulls, lo qual
tenia un gran bastó en la mà. E entorn de tots los dessús dits havia molts falcons, astros e cans de
diversa natura, qui cridaven e udolaven foro llejament."

as a vehicle for political criticism and a mirror of current affairs. As such, Metge's literary work is a significant critique of his late patron's actions.

In this chapter I analyze two significant sources that evidence contemporary criticisms of King Joan's problematic intellectual interests. Two individuals, Nicolau Eymerich, the inquisitor general of the Crown of Aragon during the reign of King Joan, and Bernat Metge, the personal scribe to both King Joan and Queen Yolande de Bar, composed trenchant commentaries that allude to Joan's pastimes. Eymerich and Metge had different backgrounds and personalities, which colored their texts accordingly. Their two seemingly dissimilar texts provide an opportunity for modern scholars to analyze comparable perceptions of Pere III's son and successor to the throne, Joan. The principal theme that runs through these two works is the king's interest in divining the future, especially through astrological means, which both writers view as a vanity that imperiled the king's soul. To divine the future by investigating the courses of the stars and planets that wheeled above one's head was a dangerous pursuit for anyone, regardless of whether a crown rested upon that head. It was perilous precisely because divining the course of the future was in fact an attempt to peer beyond one's mortality, to know what was meant to be unknown—the will of God.

A major difference between the two works is that Eymerich criticized the king in a seemingly detached, almost clinical manner, whereas Metge was more direct in his criticisms, having the king suffer explicitly for his actions. Granted, the king was dead at the time Metge was writing, but Eymerich wrote his treatise while in exile, so both texts could be, and were, read through a lens of relative safety. With these two texts we have some of the clearest depictions of how members of the ecclesiastical and secular elite viewed the act of divining the future during the later Middle Ages.

Joan *el Caçador*, the Hunter, reigned as king of the Crown of Aragon from 1387 to 1396. He died prematurely on May 19, 1396, when he fell from his horse in hot pursuit of a stag in the woods of Gerona, slipping into a coma from which he would never recover. His death set into motion a series of events that would be unfortunate for Bernat Metge, as well as for the other "new men" who packed the royal court of Joan and Yolande de Bar. Among these individuals were the astrologers who were an integral part of the royal household and court and who were actively patronized by the sovereigns, themselves interested in books of prophecy and astrology.

Joan's interest in astrology was not without suspicion. Some of his critics charged that he was overly preoccupied with it, as well as with other "frivolities."[2] Nor was Joan the most financially savvy of monarchs; his lavish appointments to court seers, musicians, and poets, as well as his passion for hunting, nearly brought the court to financial ruin. His predilection for divination and astrology has led some modern scholars to label the king "a featherheaded escapist" or "extraordinarily unstable and superstitious."[3] To discredit Joan as such, however, misses the historical importance of astrology and divination at a time when the occult was viewed as a tool for gaining access to powerful and privileged knowledge.

Nicolau Eymerich and Bernat Metge were closely linked to the network of royal power within the Crown of Aragon and, as such, held unique positions from which to offer telling critiques of Joan's problematic practices. Eymerich had a volatile relationship with both Joan and his father, King Pere III. In 1375 Pere had banished the inquisitor Eymerich from his realms, and a similar fate would befall him during Joan's reign.[4]

Eymerich's relationship with King Pere had always been tense, principally because of the inquisitor's condemnation of twenty books authored by the Majorcan philosopher and mystic Ramon Llull (1232–1315). Eymerich had persecuted a group of Valencian Llullists who were inspired by the ideas of the heretical Spiritual Franciscans and who adhered to the controversial messages contained within Llull's alchemical and divinatory writings, which they read in an eschatological manner. Eymerich's dogged hounding of these Valencian Llullists culminated in his condemnation of Llull's many, especially occult, works.[5] These actions, however, brought

2. See ACA, CR, R. 1955, ff. 108v.; R. 1956, ff. 73, 185; R. 1958, ff. 22, 188. See also Kagay, "Poetry in the Dock," 10 n32.

3. Kagay, "Poetry in the Dock," 2, references J. N. Hillgarth, *Spanish Kingdoms*, 2:223, and Tasis i Marca, *Pere el Cerimoniós i els seus fills*, 141. See also José María Roca, "Johan I y les supersticions," *Boletín de la Real Academia de Buenas Letras de Barcelona*, 10 (1921): 125–69.

4. Rubió i Lluch, *Documents*, 1:261–62. For exile, see the work most recently by Stephen J. Milner, "Exile, Rhetoric, and the Limits of Discourse," in Stephen J. Milner, ed. *At the Margins: Minority Groups in Premodern Italy* (Minneapolis: University of Minnesota Press, 2005), 162–91.

5. Anthony Bonner, ed. and trans., *Doctor Illuminatus: A Ramon Llull Reader* (Princeton, NJ: Princeton University Press, 1993), 57–58. See also Eufemià Fort i Cogul, *La inquisició i Ramon Llull* (Barcelona: Rafael Dalmau, 1972); and, more significantly, the many works of Jaume de Puig i Oliver, "El procés dels lul·listes valencians contra Nicolau Eimeric en el marc del Cisma d'Occident," *Boletín de la Sociedad Castellonese de Cultura* 56 (1980): 319–463; Puig i Oliver,

anger from all levels of Catalan society, including from King Pere, who had many of his own difficulties with Eymerich, known for his zeal in pursuing individuals suspected of heterodoxy, including those close to the crown. In 1371, for instance, Pere commanded the councilors of Barcelona to prohibit Eymerich from preaching against Micer Francesch Roma, a royal chancellor who had fallen afoul of Eymerich, in the city's cathedral.[6]

Unlike his father, Joan had managed to maintain a cordial relationship with Eymerich and, upon Eymerich's return to the kingdom in 1381, supported him in his capacity as *inquisitor haereticae pravitatis* (inquisitor of heretical depravity). Joan's backing of Eymerich displeased Pere, who, when he learned of it, sent his son a heated missive. Appalled at Joan's audacity in permitting Eymerich to be present in Barcelona against his wishes, Pere commanded his son to imprison Eymerich and not to give him any assistance ever again.[7]

Exactly what impact Pere's directive had on Joan and Eymerich's relationship is unclear, but in 1387, at the start of his reign as king, Joan supported Eymerich's stances by prohibiting the teaching of Ramon Llull's doctrines throughout his domain.[8] By 1393, however, the relationship between the two men had fractured completely, leading to Eymerich's second exile from the kingdom. Writing to his secular and ecclesiastical administrators across his domains, Joan referred to Eymerich as a pestilential man and a public enemy, a wolf from whom the shepherds of the Church must protect their flocks, and, most damning of all, a "son of wickedness" and

---

"El '*Dialogus contra lluistas,*' de Nicolau Eimeric, O.P. Edició i estudi," *Arxiu de textos catalans antics* 19 (2000), 7–296; and Nicolau Eymerich, *Diàleg contra els lul·listes,* ed. Jaume de Puig i Oliver (Barcelona: Quadrens Crema, 2002). For the ultimate position on the orthodoxy of Llullist doctrine, see Puig i Oliver, "La 'Sentència definitive' de 1419 sobre l'ortodòxia lul·liana: Contextos, protagonistes, problemes," *Arxiu de textos catalans antics* 19 (2000): 297–388.

   6. Rubió i Lluch, *Documents*, 1: 234–35. Eymerich continued this practice upon his return to the kingdom. See Richard Kieckhefer, *Repression of Heresy in Medieval Germany* (Philadelphia: University of Pennsylvania Press, 1979), 6–7.

   7. Eymerich, as a Dominican, was part of an order known for producing inquisitors. For a good survey, see Edward Peters, "*Quoniam abundavit iniquitas:* Dominicans as Inquisitors, Inquisitors as Dominicans," *Catholic Historical Review* 91, no. 1 (2005): 105–21. Jaume de Puig i Oliver, "Documents inèdits referents a Nicolau Eimeric i el Lul·lisme," *Arxiu de Textos Catalans Antics* 2 (1983): 319–16, here 328.

   8. Rubió i Lluch, *Documents*, 1:347–48.

"venomous viper."⁹ The monarch warned his administrators against providing any solace or assistance whatsoever to the exiled friar, lest they earn
the king's full wrath and indignation.¹⁰

Who, then, was this Dominican inquisitor who earned the wrath of
kings? Born in 1320 in Gerona, an important intellectual center of the
Crown of Aragon located approximately one hundred kilometers north-
east of Barcelona, Nicolau Eymerich entered the Dominican Order at
fourteen years of age.¹¹ In 1357 he was appointed inquisitor general of the
Crown of Aragon after the departure of his predecessor, Nicolau Rossell,
who vacated the position upon his elevation to the rank of cardinal. As
inquisitor general of the Crown of Aragon, Eymerich held jurisdiction in
Catalonia, Aragon, Valencia, and the Balearic Islands, a position he re-
tained until the time of his second exile, in 1393.

Although inquisitors did not reach the same levels of power and influence in the Crown of Aragon as they did in other regions of Europe,
there was still plenty of anti-heretical activity to keep inquisitors engaged
throughout the fourteenth century.¹² Starting in 1325, during the reign of
Jaume II, increased inquisitorial proceedings took place against the radical
supporter of the Spiritual Franciscans and resident of Montpellier, the supposed "heresiarch" Na Prous Boneta. Boneta came under the inquisitors'
gaze after she housed persecuted Spiritual Franciscans and denounced
Thomas Aquinas and Pope John XXII, both of whom attacked the writings of Peter John Olivi, as malicious and diabolic figures.¹³ Olivi was a

9. ACA, CR, R. 1927, ff. 97v.–98v.: "ipsum iniquitatis filium ymo potius venenosam viperum."

10. The scribe who copied down Joan's decree was none other than Bernat Metge. ACA, CR, R. 1927, f. 98v.

11. For the most recent biography of Eymerich and an assessment of his body of works, see Heimann, *Nicolaus Eymerich (vor 1320–1399)*.

12. The subject of medieval heresy and orthodoxy is one about which scholars have spilled gal-lons of ink. Some overviews of the subject include, but are not limited to, Henry Charles Lea, *History of the Inquisition*, 3 vols. (New York: Macmillan, 1887–1922); Gordon Leff, *Heresy in the Later Middle Ages: The Relation of Heterodoxy to Dissent, ca. 1250–ca. 1450*, 2 vols. (Manchester: Manchester University Press, 1967); and Edward Peters, *Heresy and Authority in Medieval Europe* (Philadelphia: University of Pennsylvania Press, 1980). For Iberia, see Marcelino Menéndez y Pelayo, *Historia de los heterodoxos españoles* (Madrid: Librería católica de San José, gerente V. Sancho-Tello, 1880–1881); and Julio Caro Baroja, *Vidas magicas e inquisicion*, 2 vols. (Madrid: Taurus, 1967).

13. At this time, Montpellier had been part of the Crown of Aragon for a while, since the 1204 marriage between Pere of Aragon and Marie of Montpellier. For more on Na Prous Boneta,

central figure for the Spiritual Franciscans and was roundly damned by some members of the Church because of his support of the controversial doctrine of apostolic poverty, which he contextualized within an apocalyptic framework. As a result, in 1326 Pope John XXII condemned him posthumously as a heretic. Around the time of Boneta's Inquisition trial, an inquisitorial commission in the Crown of Aragon indicated that a notary in Gerona, a certain Guillem de Quer, had decided to destroy his copy of Olivi's commentary on the Apocalypse when he heard that the Church had condemned it.[14]

Edward Peters has claimed that the Crown of Aragon was unique among other contemporary medieval states, since there had been comparatively less recorded activity of persecuting heretics in that kingdom. He has also argued that the papacy's focus on establishing an inquisitorial apparatus in this Iberian kingdom, accomplished in 1254 with the support of King Jaume I, was because of its geographic proximity to Languedoc, from which Cathar heretic refugees might flee into the Crown of Aragon, "and not the consequence of any noticeable Iberian divergences from the faith."[15] Peters further suggests that the system of the Inquisition did its work so well that from the later thirteenth century onward, "there is little trace of heresy of any kind in the Iberian peninsula."[16]

---

see Louisa A. Burnham, "The Visionary Authority of Na Prous Boneta," in Alain Boureau and Sylvian Piron, eds., *Pierre de Jean Olivi (1248–1298): Pensée scolastique, dissidence spirituelle et société: actes du colloque de Narbonne, mars 1988* (Paris: J. Vrin, 1999), 319–39; Burnham, *So Great a Light, So Great a Smoke: The Beguin Heretics of Languedoc* (Ithaca, NY: Cornell University Press, 2008); and David Burr, *The Spiritual Franciscans: From Protest to Persecution in the Century after Saint Francis* (University Park: Pennsylvania State University Press, 2001), 230–37.

14. Burr, *Spiritual Franciscans*, 233. For this, Burr relies on Josep Perarnau, "Opere di Fr. Petrus Johannis in processi catalane d'inquisizione della prima metà del XIV secolo," *Archivum franciscanum historicum* 91 (1998): 505–16.

15. Edward Peters, *Inquisition* (Berkeley: University of California Press, 1988), 76–77.

16. Ibid., 76. Along with Richard Kieckhefer, "The Office of Inquisition and Medieval Heresy: The Transition from Personal to Institutional Jurisdiction," *Journal of Ecclesiastical History* 46 (1995): 36–61, here 56–57; Henry Ansgar Kelly, "Inquisition and the Prosecution of Heresy: Misconceptions and Abuses," *Church History* 58 (1989): 439–51; and Mark Gregory Pegg, *The Corruption of Angels: The Great Inquisition of 1245–1246* (Princeton, NJ: Princeton University Press, 2001), 32–34, Peters has stated that "the Inquisition" is reserved for standing early modern organizations, such as the Spanish Inquisition, whereas looser structures of the Middle Ages should use the lowercase "inquisition." Even though the Crown of Aragon's Inquisition would disappear, to be reconstituted under the offices of the Spanish Inquisition in early modernity, it nevertheless had a standing inquisitorial apparatus supervised by different official inquisitor generals during the

The records from the diocesan archive in Barcelona, however, demonstrate significant inquisitorial activities taking place within the kingdom. In 1330 two women, Na Guillelma and Na Geralda, were brought before the inquisitorial apparatus for engaging in various suspect activities, including *sortilegia*, or divining the future via lots.[17] In 1345, inquisitorial proceedings started against the wife of one Ramon de Campis, who was suspected of heretical depravity and ordered to be imprisoned.[18] In addition, in 1354 a group of Franciscan friars suspected of heresy stood before the bishop of Barcelona and other secular and ecclesiastical administrators to have their orthodoxy investigated.[19]

Such activities were not restricted solely to the city of Barcelona, for it is evident that ecclesiastical authorities scoured the surrounding areas in search of heretics and Spiritual Franciscan sympathizers. Yet those were not the only individuals for whom authorities searched: reports of local officials' visits to various parish churches show their concerns about the possibility of public divination and witchcraft taking place within their parishes, practices they considered *peccato publico*. In 1366, for example, a local man named Ramon Cauleroni was reported to be a seer, and in 1378, 1382, and 1388 the bishop of Barcelona visited the parish churches of Panades, Ecclesia de Gavano, and Santa Maria de Cubellis where he had reportedly learned of individuals engaging in divinatory activities.[20]

Middle Ages. I thus use the capitalized form of the word. For the payment to these medieval inquisitors in the Crown of Aragon, see Jaume de Puig i Oliver, "El pagament dels inquisidors en la Corona d'aragó els segles XIII i XIV," *Arxiu de textos Catalans antics* 22 (2003): 175–222.

17. Arxiu Diocesà de Barcelona (ADB), Notularum Communium, 10 mai 1325–13 augusti 1330; R. 4, f. 251. By the later Middle Ages, *sortilegia* would be applied almost universally to any cases involving suspected magic. See G. R. Owst, "Sortilegium in English Homiletic Literature of the Fourteenth Century," *Studies Presented to Sir Hilary Jenkison*, ed. J. Conway Davies (London: Oxford University Press, 1957), 272–303.

18. ADB, Notularum Communium, 9 kalendas martii 1344–13 kalendas decembris 1345; R. 13, ff. 102v.–103v.

19. ADB, Notularum Communium, 27 iunii 1353–14 februarii 1355; R. 18, ff. 131v.–132.

20. I consulted these specific registers at the Hill Monastic Manuscript Library at St. Joseph's University in Collegeville, Minnesota, and so I have included their HMML accession numbers in the citation. For Ramon Cauleroni, see ADB, Visitations 5 bis, f. 30v. (HMML Source: 31957), and for the later fourteenth-century visits, see ADB, Visitations, 7, ff. 47, 242, 263, 274v.–275v. (HMML Source: 31959). For references to divination as *peccato publico*, see ADB, Visitations, 8 (HMML Source: 31960).

The Inquisition was no doubt a powerful vehicle that enabled the Church to impose its authority over the less powerful, but it was also more than that. It was, in fact, a complex system that functioned within specific religious and cultural parameters, of which the occult arts played an important part.[21] Because members of the social and cultural elite were presumed to be proponents of orthodox behavior and practice, their dabbling in practices that clerical authorities viewed with suspicion thus tested the limits of what was considered orthodoxy.

Returning to Eymerich, what appears to have concerned him specifically about Ramon Llull was Llull's construction of a unique and original body of thought that purported to comprehend the totality of existence, as seen in his *Ars compendiosa inveniendi veritatem* (Compendious Art of Finding Truth). Provided one understood Llull's elaborate system, it is possible that the universal and divine secrets of Christianity could be unlocked.[22] This system, according to Llull, was divinely inspired, as his art came to him in a sudden flash of insight, not unlike that of John of Rupescissa's visionary understanding about the course of the future. Before receiving his divine revelation, Llull sequestered himself physically from society by ascending a mountain. There he spent almost an entire week in meditation, when "the Lord suddenly illuminated his mind giving him the form and method for writing the aforementioned book against the errors of the unbelievers."[23] Llull's writings could be, and were, read within an occult framework; consequently, Llull's name became linked to magic and the occult, a connection that endured long after his death. In the sixteenth century, John Dee, personal mage and adviser to Queen Elizabeth

---

21. Christine Caldwell Ames, "Does Inquisition Belong to Religious History?" *American Historical Review* 110, no. 1 (2005): 11–37; and Ames, *Righteous Persecution: Inquisition, Dominicans, and Christianity in the Middle Ages* (Philadelphia: University of Pennsylvania Press, 2009).

22. Bonner, *Doctor Illuminatus*, 18. See also the works by Mark D. Johnston, *The Spiritual Logic of Ramon Llull* (Oxford: Oxford University Press, 1987); and Johnston, *The Evangelical Rhetoric of Ramon Llull: Lay Learning and Piety in the Christian West around 1300* (New York: Oxford University Press, 1996). See also Erhard-Wolfram Platzeck, *Raimund Lull, sein Leben, seine Werke, die Grundlagen seines Denkens (Prinzipienlehre)*, 2 vols. (Düsseldorf: L. Schwann, 1962–1964); and Anthony Bonner and Lola Badia, *Ramon Llull: Vida, pensament i obra literària* (Barcelona: Empúries, 1988).

23. Anthony Bonner, *Selected Works of Ramon Llull (1232–1316)*, 2 vols. (Princeton, NJ: Princeton University Press, 1985), iii, 14. This passage is also cited in David Abulafia, *A Mediterranean Emporium: The Catalan Kingdom of Majorca* (Cambridge: Cambridge University Press, 1994), 13.

I of England, owned a compendium of Llullist works that focused on a variety of alchemical and magical matters.[24]

In 1376 Eymerich wrote his most famous work, the *Directorium Inquisitorum* (The Manual for Inquisitors), a text so popular during the period of European inquisitorial proceedings in the late sixteenth and early seventeenth centuries that it was reedited five times in a span of less than thirty years.[25] It was not his sole written work, however. During the last decade of the fourteenth century, when Joan reigned, Eymerich leveled some of his most vitriolic criticism against practitioners of the occult, especially alchemists and astrologers.[26] In 1395, while residing in Avignon, Eymerich sent to Thomas Ulzine, a Franciscan friar who was King Joan's confessor, the missive *Contra astrologos imperitos et nigromanticos* (Against Foolish and Necromantic Astrologers).[27] In this unpublished work, which spans fourteen folios, Eymerich carefully and deliberately details the composition of the celestial spheres and the nature of the heavenly bodies that dwell within them. He closely links the practice of using astrology to divine the future with twenty other divinatory arts, all of which rely upon demonic aid and agency.[28] In the prologue to the treatise, the letter to Ulzine that directly concerns the subjects that interested King Joan, he writes that those who would perceive the hidden things of both past and future did so in vain. Neither science, nor experience, nor astrology could permit the revelation

---

24. Beinecke Rare Book and Manuscript Library, Mellon Collection of Alchemy and the Occult, Yale University, Ms. 12. ff. 168–168v. and ff. 217–18 concern, respectively, the *secreti oculti* and the *magna magica* of Llull's alchemical writings. Before entering Dee's hands, it had been owned by George Ripley in 1473 and was then passed to Sir Robert Greene of Welbe.

25. Nicolau Eymerich and Francisco de la Peña, *Le manuel des inquisiteurs*, trans. and ed. Louis Sala-Molins (Paris: Mouton Éditeur, 1973), 14. Between 1578 and 1607, Eymerich's work was reedited three times in Rome, in 1578, 1585, and 1587, and twice in Venice, in 1595 and 1607.

26. Thorndike, *HMES*, 3:515. See also Heimann, *Nicolaus Eymerich*, 151; and Sylvain Matton, "Le traité *Contre les alchimistes* de Nicholas Eymerich," *Chrysopoeia* 1 (1987): 93–136. See chapter 6 for more on Eymerich's attack against alchemy.

27. BnF, MS lat 3171, ff. 81–90v.

28. BnF, MS lat 3171, f. 87v.: "Sed quod .xx. artes diuinandi seu de occultum judicandi amet habeatur seu magis demonum consilio sunt reperte que artes sunt ipse ars nigromancie ars phitomancie ars aereomancie ars ydromancie ars piromancie ars aeromancie ars geomancie ars ydolomancie ars ymagionmancie ars spaculomancie ars prestigiomancie ars sompniomancie ars notomancie ars auguriomancie ars aruspiomancie ars sorciomancie ars purgomancie ars onomancie ars ciromancie ars geomedomancie/hec sunt artes seu modi xx de occultum huiusmodi."

of the occult, which remained hidden from human perception by divine necessity.[29] Indeed, attempting to rely upon the heavenly signs to ascertain future events brings people directly into congress with the demonic, and anyone who would encourage people to engage in this tendentious practice would merit being judged a necromancer.[30]

Another important treatise that Eymerich wrote while in exile presents a rich source for the history of apocalypticism and discernment in late medieval Europe: *Contra praefigentes certum terminum fini mundi* (Against Those Who Appoint a Certain Fixed Date for the End of the World).[31] This particular work, which I discuss at length, reflects Eymerich's criticism of a practice to which Joan was enamored and that Bernat Metge refers to in *Lo Somni:* that of attempting to peer beyond the veil during a time of widespread crisis to perceive, and thus prepare for, the future end of the world. This was undoubtedly a widespread practice in Eymerich's day, one that would soon attract serious attention from the Church; indeed, at the Fifth Lateran Council of 1516, with the promulgation of the decree *Supremae majestatis praesidio*, any and all attempts to ascertain the arrival of the Antichrist or the date of the end of the world were condemned formally.[32] But Eymerich's treatise predates this bull by almost 125 years. Eymerich wrote *Contra praefigentes* during his second exile, addressed it to Bernardus Strucci, the abbot of the Benedictine monastery of Rosis, and finished it on March 25, 1395. Using biblical exegesis and the writings of the doctors of the Church to support his arguments, Eymerich tackled twenty questions concerning themes such as the world's eternality and endurance, the presence of the Antichrist in the world, and the outcome of the Final Judgment.[33] He railed against people who tried to peer

29. BnF, MS lat. 3171, f. 81: "Occultis preteritis et futuris nouit que nos homines. Neque experiencia neque sciencia. Neque asencia. Neque astrolegia nostra possimnus penetrare."

30. BnF, MS lat. 3171, f. 81: "Incidant in nigromanciam vt merito magis nigromantici quod astrolegi sint censendi."

31. I am doing a critical study of this treatise, which remains unedited. There are two copies, in Biblioteca Nacional de España (BNE) MS 6213, ff. 217r.-242r, and BnF, MS lat. 3171, ff. 58–75. Eymerich's treatise *Contra astrologos imperitos* follows, BnF, MS lat. 3171, ff. 81–90v. See also Thorndike, *HMES*, 3:513–15.

32. McGinn, *Antichrist*, 189.

33. Nicolau Eymerich, *Contra praefigentes certum terminum fini mundi:* Biblioteca Nacional de España (BNE) MS 6213, f. 218.

into the future and comprehend the divine course of events. He began by citing Paul's Epistle to the Romans:

> O height of knowledge of divine matters and of the wisdom of God, how incomprehensible are His judgments and searchable His ways. For indeed, by clerical witness, we are not able to penetrate the height of the sky, the breadth of the earth, and the depth of the ocean. How, then, may we understand with apostolic chanting the infinite divine wisdom that is its height, breadth, sublimity and depth? For it dwells within an inaccessible light into which no one of man was able to insinuate himself.[34]

To divine the future, according to Eymerich, was the height of hubris for humans, whose intellect necessarily functioned within divinely prescribed parameters. Seeing into the future denied those parameters and granted people the illicit opportunity to glimpse the ineffable plan of God.

Eymerich's treatise drew upon a long tradition of Christian proscriptions against attempting to ascertain the exact date of the End Times. Patristic authors, including Augustine and Jerome, used the biblical passage from Acts 1:6–7 as the primary biblical reference to reject divinatory endeavors.[35] Following in their footsteps, Eymerich offers a substantial text, divided into twenty *quaestiones* and covering some twenty-five folios.[36] Throughout the work, he touches upon apocalyptic themes and refers to apocalyptic rhetoric and imagery as it concerns people's attempts to ascertain information about the end of the world and the arrival of the Antichrist. For Eymerich, these "secret mysteries of the height of divine knowledge and wisdom are hidden from human notice," and such mysteries include the knowledge about the end of time, the arrival of the Antichrist, and the consummation of the world. Those who would attempt to divine those secret mysteries did so in grave error. They were, in Eymerich's estimation, engaging in a fundamentally diabolic practice, and the artificial information that they offered made them deceivers and seducers of others.[37]

---

34. Romans 11:33; and Eymerich, *Contra praefigentes certum terminum fini mundi*, BNE MS 6213, f. 217r.

35. Pascoe, *Church and Reform*, 28. Acts 1:6–7: "Therefore those who had convened asked him [Jesus], saying 'Lord, if you will restore the kingdom of Israel in this time?' He said to them, 'It is not yours to know the times or the moments which the Father placed in his power.'"

36. Emmerson, *Antichrist in the Middle Ages*, 74–107.

37. BNE, MS 6213, f. 217v.

In the first two *quaestiones*, Eymerich addresses the matter of the eternality of the world. This topic is of singular importance within an apocalyptic and teleological framework, as the birth of the world functions as a natural *terminus post quem*. If the world were to have no beginning, it could be said to exist eternally, which means that it could have no end. Thus, the Apocalypse could not happen and the Scriptures would be mistaken. After citing Genesis, the Psalms, and the Gospels, and declaring Aristotle and Plato to be deceived in their opinions, Eymerich comes to the conclusion that "the world was not eternal, but [created] from the beginning of time," thus allowing for its ultimate, and unknowable, future destruction.[38]

In his discussion of the end of the world, Eymerich regards both astrologers' and theologians' positions concerning the physical makeup of the cosmos when he discusses the details and composition of the celestial spheres. Their existence, as well as that of the sphere of fixed stars and the Empyrean sphere, serves to support the creation of the universe ex nihilo, as well as the certain destruction of that universe, because they will cease their heavenly motions upon Judgment Day.[39] Eymerich then proceeds to his third and fourth *quaestiones*, which concern the fundamental nature of the Antichrist and whether he will appear in the world. After considering the Latin and Greek parts of the name of the Antichrist, Eymerich defines this entity as the adversary of Christ and then segues into a discussion of his arrival. The Antichrist will come because of the existence of Christ; he functions as a foil to the divinity of Christ and, as such, must appear in the world according to the divine plan. Eymerich discusses further the nature of the Antichrist and, citing the Evangelist John's ascription of the number 666 as the number of the Beast, applies biblical mathematics to the Greek name *Antichristos*, thus arriving at the sum of 666 and proving his identity as the great foe.[40]

Over an additional sixteen questions, Eymerich discusses the ills that will accompany the Antichrist's arrival, including the cooling of ardently charitable intentions, the rise in general iniquity, an increase in the number of flagellants, and the growth of blasphemers, reprobates, and sinners.

---

38. BNE, MS 6213, f. 219–219v.
39. BNE, MS 6213, f. 219v.
40. BNE, MS 6213, f. 220v.–221v.

In his fifth and sixth *quaestiones* he considers whether the Old Testament prophets Elias/Elijah and Enoch will return to preach at the End Times and will witness the arrival of the Antichrist. According to the Christian understanding of the Apocalypse, Elias/Elijah and Enoch were linked closely with the events of the Apocalypse, as they were corporeally assumed into heaven and will not return to the world until the sounding of the trumpets of the Apocalypse.[41] Eymerich proves the sanctity of these biblical prophets, determines that they ascended into heaven and stood beside God in paradise, and, citing the books of Ecclesiastes and Malachi, that they will indeed return on that "great and horrible Day of the Lord" to minister to the populace.[42] Eymerich then discusses whether it is possible to ascertain the time, day, and month of the prophets' arrival. As Elias/Elijah and Enoch were the heralds of Judgment Day, attempting to establish the time of their appearance would be tantamount to discovering the time of the Apocalypse, and, as such, Eymerich takes care to neither offer precise information nor support that endeavor, merely mentioning that they will come "with the Antichrist."[43] The Antichrist, true to form as being the opposite of Christ, will appear when he—The Antichrist—turns thirty years old and enter Jerusalem. There he will preach against Christ's doctrines and the words of Elias/Elijah and Enoch. Eymerich turns to the matter of the Antichrist's struggles against the prophets and discusses how, in accordance with apocalyptic expectations, the Antichrist will have a terrible, but brief, reign, spanning three and a half years. During that time, he will subjugate ten kings of the world, many people will revere him as a king in his own right, and he will cause an abundance of sins, intolerable wickedness, and an increase in the number of heretics and schismatics in the world.[44] The Antichrist will ascend the Mount of Olives, where ultimately "a fire will descend from the sky and consume him."[45] Enoch and Elias/Elijah will continue to preach against the son of perdition and show how his destruction via this divine fire attested to his status as the

41. Emmerson, *Antichrist in the Middle Ages*, 95–101; and Maria Magdalena Witte, *Elias und Henoch als Exempel, typologische Figuren und apokalyptische Zeugen: Zu Verbindungen von Literatur und Theologie im Mittelalter* (Frankfurt: Lang, 1987).
42. BNE, MS 6213, ff. 225v.–226v.
43. BNE, MS 6213, ff. 226v.–229v.
44. BNE, MS 6213, f. 231v.
45. BNE, MS 6213, ff. 230.

Antichrist. After the destruction of the Antichrist, many will see the errors of their ways, heeding the words of these biblical prophets and ultimately abandoning the Antichrist.[46] After a devastating earthquake levels a tenth of the city and kills many people, the survivors will physically whip themselves in repentance for their fallen ways before ultimately converting. Eymerich states that those who will have remained faithful to Christ throughout the period of tribulations will never deviate from their path.[47] Via a series of twelve conclusions, Eymerich then determines that Christ will be physically present at the Final Judgment to determine people's salvation or damnation.

Eymerich's twelfth *quaestio* is the longest, most substantial piece of his treatise. In it he tackles the difficult issue of whether or not it is possible to establish the precise time when Christ will return to judge the world. He carefully considers people's attempts to divine the future in general and singles out for particular scorn the attempts of astronomers and astrologers to discover the month, day, and hour of Christ's arrival. For the inquisitor, no one, neither celestial angels nor terrestrial kings, "knows about that day or hour of time or moment when [Jesus] will come."[48]

In the remaining *quaestiones*, Eymerich addresses such matters as the ontology of Christ (will he judge the world as man or god at the time of the Second Coming?), the Final Judgment (will there be an increase in physical deformities among both the elect and the damned?), and the fate of the damned. Those who will be found wanting at the End Times will be cursed and condemned to burn for all eternity in a pit of unquenchable fire with the devil and his angels. Those who believe, moreover, that the Virgin Mary will intercede and redeem the damned by liberating them from the inferno and gathering them together under the stars are incorrect in that assumption and adhere to a most grave heresy.[49] From the pits of hell

---

46. BNE, MS 6213, ff. 230v.

47. BNE, MS 6213, f. 232v.

48. BNE, MS 6213, f. 235: "Nec habetur ex alicuius sciencie demostratione hoc enim magis fuissem presumptum uel de sciencia astronomie uel astrologie et tamen ex illis nullatenus possimus iudicare minus demostrare nam aduentus de quo loquimur et quantum ad tempus et quantum ad modum dependet totaliter et ex toto ex mea diuina uoluntate et non corporum celestium neccesitate uero enim constellatio xpistem ad ueniendum tali tempore impegit sed ipse quando uenit uel ueniet tempus elegit."

49. BNE, MS 6213, f. 240v.

Eymerich then proceeds to the heavenly heights in his eighteenth *quaestio*, in which he discusses whether the saved will dwell eternally within the Empyrean sphere. Citing the Evangelist Matthew, Eymerich states that the blessed will gather in the "heaven of heavens, that is, the Empyrean heaven."[50] As the damned will dwell eternally in fire, so will the saved forever inhabit the Empyrean sphere.

For his final *quaestio*, Eymerich asks if the world will be restored after the events of the Final Judgment. If the world is restored, Eymerich argues, the sky will not appear as a new diaphanous or luminous creation, but will instead stay the same form and be of the same materials as it was before Judgment Day. Even though the earth might be restored in its form and substance, it most likely will not be restored to its former state, because the mountains, hills, plants, flowers, and animals will be consumed by a divine apocalyptic fire. Eymerich continues further that if the earth is ultimately to be restored, it will not be for the service of humanity, but rather to stand as an eternal testament to the honors and glory of its divine creator.[51] In concluding his treatise, Eymerich reaffirms the fundamental uncertainty about the time of the Antichrist's advent and subsequent consummation of the world and argues that he wrote his treatise to bolster the doctrines of the faith; to reject the claims of the liars, frauds, and delusional; and to extirpate the erroneous and heretical arguments of Ramon Llull.[52]

Upon Martí's ascension to the throne of the Crown of Aragon, the new king granted Eymerich the right to return to the kingdom. Eymerich indeed returned, settled in his hometown of Gerona, and lived there until the end of his days, in 1399. We now see the disposition of Eymerich, who is a trained theologian, toward King Joan's interest in divination. Although Eymerich earned the wrath of King Joan by attacking the pastimes that were dear to him, and had to depart the court as a result, he was not the sole critic of the sovereign. Others, such as Bernat Metge, closely moved within the king's circle and thus occupied a unique position to criticize Joan's interests.

---

50. BNE, MS 6213, f. 240v.
51. BNE, MS 6213, f. 242.
52. BNE, MS 6213, f. 242: "pro fidei defensione et herorum Raymundi Lull extirpatione quorumdam lulistarum hereticorum uehemencia et impulsu."

What did Bernat Metge think? Certainly no theologian, Metge was nevertheless a highly educated and accomplished man. A royal notary employed in the service of the House of Aragon during the reigns of Joan and his successor Martí, Metge occupied a significant position within the royal bureaucracy. Moreover, as a direct witness to the king's interaction with the occult, he had important things to say about Joan's astrological proclivities and their impact on his reign.

Metge's *Lo Somni* is an important source for understanding Joan's reign. Metge wrote *Lo Somni* to exonerate himself during his period of house arrest in 1396, immediately following King Joan's death. The resulting text is substantial, spanning four books, and in it Metge touches upon a number of themes, including current political developments in the Crown of Aragon, the resurgent humanist movement among members of the social and cultural elite in Barcelona, and contemporary patterns of fashion and taste. While one cannot assume that texts such as *Lo Somni* accurately depict real events and social relations, they are important sources for understanding contemporary concerns and social preoccupations. In *Lo Somni* we have a record that both matches with the extant historical data and reveals Joan's profound preoccupation with divining the future.

Lo Somni further illustrates the dangerous space that astrology and divination occupied within late medieval culture. Metge claimed to have had a divinely inspired dream that gave him access to a body of hidden knowledge. He goes on to argue that the sidereal disciplines of astrology and astronomy in King Joan's court, when used in an attempt to foresee future events, transgressed the border between religious orthodoxy and heterodoxy, and between sound political governance and flagrant mismanagement. Especially fascinating was Metge's use of the powerful genre of the dream allegory as a vehicle for his criticism against Joan's activities. The dream in the Middle Ages occupied its own liminal space, allied with both the ordinary and the supernatural, functioning as a revelation that proceeded externally and internally.[53] Through

---

53. Steven F. Kruger, *Dreaming in the Middle Ages* (Cambridge: Cambridge University Press, 1992), 17. Barbara Newman has also discussed the duality and liminality of medieval visions, categorizing them as having both rhetorical and theological functions. See *God and the Goddesses*, 300: "visions, so ubiquitous in medieval literature, could function as both rhetorical device and theological method."

the power behind the dream allegory, Metge had the character of the late King Joan suffer for his interest in the occult. Ironically, Joan had lent Metge a copy of Macrobius's *Dream of Scipio* while the two men were together in Majorca in 1395, and undoubtedly Metge was drawing upon Macrobius's text when he wrote his own dream allegory. And by using the voices of authoritative figures from ancient mythology to deliver indirectly his own withering critiques of the king's actions, Metge avoided the dangerous situation of using his own voice to denounce the late king.[54]

Before turning to *Lo Somni*, it is important to understand more about Bernat Metge, whose life would become intertwined with the lives of the princes of the court.[55] Born in 1346, he was the son of Guillem Metge, royal apothecary to the House of Aragon.[56] Guillem ascended socially because of his service to the young Joan, Duke of Gerona and heir to the throne. As a sickly boy, the prince had to spend his summers staying put in his ducal city of Gerona, in order for his guardians to monitor his health.[57] Whenever the young prince was in Barcelona, Guillem created potions and tonics in his shop in the Carrer de Espèciers and brought them to the frail prince.[58] Because of his service to the court, Guillem Metge was granted the right to display arms in 1351, and in 1356 Queen Elionor named him as a "domestic and familiar" and made him a regular member of the royal household.[59]

---

54. Metge's work is not the sole example of this type of literature. The use of the dream vision as a vehicle for criticizing the inhabitants of a ruling dynasty had ancient roots. For the Early Middle Ages, see Paul Edward Dutton, *The Politics of Dreaming in the Carolingian Empire* (Lincoln: University of Nebraska Press, 1994).

55. Lola Badia has conducted the most significant research about Bernat Metge. See her critical edition of Metge's fourteenth-century "dream," *Lo Somni* (Barcelona: Quaderns Creama, 1999). See also Badia, "Fa che tu scrive: variaciones profanas sobre un motivo sagrado, de Ramon Llull a Bernat Metge," *The Medieval Mind: Hispanic Studies in Honour of Alan Deyermond* (London: Tamesis Books, 1997), 3–20.

56. Michael R. McVaugh, *Medicine before the Plague: Practitioners and Their Patients in the Crown of Aragon, 1285–1345* (Cambridge: Cambridge University Press, 2002). With a brief exception, McVaugh does not discuss in great detail the roles that astrology and divination played for medical science. He writes, "It is difficult not to conclude that a more technical astrology (and the 'occult sciences') played very little part in medical practice during the first half of the fourteenth century," 164. See also Joseph Ziegler, *Medicine and Religion c. 1300: The Case of Arnau de Villanova* (Oxford: Oxford University Press, 1998).

57. José María Roca, *Johan I d'Arago* (Barcelona: Institució Patxot, 1929), 419–20.

58. Metge, *The Dream*, x.

59. Ibid.

Not surprisingly, Guillem's fortunes facilitated the younger Metge's proximity to the throne. After Guillem's death in 1359, Metge's mother married a man named Ferrer Sayol, who worked for the royal chancellery and fancied himself a humanist.[60] Richard Vernier has supposed that Metge's stepfather guided him, helping him to make the transition into the royal bureaucracy. This would result in the young Metge's becoming a junior scribe in the queen's household by 1371, with an annual salary of 750 Barcelonan sous, a substantial sum.[61]

By the time Queen Elionor died in 1375, Metge was already a member of the Duke of Gerona's retinue, and within Prince Joan's "glittering circle of courtiers," in which skill in the humanistic arts was well rewarded, Metge flourished.[62] His pay increased steadily and substantially to the point that soon the junior scribe's annual salary was 3,300 sous. Such an increase pointed to a close, personal relationship between the prince and the secretary that blurred the lines between public service to the government and private service to Joan. This relationship between the scribe and the king could not help but attract the attention of rivals in the royal demimonde of the Crown of Aragon.

There was also personal turmoil within the ruling family. Joan chose as his wife Yolande de Bar, a decision that displeased his father, Pere, who did not favor the French queen.[63] There was much at stake in this politically significant union. The arrangement of a marriage between the French and the Aragonese royal houses was in the interest of the king of France, who hoped that the Aragonese would stay neutral in their conflict with the English during the Hundred Years' War.[64] The effects of the entrance of the French queen rippled throughout the Catalan court. Upon Yolande's arrival there was a reinvigorated French cultural influence in

---

60. Ibid.

61. Ibid., xi.

62. Kagay, "Poetry in the Dock," coined the phrase "glittering circle of courtiers" to describe the people skilled in the arts and letters who populated Joan's court.

63. Tasis i Marca, *Pere el Cerimoniós*, 112. See also Pere el Cerimoniós, *Chronicle*, trans. and eds., Mary Hillgarth and Jocelyn N. Hillgarth, 2 vols. (Toronto: PIMS, 1980), 2:594.

64. For more on the Hundred Years' War (1337–1453 C.E.), see Jonathan Sumption, *The Hundred Years War*, 2 vols. (London: Faber and Faber, 1999); and Jean Favier, *La guerre de Cent Ans* (Paris: Fayard, 1980). For events in Iberia during the Hundred Years' War, see Luis Suárez Fernández, *Intervención de Castilla en la Guerra de los Cien Años* (Valladolid: Industrias Gráficas ESPE, 1950).

Barcelona. French fashion, music, letters, and art thrived within this atmosphere, and Yolande was instrumental in this cultural development.[65]
However, the imported culture was not without its critics. At the beginning of the fifteenth century, the stoic and pious King Martí reportedly
stated that the pervasive French influence within the higher levels of Catalan society was "conducive to depravity," a direct attack upon his brother's
and sister-in-law's interests.[66] The decadent influences of French culture
notwithstanding, it is evident that the demimonde of Joan and Yolande
encouraged the study and pursuit of letters in which a man such as Bernat
Metge would thrive.

Joan's reign over the Crown of Aragon was troubled. Among both the
popular and the elite there was widespread anger against the court, but it
was directed not against the person of the king himself, which would have
been impolitic, but against his queen and courtiers, who were viewed as
domineering and selfish.[67] Critics of the court argued that greed, moral
turpitude, and corruption were rampant among the queen and the councilors and that this in turn accounted for the treasury's poor state.[68] Metge was
embroiled in this fiscal situation. Papal revenues that were in Metge's trust
and had been earmarked for an armed expedition against the rebellious
island of Sardinia had been squandered, an incident that would become a
focal point for great public dissatisfaction against the court. The genesis of
this situation lay in Joan's support of the Avignon papacy. While the prior
king, Pere, managed to remain neutral in the schism between Rome and
Avignon, Joan backed the Avignon pope Clement VII. The ties linking
the dominions of Aragon with those of the Avignon papacy became even
tighter when in 1394 the Valencian nobleman Pere de Luna ascended to
the papal throne as Benedict XIII. The heir to the throne of the Crown of
Aragon, Joan's younger brother Martí, was married to Maria de Luna, a
relative of the new pope.

When Joan died the fortunes of Metge and others of the king's retinue
changed dramatically. They no longer had the privileges and immunities

---

65. Metge, *The Dream*, xiv.
66. Ibid., xiv. See also Núria Silleras-Fernández, *Power, Piety, and Patronage in Late Medieval
Queenship* (New York: Palgrave Macmillan, 2008), 44. My thanks to both Núria Silleras-Fernández
and Brian Catlos for discussions about this matter.
67. Kagay, "Poetry in the Dark," 25.
68. Ibid., 25–26.

obtained through their close connection with the royal person. Martí, who was viceroy in Sicily, now was the new king of the Crown of Aragon, although it took him time to claim the throne. In order to rectify some of the excesses of his older brother's reign, to distance himself from several of Joan's actions, and to demonstrate himself a strong and independent monarch in his own right, Martí and his queen, Maria de Luna, named a committee to investigate charges brought against Joan's councilors. Metge's name appeared in the indictment of the trial that opened on June 2, 1396.[69]

In March and April 1396 the town councilors of Barcelona focused their anger on Joan's courtiers, whom they dubbed "cruel enemies" of the king and of God.[70] With the death of Joan, the time to exact vengeance upon the hated councilors was at hand. The councilors leveled charges of conspiracy, treason, corruption, and subversion against the courtiers. They accused the courtiers of having misused their positions by accepting bribes and of undermining the role of Joan as an agent of "divine majesty."[71]

Imprisoned from June or July 1396 until September 1397, Metge found solace in writing.[72] He composed *Lo Somni* as a plea to regain Martí's trust, and it seems to have worked.[73] On the advice of Metge's powerful friend Ramon Savall, who had seen Metge's work and had the ear of the new king, Martí wrote Metge in 1402 and requested to see a copy of *Lo Somni*.[74] Knowing this, it makes perfect sense that Metge composed his work as he did. In the atmosphere of humanism patronized within the royal court, Metge's erudition and literary sophistication would garner the attention of other powerful courtiers, as well as the king.[75] Rather than lose his life, Metge was out of prison by 1402, rehabilitated and working again as a scribe in the chancery. Metge survived King Martí, who died without a male heir in 1410, and witnessed the shift of the throne to a member of

---

69. Metge, *The Dream*, xx.

70. Kagay, "Poetry in the Dock," 22, cites Ramón d'Abadal y Vinyals, "La vida politica y sus dirigentes," *España cristiana: Crisis de la reconquista luchas civiles. Historia de España*, ed. Ramón Menéndez Pidal, 37 vols. (Madrid: Espasa-Calpe, 1935–1984), 14:558–60.

71. Kagay, "Poetry in the Dock," 28.

72. Metge, *The Dream*, xviii; xx–xxi.

73. Ibid., xxi.

74. Rubió i Lluch, *Documents*, 1:408–09 and Vernier, *The Dream*, xxi.

75. Metge, *The Dream*, xxxi.

the Castilian Trastámara dynasty, Fernando de Antequera, in 1412. Metge himself died in 1413.

In *Lo Somni* Metge recounts his vision in which King Joan is suffering in Purgatory, and one of the reasons for this is his former dallying in astrology and divination. After Metge falls asleep, King Joan appears as "a man of middling stature and noble visage, dressed in crimson plush embroidered with double crowns of gold, and with a red hat on his head." Along with the shade of the dead monarch are his spiritual guides, Tiresias and Orpheus, and all of his hunting animals, which create a frightening din. Metge recognizes the king, which leads him to panic. Joan seeks to assuage the shaken scribe and tells him, "Leave off being afraid, for I am the one you think." When the scribe asks the king why he is present before him, for he has heard that the king had died, the king responds: "I did not die . . . but only left the flesh to its mother, and returned the spirit to God who had given it to me."[76] After that statement Metge and the king engage in a lengthy debate, which spans the rest of the first book. They cover several topics, including the ontology of the soul, its immortality, and what happens to the soul after death, a discussion initiated by Joan. The debate is long and pedantic, with frequent references to scriptural and classical authorities, as the two men trade opinions on the eternity of the soul and the necessity of reason. It also demonstrates Metge's erudition. Writing while imprisoned, he knew that his future was uncertain. Were he to be executed, this work would be a final testament to his intelligence through both his own voice and that of the dead king Joan.

After discussing some of the ancient philosophers' ideas about the immortality of the soul, Metge becomes impatient and entreats Joan to "go on to the sayings of the Christians, as you promised me you would" (17). To demonstrate that the soul does not die with the passing of the body, Joan offers Metge examples of Jesus's raising Lazarus from the dead, as well as Jesus's own resurrection. Metge then asks the king to discuss Muslims' understandings about the eternality of the soul, but Joan dismisses Islam. He calls the "Alcoran [*sic*] . . . all bad . . . for there are countless errors and monstrous things," and paints the Muslim paradise where souls dwell as opulent, decadent, and lecherous. In it rivers of milk, wine, water, and

---

76. Metge, *The Dream*, 3.

honey flow freely, and it is filled with an abundance of women, sweets, fruits, and luxurious silks. It "favors and predisposes to . . . carnal sins" and thus, in his estimation, has nothing to offer (18).

Joan then asks Metge if they might switch subjects, to discuss "the rest of the definition of the soul, namely that the soul can be turned towards good or evil" (18). With the debate between Joan and Metge about all things spiritual over, Metge requests that Joan then answer some of his additional questions, to which Joan agrees, with one warning: "Tell me what you want to know, but briefly, for I shall not be able to remain here very long" (22).

In the second book of *Lo Somni*, Metge takes the specter of the dead king Joan to task for his dedication to prophecy, astrology, hunting, and literature, at the expense of rectifying the Great Western Schism or ruling his kingdom effectively. The second book thus stands as a more blatant attempt at self-vindication. Metge begins by trying to remove the taint from his name as a corrupt adviser to the king. Indeed, the first of the four questions Metge asks of the shade concerns the death of the king. Joan exonerates Metge, stating that neither Metge nor the rest of the councilors were responsible for his death, in spite of what their detractors, "harboring evil and envious designs against you and some of my other servants and familiars . . . [who] desired that . . . you should be purged from the face of the earth," argued (25). The king died because "the end of the life allotted to me by Our Lord God had come at that hour" (25). His death has served three purposes: to make evident the motives of those jealous of Metge and the other councilors; to exonerate those disgraced councilors publicly and legally; and so that the successful completion of those first two purposes would not be impeded (26).

When Metge asks the king what he means by this third purpose, the king explains that if he had not died suddenly: "I would have come straight to Barcelona and I would have done everything that city advised me to do concerning justice and the defense of our lands. . . . I would have given to all my servants and familiars a general pardon, although such was not necessary. . . . [Thus] great infamy would have befallen all of you" (26). His sudden death was thus necessary to prove the innocence of his councilors. Additionally, since God appointed that particular time for the king to die, neither beneficent nor malicious actions on the part of the councilors would have prevented it from occurring.

It is in the second book where Metge deals extensively with the tendentious topic of divination. After a discussion concerning Paradise and one's need for God's grace to be able to enter it, Joan relates that he will be able to enter Paradise only when he has fulfilled his penance, and that only the miraculous intercession of the Virgin Mary prevented him from falling into the pit of hell. Metge, surprised at the king's admission, replies: "I am very amazed, for in your life I was very close to you, my lord, as you well know, and I never saw nor heard it said that you were a bad Christian or impious. I could plainly see that you were inclined to some pleasures that did not look very sinful to me" (28). It is at this point that Joan sternly corrects the scribe:

> "The pleasures," he said, "to which I was inclined were not in themselves enough to hurl me into Hell, for they did not any harm or wrong to anyone except myself. I took more pleasure than one should in the hunt, and in listening to singers and minstrels, in gifts and spending too much, and sometimes I sought (as great lords are wont to do) ways to know of events to come in the future, so that I could foresee and forestall them. All those deeds were bad, but I often confessed them and received the Sacrament, and I repented of my sins but not enough to keep me from returning sometimes to them. That is why Our Lord God wants me to bear the penance for them which I did not accomplish wholly while I lived." (28)

The penance that Joan has to suffer is to have as his constant companions his baying hounds and screeching hawks, as punishment for engaging in the hunt too much; for his love of music and poetry, Orpheus must play discordant melodies on the lyre; and, finally, in relation to the king's inordinate interests in divination, Joan must suffer the domineering presence of the distasteful Tiresias:

> Because I sought to know events in the future . . . He [God] has put in my company this old man who incessantly reminds me of all the unpleasant things that ever happened to me. He makes me remember the vanity I pursued, and says to me: "For the things of the future that you wanted to know, Our Lord God wants you to remember the past ones, so that they will be occasion of grief and pain to you, because your sins deserve Hell."[77]

---

77. Ibid., 29. See also Metge, *Lo Somni*, 96: "Per l'encercar com poguera saber algunes coses esdevenidores . . . ha mès en ma companyia aquest hom vell, qui incessantment me redueix a memoria tots quans desplaers jamai haguí, faent-me retrets de la vanitat que jo seguia, e dient-me. <<Per les coses esdevenidores que volies saber, nostre senyor Déu vol que records les pasades, per tal que et sien ocasió de dolor e pena, car per ta culpa mereixies infern.>>"

It is clear that Metge paints Joan's predilection for divination and astrology as no small matter. Though Richard Vernier has asserted that Joan dwells in Purgatory for "some illicit dabbling in the forbidden art of divination . . . which ha[s] no impact on public affairs," this assessment is not entirely correct.[78] In the beginning of the second book, Metge tacitly condemns Joan's divinatory proclivities for this very reason. Yet, as seen in the first book of *Lo Somni*, Metge himself dabbles in heterodox behavior, especially concerning the eternality of the soul. Only after reestablishing his own orthodoxy in the first book is Metge able to criticize Joan's problematic behavior and borderline heterodoxy in the second.

After describing his punishments, Joan then explains why he has avoided the infernal fires of hell: "no sooner had I abandoned my body . . . than I was brought before the judgment of Our Lord God. And the prince of evil spirits, accompanied by his terrible cohorts, presented himself and claimed that I belonged to him by right because I had been one of the principal caterers to the Schism which is in God's Church."[79] Christ serves as judge for this dramatic trial. Throughout the scene of the king's divine trial, Metge, through the voice of the devil, lambastes Joan because of his prolongation of the Great Schism through his tacit support of the Avignon papacy.[80] Joan's relative indifference to healing Christendom, compared with his interest in less important and unsavory affairs, such as divination, prophecy, and astrology, would have damned the sovereign if the devil had prosecuted him successfully.

Joan explains that the Virgin Mary suddenly appeared during his trial to intercede on behalf of the dead king. Mary pleaded to Jesus that he have mercy upon the dead king's soul because Joan engaged in a series of pious, if not wholly canonical, actions while he was alive: he was a vocal and active proponent of the Cult of the Immaculate Conception in the Crown of Aragon. Members of the royal family, including Joan and later his younger brother, Martí, were inspired by Franciscans who preached the doctrine in their realms some five hundred years before the Church recognized it

78. Metge, *The Dream*, xxiv. Punishments meted out to souls in Purgatory reflected activities that they were overly fond of while alive. LeGoff, *Birth of Purgatory*, 180.

79. Metge, *The Dream*, 29.

80. Ibid., xxiv–xxv.

as orthodox.[81] In *Lo Somni* Joan relates that Mary told Jesus the king "had ordered and commanded that it should be celebrated every year by a perpetual and solemn feast in all the realms . . . possessed and . . . forbade anyone to dare say, dispute, preach or sustain the contrary."[82] Because of the king's support of the Immaculate Conception, Mary convinced her son to show mercy and prevent the king from being damned. This, however, came at a cost. Joan tells Metge that Christ ruled "that I should suffer the penance of which I have already told you, and that I should not be able to enter the celestial glory until the said Schism is uprooted from His Church, since by my own negligence I had allowed it to grow."[83]

Metge played his own perilous game, however, in his condemnation of Joan's support of Benedict XIII. Even though Metge "pretended to hide behind the persona of the Devil,"[84] the potential danger was very real for him. Not only did he imply the future torments that Martí could face in dying, or worse, taking an indifferent position on the restoration of the Church's unity, but he also criticized an immediate family member of Queen Maria de Luna. Despite Metge's running a huge risk, the result was ultimately positive.

The final part of the second book sees Joan test Metge. Metge asks the dead king why he has not sought information about the welfare of other members of the royal household, especially Queen Yolande and their daughter, "both of whom should, to my mind, come before all your friends

---

81. Faustino D. Gazulla, "Los reyes de Aragon y la Purísima Concepción de María," *Boletín de la Real Academia de Buenas Letras de Barcelona* 3 (1905–1906): 1–18, 49–53, 143–51, 224–33, 258–64, 388–93, 476–83, 546–50, and 4 (1907–1908): 37–41, 116–22, 137–46, 226–34, 298–303, 408–16; Basilio de Rubi, "La escuela franciscana de Barcelona y su intervención en los decretos inmaculistas de la corona de Aragón," *Estudios franciscanos* 57 (1956): 363–405.

82. Metge, *The Dream*, 31. On December 8, 1854, Pope Pius IX pronounced the Immaculate Conception in his *Ineffabilis Deus*. For more on the medieval concept of the Immaculate Conception, see Jaroslav Pelikan, *The Growth of Medieval Theology (600–1300)*, 3 vols. (Chicago: University of Chicago Press, 1978), 3:70–72; Edward D. O'Connor, ed., *The Dogma of the Immaculate Conception: History and Significance* (Notre Dame, IN: University of Notre Dame Press, 1958); and Kagay, "Poetry in the Dock," 32 n106. No less a theologian than Jean Gerson himself supported the doctrine of the Immaculate Conception, as evidenced in his French sermon from 1401. See Daniel Hobbins, *Authorship and Publicity before Print: Jean Gerson and the Transformation of Late Medieval Learning* (Philadelphia: University of Pennsylvania Press, 2009), 59.

83. Metge, *The Dream*, 31.

84. Ibid., xxv. Pere also appeared unconcerned with the matter of the Schism. P. Ivars Andrés, "La 'indiferencia' de Pedro IV de Aragon en el Gran Cisma de Occidente," *Archivo iberoamericano* 29 (1928): 21–97 and 161–86.

and servants."[85] Joan replies that he has avoided asking about them "to test if you still have for my family the same love you used to have. . . . I give you the special charge of revealing all of this to them, for they will take great solace from it."[86] Joan, pardoning Metge, allows him to share this information with other members of the late sovereign's family, which would presumably include Martí. When the king moves to speak further, one of his ethereal companions rudely interrupts him, ordering him to be silent. Joan explains to the appalled scribe that his spectral guides were Tiresias and Orpheus, and that Tiresias was the one who told the king to still his tongue. With that, the second book ends and, for the rest of the allegory, King Joan speaks no more.

The speeches of Orpheus and Tiresias dominate book 3. Indeed, it is there that their characteristics, respectively reflective and abrasive, shine forth. For the rest of Metge's work the only individuals who speak are Metge and Joan's two companions. In the third book, Metge shows that not only is divination bad, meriting hell or at the very least, Purgatory, but he also depicts women as being especially inclined toward divinatory practices. Additionally, the structure of the debate between Metge and Tiresias, which spans the third and fourth books of *Lo Somni*, mirrors the debate between Cicero and his brother, Quintus, in *De Divinatione*.[87]

Closely linked with magic and the occult in premodernity, Orpheus relays to Metge the tragic tale about his lost love, Eurydice.[88] In the myth of Orpheus and Eurydice, the shepherd Aristeus assaulted Eurydice and attempted to rape her. As she fled from his lecherous advances, she stepped on a poisonous snake that was hiding in the grass, which bit and killed her. Orpheus relates to Metge that he then descended into the Underworld in an attempt to bring his wife back with him to the world above. Being a skilled musician, Orpheus played his lyre until the infernal hosts began to weep. Eurydice was returned to him with the promise that as they ascended to the world of the living, he must not turn back to see if she followed, "for

---

85. Metge, *The Dream*, 34.

86. Ibid., 34.

87. Cicero, *De Divinatione*, trans. and ed. William Armistead Falconer (Cambridge, MA: Harvard University Press, 1927).

88. See D. P. Walker, "Orpheus the Theologian and Renaissance Platonists," *Journal of the Warburg and Courtauld Institutes* 16, no. 1/2 (1953): 100–120; and John Block Friedman, *Orpheus in the Middle Ages* (Syracuse, NY: Syracuse University Press, 2000).

if I did, I should lose her."[89] As they almost reached the outside world, Orpheus, doubting that Eurydice followed, turned back to see if she was there, only to see her snatched back into the Underworld. Inconsolable, Orpheus exiled himself to a mountaintop, where the maenads, female followers of Dionysus, descended upon him and tore him apart.[90]

Tiresias, whom Metge depicts as a dyspeptic character, negates the tragedy of Orpheus and Eurydice by comparing it with a "more important" loss that impacted Christendom, that of the 1291 fall of the crusading outpost of Acre: "When the Moors took the city of Acre . . . the Christians lost more than you did when you lost your wife, or than you would if you lost her now. It often happens that one gains by losing; but not everyone is good at arithmetic!"[91] Tiresias demonstrates no remorse when Metge chastises him for his prickly behavior and responds, "Like a good doctor, who does not look to the pleasure of the patient, but to his well-being . . . so shall I do with you, for my office is not to say pleasant or flattering things, but to disabuse."[92] The scribe and the seer get into a heated exchange, and, turning his back on Tiresias, Metge asks Orpheus to describe the Underworld. Orpheus casts the deities and supernatural beings that inhabited the infernal realms as nothing less than demons from hell.[93] His vivid and detailed description of the Underworld is significant, as it evokes those descriptions of hell that appear in Dante Aligheri's *Inferno*.[94] Shades of Dante echo throughout Metge's allegory. As seen in the twentieth canto of the *Inferno*, prophets, astrologers, and soothsayers of all types were damned in a most disturbing way. For daring to peer into the future, they were condemned to regard the past eternally, their heads twisted on their spines. Metge was wise enough not to have the ghost of King Joan suffer the same torment. Still, the idea was mirrored in Metge's allegory.[95]

---

89. Metge, *The Dream*, 38.
90. Ibid., 37–39.
91. Ibid., 39.
92. Ibid., 39.
93. Metge, *The Dream*, xxvii. Vernier has suggested that Orpheus's philological treaty derived from Boccaccio's *De genealogia deorum*.
94. For Dante's *Commedia Divina*, the standard work remains the translation by Charles Southward Singleton, ed., *The Divine Comedy*, 6 vols. (Princeton, NJ: Princeton University Press, 1970–1975).
95. Metge, *The Dream*, 29.

Women's interest in divination, as reflected in Tiresias's misogynistic speeches, becomes a dangerous way of seeking access to hidden knowledge. As already seen in this chapter, Metge's voice, divided among various characters, reflects his opinion of what constitutes heterodox behavior. Through the dead king Joan and Tiresias, Metge provides a glimpse into either his personal beliefs concerning the dangers of divination and the occult, or a crafty ploy to appeal to the religious sensibilities of the new king and queen. In doing this, Metge assesses the personal character of those who consult seers and fortune-tellers. Speaking through the voice of Tiresias, Metge attacks women's supposed obsession with divining the future. According to the cantankerous seer, this deed is connected to the purportedly female appetite for being unfaithful and scheming:

> All their thoughts and efforts tend to no other thing than to rob and deceive men. To that end, and also to know if they can expect good or bad fortune, or if their husbands or lovers will die before them, they consult and hold in great esteem astrologers, necromancers, witches and soothsayers, especially those who have often been arrested and punished for divining, and they enrich them with the wealth of their husbands. . . . Do you know in what they are generous? Not in spending, but in squandering on clairvoyants, especially if they can bamboozle their husbands.[96]

In this section from Metge's work, the disdain Tiresias feels for prognosticators of all kinds is clear; in his estimation, they are nothing more than quacks. Even worse, Metge hints at the potential crime of popular divination. He gathers astrologers, necromancers, witches, and seers under one umbrella and intimates that they associate with malevolent women who reward them with the hard-earned money of their hapless spouses and lovers. Clearly, for Tiresias, divining future events and gaining access to privileged knowledge was solely the provenance of the male, the authoritative, and the powerful.

---

96. Ibid., 50 and 52; and Metge, *Lo Somni*, 133: "Tot llur estudi e pensament e altres coses no giren sinó a robar e enganar los hòmens. E sobre açò, e per saber semblantment si els deu venir bona ventura o mala, o si morran llurs marits abans que elles, o llurs amadors, consulten e han fort cars los astròlegs, los nigromàntics e les fetillers e los devins, e especialment aquells qui moltes vegades són estats presos e punits per divinar, los quals enriqueeixen dels béns de llurs marits."

In addressing Tiresias's claims against women, Metge nonetheless remains strangely silent concerning one specific criticism that Tiresias leveled: that of women's superstitious nature and their excessive interest in divination. The answer lies in the presence of the mute king, Joan, who functions as a response to Tiresias. Although Joan was a representative of supreme male and temporal authority, he nevertheless engaged in the "womanly" pursuit of divination. As Pierre d'Ailly argued that prophets and soothsayers frequented the homes of women and effete men, Joan's undue interest in these themes, especially at the expense of ruling his kingdom, placed him squarely in this second category. King Joan thus stands as an emasculated sovereign in *Lo Somni.*

Tiresias, though pleased with Metge's refutation of his position concerning women, remains unconvinced. Indeed, the seer tells the scribe in the final pages of the work to "Give up the love of women . . . avoid them like lightning . . . most of the evils and troubles that occur in the world came from women." Those themes of trouble and its avoidance are the final points that Tiresias discusses with Metge. He tells the scribe, "to give your thoughts to your own affairs . . . the spiritual and durable ones, and especially to knowing and improving yourself . . . since you have lived in the midst of stormy seas, do all you can to die in a calm and secure port." When Tiresias utters these final words, the dogs and falcons howl and shriek, waking Metge from his dream and leaving him "very sad and depressed, and until morning deprived of the strength of my limbs, as if my spirit had deserted them."[97]

In both Nicolau Eymerich's theological treatise and Bernat Metge's dream allegory, divining the future was depicted as dangerously improper and unorthodox. Both men, who wrote their works while in a state of disgrace with the royal household, were able to give voice to their opinions regarding this practice beloved by Joan. In the case of Metge, himself charged with impropriety and viewed as a wicked councilor, it comes as no wonder that he would have taken a stance against unorthodox behavior. Even if his name was linked to bureaucratic and financial malfeasance, at least the scribe could redeem himself through his art. In his vernacular masterpiece, he recognized the "wickedness" that characterized Joan's

---

97. Metge, *The Dream*, 75.

reign and addressed it accordingly. To Metge, it was small wonder, then, that fortune did not shine on the later years of his reign and brought the king to a most ignoble end. Metge sought to exonerate himself with his work and implied that illicit behavior such as fiscal mismanagement was less a crime than dabbling with books of prophecy or gazing at the stars to ascertain future events. He manipulated the power behind dream texts both to rehabilitate himself and to comment on the dead king's interest in divination; by having the shade of the king suffer for his sins, and by uttering criticisms against Joan through the voices of literary figures, Metge redeemed himself. The dead king's punishment in this story is significant because although the disgraced notary wrote this work ostensibly for one set of eyes, his own, he knew that the new king Martí, whose reign was characterized by a return to religious piety, orthodox behavior, and fiscal conservatism, would find many of the themes within *Lo Somni* appealing. Although astrology and magic flourished within the cultures of many royal demimondes across medieval Europe, Eymerich's and Metge's texts functioned as mirrors of the culture of King Joan's court. They both suggest that the monarch should have spent his time addressing more pressing and practical matters while alive, rather than spending his time at the hunt and attempting to peer into the future. And in *Lo Somni* no less a person than the dead king himself issues a warning to the careful reader in order to steer that reader away from the brink of damnation: "'Mind the present,' he said, 'and leave the future alone. What Our Lord God has ordained must come to pass of necessity, and it is not permissible for me to foresee it.'"[98]

---

98. Ibid., 35.

6

A RETURN TO ORTHODOXY

The Ascension of Martí I and the End of an Era

On October 4, 1399, three years into his reign as count-king of the Crown of Aragon, King Martí wrote to Berenguer de Montagut, his lieutenant governor in the kingdom of Majorca. The king told his administrator he had received a letter from one Jaime Lustrach, an alchemist from the island. In his letter to Montagut the king wrote that Lustrach, commissioned by King Joan to write a brief treatise on the search for the philosopher's stone, had some misgivings about completing his alchemical work and that he proposed to abandon the project. Martí urged both Berenguer de Montagut and the royal procurator on the island, Mateo de Lostos, to prevent Lustrach from leaving his work, especially since it had been commissioned during the reign of his predecessor.[1]

---

1. José Ramón de Luanco, *La Alquimia en España* (Madrid: Editorial "Tres, Catorce, Diecisiete," 1980), 125–32. My translations follow.

Martí also decided to write the alchemist, telling him he had received his letter as well as "the little book that you sent us on the work on the philosopher's stone, which you had continued in Majorca by the command of the Lord King don Joan, our brother in good memory."[2] King Martí told Lustrach that he had let his royal procurator know about the matter regarding this commissioned work and to make sure that the procurator continued to receive faithfully, without any delay, the work that was owed to him by Lustrach.

A little more than three months later, on January 26, 1400, King Martí sent a missive to both his lieutenant governor and the royal procurator, commanding them to imprison Lustrach. Martí thundered:

> Having received a letter from you, procurator, about the work of Lustrach, and understanding what is contained within it . . . and also what he himself has written to us, We see that his work has been *all vanity mixed with great temerity*, and that for good reason he would be worthy of being well punished [to serve as an example]. . . . We want, at the very least . . . that . . . he cease the said work entirely and immediately and that you not waste any more time in enacting this.[3]

Although Lustrach was an alchemist and not an astrologer, Martí's comment dismissing Lustrach's work as "all vanity mixed with great temerity" illustrates well the monarch's complex position regarding the occult sciences. Known frequently as Martí *l'Humà*, the Humane, his other, lesser-known sobriquet is that of *l'Ecclesiàstic*, the Priest. This was appropriate, as the new sovereign was extraordinarily devout. Martí's dismissal of Lustrach's work is a bit surprising, because some three months earlier the king had supported the alchemist's continued work on the treatise. Yet Martí's encouragement of Lustrach's work more likely functioned as a token remembrance of his fraternal predecessor's interests. Despite the

---

2. Ibid., 128.

3. Ibid., 129: "Reebuda una letra de vos procurador sobre la obra den Lustrach et entes ço quen es contengut. E entes encara ço que ell matex nos ha scrit veem quel seu fet es estat tot vanitat mesclada ab gran temeritat de que per bona raho serie digne de bon castich. E come se vulla sia de aço almenys volem pus axi es que façats tantost cessar del tot la dita Obra et no si perda temps pus avant." Emphasis mine.

king's earlier supposed backing of Lustrach's work, his dismissal of that same work just three months later demonstrates both the liminal position the king held regarding the occult arts and his great pains to imprint his religious character on the culture of the court and in the administration of his domains. Perhaps Lustrach suggested abandoning his work to King Martí because he foresaw the warnings and tried to stave off what he feared would be the king's wrath. By 1399, however, it was too late. The alchemist was forced to continue the alchemical work, submit it to Martí's review, and await the royal word, which he received a year later. Lustrach could have been punished severely for incurring the king's ire were it not for the intercession of Queen Maria de Luna. Her request for mercy for the imprisoned alchemist apparently encouraged Martí to reevaluate his decision to have Jaime Lustrach imprisoned, for on May 18, 1400, the king wrote the *veguer* of Barcelona and commanded him "to set Lustrach free . . . with all his goods . . . [and] we ordain the said parole by the supplication, graciously given, of our beloved wife, the Queen."[4]

This interaction between the king and the alchemist reflects the central theme of this chapter: that Martí's personality and religious proclivities permeated the culture of his court and represented a distinct shift from the intellectual pursuits and administrative approaches of his older brother. Within medieval reckoning, the positions in support for or against occult matters were contested hotly and in continual flux. Martí, who operated within this intellectual system, could not completely escape this tension over the occult. However, in contrast to his father's and elder brother's interest in the occult, Martí appeared to be more aligned with those principles that took a more hostile view of the disciplines. Martí's approach was thus considerably different from Joan's.

Also unlike Joan, Martí had no smooth transition to the throne of the Crown of Aragon. Martí's tenure as king began precariously, as Martí could claim his birthright only after he and his queen, Maria, repelled the forces of Matthieu de Castelbon, the Count of Foix. Like his father and brother before him, Martí was compelled to use his personal character

---

4. Ibid., 159–60: "Beguer manam uos que entost Deliurets anar ab tots sos bens franchament on uolra en Lustrach . . . nos haiam lo dit relaxament a supplicació de nostra cara muller la Reyna graciosament ortogat."

and devotion to religion to stamp the culture of his court and ensure his role as legitimate sovereign. Ruling in conjunction with Queen Maria, the new king actively sought to enact a change in both his kingdom and the culture of the royal court, marking them with a return to orthodoxy and a partial rejection of the occult that his fraternal predecessor so favored. Thomas Bisson has described Martí in glowing terms as being "deeply cultivated like his father and brother, he was more civilized than either, well versed in the records and history of his house, responsive to the prevailing sentiments of his peoples . . . more pious than his predecessors, given to contemplative reading and private devotion, influenced by the fervent Dominican Saint Vincent Ferrer, and regarding himself the defender of the churches (as well as of the pope) in his realms."[5] Martí's devotion to religious orthodoxy and the Church, which at times bordered on the obsessive, thus earned him his sobriquet *l'Ecclesiàstic.* As a striking display to his religiosity, and as an additional testament of legitimacy, when Martí entered the Crown of Aragon for the first time as king, in May 1397, after having sojourned in Avignon to meet with Benedict XIII, he brought with him the spiritually powerful relic of a piece of the True Cross.[6] Within the hierarchy of medieval relics, those affiliated with the narrative of the Passion were particularly important, and a sliver of the True Cross was no trifling relic.

Martí was also a prudent and cautious king, possibly because he was a forty-year-old man when he inherited the throne. He had plenty of experience with the poor administration of Joan's realm. Rather than being overly generous with lavish salaries and appointments, Martí made fiscal conservatism the watchword of his kingdom and curtailed court and state expenses in order to refill the royal coffers after the reign of Joan and Yolande.[7] Unlike his brother, Martí did not spend large sums of money on prophetic, astrological, and divinatory treatises.

One of the reasons Martí and Maria sought a return to stability was because of the perceived excesses of Joan and Yolande's reign. They began this process through the aforementioned purge of Joan's councilors. Martí and Maria, however, knew the worth of keeping some of Joan's former

---

5. Bisson, *Medieval Crown of Aragon*, 130.

6. Ibid., 127.

7. Ibid., 126–29.

assistants in helping smooth the transition to their reign. Of Joan's thirty-four accused courtiers, twelve were reinstated to serve in Martí's court, including the vice chancellor of Catalonia, Esperandéu Cardona; the chamberlain to Yolande de Bar, Ponç de Perellós; and, of course, Bernat Metge.[8] In tandem with the purge of the royal household, however, was a deliberate search for a return to orthodox practice and moral regulation.

Despite King Martí's religiosity, the occult still whispered within the culture of his courtly demimonde. Important occult texts were contained within Martí's royal library, which is why I have considered Martí's rejection of the occult sciences partial. Of some 340 books, 52, or 15 percent, dealt with sidereal matters.[9] On one level the possession of these texts in his library pointed to Martí as intellectually well rounded, although there is no indication in the historical record that Martí actually read those texts. More likely these were texts he had inherited from the libraries of his father and brother. As such, he might not necessarily want to purge them from his own royal library despite his religious leanings. Even if Martí never embraced occult matters as completely as had Joan, it appears he was not completely distanced from the occult. One of the strangest texts to appear to be written for Martí was an anonymous alchemical work, the *Tractatus compositus super lapidem philosophorum que fenix intitulatur*, or simply, *The Phoenix*.[10]

This seeming disconnect reflected in Martí's intellectual and religious interests had been seen in other instances. Even though notions of religious orthodoxy and moral rectitude were central aspects to Martí's regnal style, during his principate Martí appeared at times to not enforce religious demands as strictly as he would when he became king. For example, Martí's shifting position concerning the local Muslim pilgrimage site of Atzeneta, located in the municipality of Guadalest in the kingdom of Valencia, reflects this. At the Council of Vienne in 1311, Pope Clement V told the assembled ecclesiastics that Christian religious and secular authorities were to

---

8. Kagay, "Poetry in the Dock," 40–41.

9. See Jaume Massó Torrents, "Inventari dels Bens Mobles del Rey Martí d'Aragó," *Revue Hispanique* 12 (1905): 413–590; and Boudet, *Entre science et nigromance*, 305. Such texts of an astrological and/or prophetic nature included, among others, *los juys de Stronomia de mestre Johan de Sibilia; Almanach; la stralabria; De la proprietat de les planetes; Libre de les ymages del cel destres et sinestres; profacies de Merli*, and *De Strologia*.

10. De Luanco, *La Alquimia*, 225–37.

prohibit their Muslim vassals from engaging in their individual and collective religious practices, such as publicly invoking the name of Muhammad, announcing the call to prayer, and going on pilgrimage to local saints' sites, as such acts were considered "an offense to the Christian community."[11] Regarding the latter act, local administrators in the kingdom of Valencia, who were subject to the authority of the king of the Crown of Aragon, attempted to prevent *mudéjares*, those Muslims who lived under Christian dominion in the Iberian Peninsula, from going on pilgrimage to the local site of Atzeneta. This was the location of the grave of the widely venerated prophet Galib ibn Hasan ibn Ahmed ibn Sid Buna al-Juzai and was a popular destination for many *mudéjares*. Understandably, the *mudéjares* chafed at this restriction, and Prince Martí commanded the local authorities to permit members from some twenty-five *mudéjar* families from the towns of Sogorb and d'Eslida to go on pilgrimage to the site, despite the restrictions imposed on them by local authorities.[12]

When he became king, however, Martí changed his position regarding Atzeneta. Appearing to recall the prescription against Muslim pilgrimage as issued by the Council of Vienne in 1400, King Martí wrote his administrator, Guillem Martorell, and commanded him to punish those *mudéjares* who continued to visit Atzeneta and leave votive offerings despite royal prohibition.[13] The situation, which Martí called "an affront to the Christian community," infuriated the king to such a degree that he commanded that the mosque at Atzeneta be razed and that the body of Sid Buna al-Juzai be exhumed, pulverized, and the ashes cast into the sea.[14]

As king, Martí was a staunch champion of religious orthodoxy. Yet the presence of *The Phoenix* in the king's library is problematic, as alchemy was

---

11. María Teresa Ferrer i Mallol, *Els Sarraïnes de la Corona Catalano-Aragonesa en el Segle XV: Segregació i Discrimació* (Barcelona: Consell Superior d'Investigacions Científiques, 1987), 95. See also John Boswell, *The Royal Treasure: Muslim Communities under the Crown of Aragon in the Fourteenth Century* (New Haven, CT: Yale University Press, 1977), 262. See also Francisco A. Roca Traver, "Un siglo de vida mudéjar en la Valencia medieval (1238–1338)," *Estudios de Edad Media de la Corona de Aragon* 5 (1952): 115–208; and the *Corpus Iuris Canonici, Clementinarum* V, I.1.26 (Antwerp: Apud Ioannem and Iacobum Meursios, 1648).

12. Ferrer i Mallol, *Els Sarraïnes*, 97 and 322.

13. Ibid., 364–65.

14. See Daniel Girona i Llagostera, *Itinerari del rey en Martí (1396–1410)* (Barcelona: Henrich y Compania, 1916), 112; and Michael A. Ryan, "Power and Pilgrimage: The Restriction of *Mudéjares*' Pilgrimage in the Kingdom of Valencia," *Essays in Medieval Studies* (2008): 115–28.

another contested discipline in the eyes of the clergy. Nicolau Eymerich had significant problems with the discipline of alchemy, which he considered "a deadly, sinful fraud," and he linked alchemists with other dabblers in the supernatural arts, including necromancers, seers, and astrologers, all of whom he believed depended upon direct or indirect demonic agency to successfully complete their tasks.[15] Writing again to Bernardus Strucci in 1395, Eymerich blasted alchemists and urged him not to consort with them, as their words pool "beneath their lips like the venom of asps."[16] For Eymerich, these individuals "fabricate lies, delude the great, empty men's purses, and defraud the poor." How do they do this? "Namely they craft artificially various and many precious stones and claim to be able to transmute by the art of alchemy lead into silver and silver into gold."[17] Alchemists represented the most iniquitous type of charlatan, as they "sin against God and their neighbors, readily degenerate into counterfeiting, and, like superstitious astrologers, are too disposed to invoke demons."[18]

Returning to *The Phoenix*, an alchemical work attributed to Arnau de Vilanova, the anonymous scribe dedicated this text to King Martí in 1390.[19] The immediate problem with this was, of course, that Martí did not begin his reign as king until 1396. It is conceivable that Martí, as prince, might have commissioned this specific work, but to my knowledge no proof of this has yet become known. *The Phoenix* is a brief alchemical guide for transmuting dust into precious metals. The process, like many alchemical procedures, relates a complex series of steps that must be done and is precise about the quantities of expensive and dangerous materials used. The

---

15. Matton, "Le traité *Contre les alchimistes*, and William R. Newman, *Promethean Ambitions: Alchemy and the Quest to Perfect Nature* (Chicago: University of Chicago Press, 2004), 91–97, here 96.

16. BnF, MS lat 3171, f. 51v.: "venenum aspidum sub labiis eorum."

17. BnF, MS lat 3171, f. 52v.: "Scilicet preciosos lapides uarios et multiplices artificialiter fabricant atque plumbum in argentum et argentum in aurum arte alchimie possint transmutare."

18. Thorndike, *HMES*, 3:515.

19. De Luanco, *La Alquimia*, 225: "ductus Ser^{mo} Regi Aragonum martino anno do^{ni} MC-CCXC." De Luanco, *La Alquimia*, 225, refers to another version of this work dedicated to King Martí, listed as "T. 284 in our Biblioteca Nacional." De Luanco quotes the dedicatory of this alternate version on page 226, but I am unsure whether he or the medieval scribe who first copied it misdated the work as 1499: "Tractatus compositus super lapidem philosophorum qui fenix intitulatur phie filium et missus per eundem ad Dominum martinum regem Aragonum año millesimo quadragentessimo nonagessimo nono et vocatur liber iste fenix."

author of the work refers to the precision necessary for every step of the process and advises the would-be alchemist to ensure that he or she garners all necessary materials in accordance with the writings of astrologers. This comes as no surprise, as the two disciplines were closely linked, and alchemical processes were dependent upon astral principles.

References to sidereal matters course throughout the text. To begin the specific alchemical process that *The Phoenix* depicts, one is to obtain a pound of mercury during the month when the planet Mercury would have its greatest influence upon the world below. This action would also preferably take place on a Wednesday, as that day was named in honor of the planet. The author continues that the first Wednesday of that month would be the optimal day to acquire said mercury for the alchemical process.[20]

These and similar prescriptions continue throughout *The Phoenix*. Concerning the creation of "the sun," meaning gold, the author urges the practitioner again to rely on astrology: "take an ounce of very fine gold, the finest that you are able to obtain, and look towards astrology for the month of the year that the sun has the best, sweetest, and most amiable influence." However, the author mentions, one has to do this in accordance with Christian tenets and tells the alchemist that the process can take place, "provided that it is not on Sunday, because it would be a sin to work with one's hands."[21]

Was *The Phoenix* an alchemical work commissioned by the young prince Martí? Did the anonymous scribe make a mistake in dating the dedication of the work? Was that mistake intentional, an attempt to discredit the king and cast doubt on his seeming orthodoxy? It is impossible to know the anonymous author's intent in dedicating this work to Martí. Despite the existence of this strange and problematic alchemical treatise dedicated to a king for whom Christian identity was significant, if not paramount, the occult sciences, overall, occupied an uneasily reconciled space within King Martí's mind. Before discussing the relationship that King Martí had with the occult, however, we must first turn our attention to the crisis that could have prevented him from wearing the crown in the first place.

20. Ibid., 228.
21. Ibid., 231: "E siuols fer sol. soes or . . . pren i oz deor molt fi lo mes fi que pugues auer eueies per estrologia en qual mes del any lo sol a millor epus dolsa influensia epus amable . . . ab que no sia dumenge car seria pecat obrar de mans."

King Joan's hunting accident set in motion a series of dramatic events. As Joan had no male heir, the throne of the Crown of Aragon was to pass to his younger brother. Martí, however, was away from the kingdom and attempting to solidify Aragonese possessions in the Mediterranean, especially Sicily. Since the throne was vacant, storms soon began to gather. With Joan's sudden death and the increasing interest of the Count of Foix, Matthieu de Castelbon, in appropriating the kingdom, Martí found himself in dire straits. Needing to remain in Sicily to enforce his claims over that island, Martí nonetheless needed an advocate, someone to defend the realms until his return. That duty fell to the new queen, Maria de Luna, who was a staunch supporter of her husband's monarchical authority.[22] Maria ruled as a sovereign in her own right during Martí's absence, and she defended the kingdom by holding off militarily the forces of the Count of Foix until Martí could return.

Matthieu de Castelbon was able to press his claim to the throne through his marriage to Joanna, the daughter of Joan by the late king's first wife, Mata d'Armagnac. Further compounding matters was Yolande's staunch refusal to give up the throne after Joan's death. Yolande wrote his administrators and urged them to continue serving her, as they had done her husband, "as good vassals and servants as always."[23] When she announced that she was pregnant with the late king's child, a claim that later turned out to be false, the issues of succession became more clouded. Upon Castelbon's invasion of the Crown of Aragon to reinforce his claims to the throne, Maria was forced to defend the kingdom.

Bernat Metge's situation sheds significant light on the matter. Metge, as previously mentioned, was under arrest by the time of the Count of Foix's invasion. In addition to being considered a treacherous courtier who contributed to the excesses and poor management style that plagued the late King Joan, it was rumored that the notary favored Matthieu de Castelbon as the new sovereign of the Crown of Aragon. Metge supposedly uttered

---

22. For more on Maria's regnal style, see Núria Silleras-Fernández, "Spirit and Force: Politics, Public and Private in the Reign of Maria de Luna (1396–1406)," *Queenship and Political Power in Medieval and Early Modern Spain*, ed. Theresa Earenfight (Burlington, VT: Ashgate, 2005), 78–90; Silleras-Fernández, *Power, Piety, and Patronage.*

23. ACA, CR, R. 2051, f. 44. See also Kagay, "Poetry in the Dock," 2 n7.

an impolitic comment about Martí in public. When Metge heard the news about the death of the Catalan knight Pedro Maça, who fell in battle against the insurgent Sardinians, Metge was reported to have said: "It would have been better for the Lord Duke [Martí] (who is today the king) rather than Pedro Maça to have died, and if the lord [Joan] would do what he should, he ought to cut off the Lord Duke's head . . . for he has not proven faithful to the Lord King."[24] Being linked with these intemperate remarks did not win the disgraced scribe any favors.

Maria was able to repel the forces of Matthieu de Castelbon, and Martí and Maria were officially crowned king and queen of the Crown of Aragon, respectively, on the thirteenth and twenty-third of April 1399 in the city of Zaragoza.[25] They began to rule accordingly and turned their attention to the matter of King Joan's supposedly wicked councilors. As seen above, in *Lo Somni* we see Metge, suspected of having not supported the ascension of King Martí, using all of his literary skills to construct an impassioned defense of Martí and to depict both Queen Maria and King Martí as the rightful and legitimate monarchs to the throne.

A unique way he did this was through his defense of women, broadly, and Queen Maria, specifically. As seen above, in the third book of *Lo Somni*, the polarizing character of Tiresias rails against Metge and his "misplaced" love and respect for women. Tiresias spins a misogynist rant that spans the rest of the third book, a screed to which Metge responds point by point in his fourth book. The seer warns the sleeping Metge, "No man can have happiness in this world if he gives his love to a woman . . . not to his wife . . . nor to any other. . . . If men saw her as they should, they would, after having done what human procreation requires, flee from her as they would from death."[26] Tiresias lists the myriad failings of women in

24. Kagay, "Poetry in the Dock," 31 n102. See also Marina Mitjà, "Procés contra els consellers, domestics i curials de Joan I, entre ells Bernat Metge," *Academía de Buenas Letras de Barcelona* 27 (1957–1858): 375–415: "Interrogat si sab o ha hoyt dir que l dit Bernat Metge haia dit en publich, en lo temps que s sabe la mort de don Pero Massa, en la ciutat de Barchinona, com playent sa de la mort del dit don Pero Massa, dient tals o semblants paraules, que. Mes volguera que fos mort lo senyor duch (qui vui es rey) que no don Pero Massa, e que si lo senyor rey hi devia fer ço que devia, que devia levar lo cap al dit senyor duch, qui vui es rey, car prou li n havia fets."

25. *Manual de Novells Ardits vulgarment apellat Dietari del Antich Consell Barceloní*, eds. Frederich Schwartz y Luna and Francesch Carreras y Candi (Barcelona: Henrich y companía, 1892), 1:77.

26. Metge, *Lo Somni*, 46.

detail, which includes such unsavory aspects as their being unclean, superstitious, and capricious, among others.[27]

Tiresias's attitude toward women is based on his own life. He relates his biography to the dreaming Metge, explaining how he once was a famous philosopher, mathematician, and father to Manto, "who in necromancy and other arts reproved by Catholics was not inferior to Medea."[28] Tiresias was therefore closely linked with the occult arts and the privileged knowledge they promise. He was also privy to another body of privileged knowledge, having lived as both male and female.

Tiresias explains to Metge that one day, while walking in the woods, he spied two snakes copulating and struck them with his staff, a deed that instantly turned him into a woman. After spending seven years as a female, Tiresias saw the same two snakes fornicating and he struck them again, which turned him back into a man. Having lived as both male and female, Tiresias was therefore in a unique position to serve as the requested judge in a postcoital conflict between the gods Jupiter and Juno, who were arguing about whether men or women were lustier. Based on the empirical evidence he had gained while living as a woman, Tiresias decreed, "the woman's lust surpasses that of the man three times over." His decision angered Juno so greatly that she tore out his eyes. Jupiter, feeling regret and sympathy for Tiresias, rectified the situation as the seer explains: "seeing that for having spoken the truth I had incurred such great damage, [that he] gave me by way of compensation the spirit of divination. And while I lived in the world, I gave many times the answers to what people asked about things yet to come."[29]

By living as both a man and woman, Tiresias gained access to another level of particular knowledge, but it was not his sole body of privileged knowledge. Tiresias received the gift of prophecy from Jupiter because of the consequences of his having drawn from this body of privileged knowledge in answering Juno. Divination, therefore, becomes linked with a

---

27. Ibid., 46–55. For more on the traditional catalog of medieval women's supposed sins, much of which Metge echoes in *Lo Somni*, see Georges Duby, *Women of the Twelfth Century: Volume 3: Eve and the Church*, trans. Jean Birrell (Chicago: University of Chicago Press, 1998), 3–28.

28. Metge, *Lo Somni*, 45.

29. Ibid., 46.

knowledge that transgresses sexuality, and in Tiresias's speeches he rails against women's attempts to use divination for multiple ends.

After Tiresias's vicious railing against women, which tickles the author, Metge tells Tiresias, "everything you have said will not go unanswered."[30] It is in the fourth book where Metge addresses Tiresias's claims, point by point. Metge speaks of the virtue of Mary, but Tiresias does not accept her as a model of virtuous womanhood for, "she . . . was a unique phoenix of virtue and holy life. A single flower does not make Spring."[31] Relying upon his humanist knowledge, and patterning his style after Giovanni Boccaccio's 1374 work, *De claris mulieribus* (On Famous Women), Metge lists virtuous women from the worlds of history and myth. Among them Metge includes the prophetic Sibyls "who . . . prophesied the coming of Christ."[32]

After praising many virtuous women, Metge then segues to the most important part of his work, the section that would ultimately determine whether his life would be spared: his defense of the royal women of the House of Aragon. He ascribes great sanctity, power, and rectitude to such luminaries as Elisenda de Montcada, the royal founder of the prestigious Benedictine convent of Pedralbes; Queen Elionor, the mother of Joan; and the widowed Queen Yolande.[33] He is most effusive, however, in his concluding praise for Queen Maria, the wife of King Martí, in whose hands his life hung. Metge celebrates Maria's defense of the realms in *Lo Somni*, and he lauds Maria as a virago, linking her with other heroic, martial, and virtuous women of myth and antiquity. Metge was careful to depict the ruling queen as a virtuous, honorable woman who defended the realms and preserved the rightful lineage of the Crown of Aragon. This comprised a significant part of his defense:

> I shall conclude briefly with our present queen, Lady Maria. Not that she deserves to be the last on account of being less virtuous, but in order to give her greater advantage and honor. She will be the key that closes the work, the signature placed at the end of the rescript, and the seal that makes its authority complete. So many are the virtues for which she deserves praise, that

---

30. Ibid., 55.
31. Ibid., 60.
32. Metge, *Lo Somni*, 62; and Metge, *The Dream*, xxviii.
33. Metge, *Lo Somni*, 65.

I do not know where to begin. . . . [The strength of her love for Martí was so pronounced] she always thought of him while he was, in extreme peril of his person, fighting to subdue the kingdom of Sicily; she waited for him, half-widowed and, by common opinion with little hope of seeing him ever again; but also, to support and help him, she sold all she owned and sent him many fresh troops and much money, while she remained, considering her station, in great want and penury. . . . the great patience she showed upon her accession to the royal dignity, when she suffered certain insolent people to say in the presence of her majesty, because she would not comply with their unjust demands. "You do not know yet if you are queen!" . . . You cannot imagine the wisdom she displayed when, in the absence of the king, she expelled from the land the count of Foix who had invaded it with a company of mighty thieves, for he claimed rights to the kingdom, of which he had no more than you do. . . . The count was defeated only by the wisdom and diligence and the good decisions of that lady. Having amply prepared for it with the help of our illustrious city of Barcelona and of Aragon, she frightened him away and put him to flight, even as the lion does the deer, and the falcon the crane.[34]

Maria's defense of the realm and the throne in the absence of her husband was thus celebrated by Metge and well remembered by the king himself, who recalled the near loss of his realms.[35] By virtue of Metge's literary prowess, it appears that Martí did not notice, or at least ignored, his heterodox stance in the first book of *Lo Somni*. This is surprising, since both the king and the queen were staunch advocates of orthodoxy, but it might be that because of the debate in the first book, Martí genuinely believed the scribe to have been rehabilitated. Whereas it might seem that the imprisoned notary was engaging in heterodox behavior, he played an intellectual game and, as is seen in his work, continually tried to pay respect to authoritative, orthodox figures and contextualize them within a wholly Christian framework.[36] Furthermore, Metge was a valuable member of Joan's coterie and would be most useful in helping the new king transition to the throne and establish his authority and legitimacy in

---

34. Ibid., 65–66.
35. Girona i Llagostera, *Itinerari del Rey en Martí*, 23.
36. Metge, *The Dream*, xxvi.

his realms. After freeing Metge, Martí employed him in his administrative service. Metge returned to service as a scribe in the chancery and by 1405 headed investigations of internal affairs in Sicily. Metge inspected agencies and administrators on the island and was later even bought as a lobbyist by the city council of Valencia, one of the most strident collection of critics of the misgovernment and corruption that plagued Joan's reign.[37]

Although in *Lo Somni* Metge depicts Joan as an emasculated and silent king, one who merited the pains of Purgatory for his interest in divination, Joan cannot be considered a fully heterodox sovereign, as he was aware of what constituted orthodox principles. In the late fourteenth century, King Joan sent the pope a missive that contained an oath of faith made on the part of the Byzantine emperor, which contained the articles of Catholic faith, as well as other tenets of faith in which an orthodox Christian should believe.[38] Yet his interest in divinatory and magical arts at the expense of other, more important duties might have led some critics to question if not his orthodoxy, then his ability to rule. If, as it was popularly believed, Joan's intemperate activities were encouraged by a coterie of corrupt officials, it made sense that Maria and Martí would not want to risk their court being similarly tainted. Maria herself shared her husband's predilections for piety and orthodoxy, and it comes as no shock that Queen Maria sought oaths of loyalty from her new domestics and familiars of the royal household.[39]

However, Martí's own excessive devotions—in his case, to religion— earned him criticism. While Martí was still a prince, a Franciscan friar contacted him to update him on Sicilian affairs. In the missive the monk criticized the prince outright for his excessive religious devotion instead of being active in the practical political and military affairs of the island.[40] Martí's religious obsessions continued well into his reign as king; as Joan had been fond of books of prophecy and astrology, so Martí was fond of religious books. In 1399 Prince Martí bought a book titled the *Catholicon*, and in 1407, as king, he paid handsomely for other religious books.[41] This is not to say,

---

37. Kagay, "Poetry in the Dock," 35.

38. ACA, CR, R. 1926, f. 89v.–91.

39. ACA, CR, R. 2354, 16v.–17. See also P. Ivars Andrés, "Franciscanismo de la reina de Aragon doña Maria de Luna (1396–1406)," *Archivo Ibero-americano* 34 (1931): 568–94.

40. Rubió i Lluch, *Documents*, 2:335–37.

41. Ibid., 1:406–7; 2:386.

however, that the new king was not wholly disinterested in the sidereal arts; nonetheless, he was not as preoccupied with them as his older brother was. In 1403 King Martí contacted the astronomer Joan Foixa about his knowledge of lunar eclipses, and two years later the monarch contacted the abbot of the royal monastery of Poblet for information about someone who knew how to read astrolabes for his son, the king of Sicily, also named Martí.[42]

Martí's devotion to his Christian faith manifested itself in his backing of his older brother's support of the doctrine of the Immaculate Conception. More practically, and with wider and more immediate ramifications for medieval Christendom, Martí was concerned about ending the Great Western Schism. Perhaps recalling the fate his brother suffered in *Lo Somni* for his apathy, Martí actively corresponded with his relative Benedict XIII in an attempt to end the crisis.

Compared with other medieval states, the Crown of Aragon navigated the politically treacherous waters engendered by the Schism in a very different way. During Pere's reign the Crown took a decidedly neutral position in regard to its relationship between Rome and Avignon. Yet the position would shift during the reign of his son Joan, who was initially indifferent to the crisis of the Schism, which was significant. Before his election as Pope Benedict XIII, Valencian cardinal Pedro de Luna had agreed to a compromise. In order to end the division of the Church, he promised that if elected pope he would abdicate the papal seat once he was in power. By a principle known as the "way of cession," the popes in Rome and Avignon would cede their power at the same time and usher in a new papal election and a new age for the Church. The leading minds of the day sought to resolve the crisis. By 1394 the faculty of the University of Paris offered three potential solutions to resolve the Schism: there was the *via cessionis*, in which both popes would abdicate; the *via compromissi*, through which an ideally impartial group of arbiters would determine the matter; and the *via concilii*, whereby a general council would convene and decide.[43] The third of these was seen as the most extreme and least desirable solution. However, Benedict XIII did not immediately fulfill his promise and postponed his abdication indefinitely. By 1395 the pope began to feel the pressure exerted upon him by the French

42. Ibid., 1:427–28 and 433.
43. Smoller, *History, Prophecy and the Stars*, 120.

monarchy to resign. Joan, however, shifted his position and actively courted the favor of the Avignonese pope; indeed, the only region that did not desert him ultimately was the Crown of Aragon. After Joan's accident, the task to make the intractable pope abdicate fell to King Martí.

The abbot of the prestigious monastery of Sant Cugat del Vallès, Joan Armengol, who would eventually become bishop of Barcelona in 1398, supported Martí in all of his endeavors to rectify the Schism.[44] Martí repeatedly wrote to Benedict, requesting various audiences for Aragonese ambassadors, as well as his other administrators, and thus put his energy and the full weight of royal diplomacy behind ending the crisis.[45] In addition to his diplomatic resources, Martí also provided military support to the besieged pontiff, dispatching eighteen galleons from Aragonese maritime bases stationed along the Rhône. However, the fact that Benedict XIII was the relative of Queen Maria generated significant popular support for the Avignonese pope in the Crown of Aragon and encouraged the pope in maintaining his position. Therefore, despite his best efforts, Martí ultimately was unable to persuade the intractable Benedict XIII to abdicate his throne and end the crisis.[46] The situation generated pronounced tension between pope and sovereign, yet Martí later permitted Benedict XIII to take up residence in Barcelona in August 1409 because of the latter's poor health.[47]

Although they were unable to affect change on a wider scale and thus help end the Schism, Martí and Maria looked to their own backyard in seeking to enforce moral rectitude among their subjects. For instance, Martí enacted legislation that would crack down on prostitution in his realms.[48] He also targeted "most wicked" blasphemers, those individuals who, "from the heart or the mouth, irreverently utter something against the goodness or divine excellence or deny its pertaining majesty."[49]

44. Delaruelle, *L'Église au temps du Grand Schisme*, 1:88.
45. Girona i Llagostera, *Itinerari del Rey en Martí*, 12–14.
46. Ibid., 14.
47. Delaruelle, *L'Église au temps du Grand Schisme*, 1:157.
48. ACA, CR, R. 2345, ff. 130–31 and ACA, CR, R. 2346, ff. 46–46v.
49. ACA, CR, R. 2166, ff. 101v.–102. The definition comes from Francesc Eiximenis's *Art de Bé Morir*, BC, Arxiu Fotogràfic Miquel i Planes (AFMP) 22.3: "E de blasfemar deu. ço es dir de cor o de boca. irreuerendment cosa alguna la qual nos couinga ala bonea o excellencia diuinal o denegar co que a la magestatse pertany o pertanga." This definition is sandwiched in the manuscript between those of "infidelity" and "schism."

Connected with these blasphemers were other unsavory characters such as prostitutes, gamblers, defilers of the Virgin Mary's name, and individuals known as *zafurs*. Deriving from the Arabic word *zuharī*, a servant of the planet Venus, these people were perceived as specialists in the occult art of geomancy.

This restriction against *zafurs* appears to reflect a perception of a body of knowledge and occult practices linked particularly with Muslims. Within the context of medieval religious polemic literature, astrological signs and planets were attributed to various peoples. For instance, Muslim polemic linked Jews to the malevolent planet Saturn because of their observation of the Sabbath. Physiological characteristics came into play within this understanding, as some Muslim polemicists declared Christians, because of their blond hair and ruddy skin, to be subject to the sun's sway.[50] Within medieval astrological reckoning, Muslims were considered to be "the people of Venus," a perception that Muslim astrologers, including the authoritative Abu ʿMashar, themselves also held, as it was linked to the Islamic practice of conducting and attending worship services on Friday.[51]

The connection of Venus with Islam within Muslim religious polemic might have served a dual purpose for the intended Muslim audience: it linked Muslim populations with a sense of purity and cleanliness that was diametrically opposed to the supposed stench and depravity of Jewish and Christian communities, and it countered Christian polemic that linked Muslim pilgrimage to the Kaʿba with the pagan worship of Venus and, therefore, sexual promiscuity. Thus, the planets and heavenly signs could also govern sexuality. Within the Islamic context, Venus represented lawful sexual purity and deeds, *turh*, and stood in contrast with Christian sexual virtue and infertility.[52]

Sexuality factors heavily in one particular fourteenth-century source against the *zafurs*. Concerned with regulating sexual immorality, in March 1397 Queen Maria wrote one of the king's administrators, Guillermo de Raiadello, regarding the matter of "detractors, blasphemers of the divine

---

50. Cuffel, *Gendering Disgust*, 183–84.
51. Ibid., 184 and 333 n135; and Peter Biller, "A 'Scientific' View of Jews from Paris around 1300," *Micrologus: Natura, Scienze e Società Medievali* 9 (2001): 137–68, here 154.
52. Cuffel, *Gendering Disgust*, 184.

name, and ruffians popularly called *alcauots* and *zafuers*."[53] Maria was concerned that these individuals not only had gaming tables and gambling implements in their possession, but they also held women as servants or captives and forced them into committing carnal acts.[54] Simultaneously establishing regnal legitimacy and enforcing orthodoxy, she commanded Guillermo to investigate the matter and ensure that the culpable parties are punished.

After such a tumultuous beginning, the remainder of Martí's reign was marked by his and Queen Maria's prudence and piety. In purging the royal court of the excesses and corruption that tarnished the glitter of Joan and Yolande's royal court, they attempted to stamp their outlook upon the culture of their court and thus establish it as part of their enduring legacy. For Martí and Maria, fiscal mismanagement and occult matters had little place in their court. Even though Martí maintained the astral and alchemical writings and commissioned works from his father and older brother, unlike them, the new sovereign was not as enamored with such subjects, relegating them to the margins of the culture of his royal courtly demimonde. Peering into the future through any number of means does not appear to have been one of his predilections. Unbeknownst to the pious monarch, Martí's reign would indeed be monumental for reasons that would have distressed him greatly had he known what would happen.

---

53. ACA, CR, R. 2346, f. 81: "contra detractores et blasfematores diuini nominis et contra ruffianos vulgariter nuncupatos alcauots et zafurerios."

54. ACA, CR, R. 2346, f. 81.

EPILOGUE

An Unfortunate Claimant: Jaume el Dissortat, the Rise of the Trastámaras, and beyond the Closing of the Ecumene

The death of the young Martí II, king of Sicily and legitimate heir to the throne of the Crown of Aragon, set into motion a grave dynastic crisis that would have profound ramifications for the ruling house. Felled by malaria in July 1409, Martí II was to become the next count-king after the death of his father, Martí *l'Humà*.[1] However, with the young prince's death, the line of the Catalan count-kings, which had been unbroken since the time of the ninth-century Guifré *el Pelòs*, risked being fractured. It is small wonder, then, why the elder King Martí scrambled to remarry Margarita, daughter of Pere de Prades, in September 1409 and produce a male heir before his life ran its course.[2]

---

1. News of the young prince's death did not reach Barcelona until August of that year. *Manual de Novells Ardits vulgarment apellat Dietari del Antich Consell Barceloní*, ed. Frederich Schwartz y Luna and Francesch Carreras y Candi, 28 vols. (Barcelona: Henrich y Companyía, 1892), 1:162.
   2. Ibid., 1:163.

This, however, was not meant to be. Upon the death of King Martí in the monastery of Valldonzella on the last day of May 1410, the original line of the House of Aragon ended.[3] Martí lacked a male heir to ascend to the throne, and the crisis became full-blown, as the throne in Barcelona was now completely vacant. Lest any usurpers seek the crown again, as Matthieu de Castelbon did upon the death of Joan, a quick resolution had to be found. Two camps for the throne stood out. One, led by Jaume, the Count of Urgell, claimed the throne based on historical tradition, as the counts of Urgell had been linked with the royal domains since the time of Guifré.[4] The restored Bernat Metge, for his part, supported the candidacy of Count Jaume. This claim, however, was disputed by the Castilian nobleman Fernando d'Antequera, the grandson of Pere III, connected to the Crown of Aragon via his mother Elionor, the spouse of King Juan I (1379–1390) of Castile.

The contest was resolved in 1412 at Caspe. One of the most important individuals who helped resolve this dynastic crisis was the apocalyptic preacher Saint Vincent Ferrer (1350–1419).[5] Ferrer moved within powerful social and religious circles in the Crown of Aragon, influencing the prior king Martí profoundly. His sermons, which were immensely popular, were also controversial. In 1416, four years after the decision at Caspe, the French theologian Jean Gerson wrote Ferrer and chastised him for not distancing himself from a turbulent group of flagellants, inspired by Ferrer's apocalyptic sermons and who followed the preacher throughout his journeys.[6]

Allies of both Jaume of Urgell and Fernando d'Antequera relied on political prophecy to help reinforce their respective claims to the throne. The countess Margaret, the mother of Jaume, "held stock to some vaticinations and prophecies from a certain brother Anselm of Turmeda" and lent her son copies of Turmeda's prophecies, in addition to other prophecies

---

3. Ibid., 1:167.

4. For more on the last Count of Urgell, see Àngels Masià de Ros, *El Dissortat Comte d'Urgell* (Barcelona: Rafael Dalmau, 1960).

5. There are many studies on this famous apocalyptic preacher. For a more recent assessment of Vincent Ferrer and his role in the Schism, see Smoller, *History, Prophecy, and the Stars*, 94–95. Philip Daeleader is currently writing a new scholarly biography about Vincent Ferrer.

6. Smoller, *History, Prophecy, and the Stars*, 116–17. On July 18, 1417, Gerson finished a colophon, *Against the Sect of the Flagellants*, and sent it to Vincent Ferrer. Hobbins, *Authorship and Publicity*, 178.

attributed to historical figures, including John of Rupescissa, and literary ones, such as Merlin and Cassandra.[7] Both Pope Benedict XIII and Vincent Ferrer, however, backed Fernando d'Antequera, and the Valencian pope placed the Trastámaran upon the throne of Aragon. Benedict's decision, known as the Compromise of Caspe, which some modern Catalan patriots have viewed as the beginning of Castilian oppression of Catalan identity and culture, hastened the process of uniting the kingdoms of Castile and Aragon under one crown. When Fernando d'Antequera ascended to the throne of the House of Aragon, the new Trastámaran kings would bring the Crown of Aragon closer to the political sphere of Castile. The 1469 marriage between Queen Isabel of Castile and King Fernando II of Aragon, a direct descendant of the Trastámara line, would formally unite the two kingdoms and forge a new Hispania. This unity, however, would appear in name alone, as the separate literary legacies and languages of the two kingdoms have endured well into the twenty-first century.

Although the House of Aragon shifted to a Castilian dynasty with the Compromise of Caspe, the widespread interest in millenarian, apocalyptic, and occult themes, and their intersection with regnal authority, certainly did not perish with the deaths of the younger and elder Martís. During the reign of Fernando I, the new Castilian king of Aragon, an anonymous cleric composed a moralistic prophecy in response to the new king's ascension to the throne.[8] In addition, throughout the course of the fifteenth century, the pan-European interest in occult and apocalyptic literature continued to flourish apace.[9]

---

7. Calvet, *Fray Anselmo Turmeda*, 11: "Valíase la condesa, para más animar al hijo, de unos vaticinios y profecías de un fray anselmo de turmeda, que se había pasado a Tunez y renegado de la fé." My thanks also go to Ronald Surtz for this reference. The prophecies of Merlin were also extremely popular in Iberia. See Pere Bohigas i Balaguer, "La 'Visión' de Alfonso X y las 'Profecías de Merlín,'" *Revista de Filología Española* 25 (1941): 383–98; Bohigas i Balaguer, "Proficies de Merlí: Altres profecies contingudes en manuscrits catalans," *Butlletí de la Biblioteca de Catalunya* 8 (1928–1932): 253–79; Sylvia Roubaud, "La prophétie merlinienne en Espagne: des rois de Grande-Bretagne aux rois de Castille," *La Prophétie comme arme de guerre des pouvoirs, XVe–XVIIe siècles*, ed. Augustin Redondo (Paris: Presses de la Sorbonne Nouvelle, 2000), 159–73; José Tarré, "Las profecías del sabio Merlín y sus imitaciones," *Analecta Sacra Taraconensia* 16 (1943): 135–71.

8. BC, MS 485, f. 263–68: "propter peccata Regum et populii succesio per lineam rectam masculinam auferetur a duo Aragonum et succedet quidam infans castelle."

9. Illustrative works on this topic include, for Iberia, Richard Kagan, *Lucrecia's Dreams: Politics and Prophecy in Sixteenth-Century Spain* (Berkeley: University of California Press, 1990); Kagan, "Politics, Prophecy, and the Inquisition in Late Sixteenth-Century Spain," *Cultural Encounters: The Impact of the Inquisition in Spain and the New World*, ed. Mary Elizabeth Perry and

In studying the late medieval experience, understanding, and application of the apocalyptic, divinatory, and occult in conjunction with constructions of kingly mien, I have provided a powerful and unique perspective on the close relationship between these two worlds. For Pere, Joan, and Martí and their reigns, the divinatory and the occult occupied liminal and ever-shifting spaces, especially in response to the kings themselves and their methods of rule. For Pere, the strong sovereign who reigned while the powerful crises of plague and religious schism affected his own dominion, and who applied his own royal power at the expense of regional nobles, his interest in astronomy, astrology, and the occult went without censure. Joan, his son, was not nearly as fortunate. Plague and schism certainly did not abate from the Crown of Aragon during his reign. Yet his interest in the occult and divination was roundly condemned by his critics, because they perceived him as a weak king, one who was more interested in the newest cultural and intellectual trends of his day rather than soundly governing his state. As such, the sidereal and occult arts became major liabilities for Joan. Martí, his younger brother and regnal successor, took great pains to impress a new, pious culture on the courtly demimonde of the late fourteenth-, early fifteenth-century Crown of Aragon, and separated himself, to a degree, from the sidereal and occult interests of his father and brother. A champion of religiosity and orthodoxy, Martí tried to resolve the Great Western Schism, even if he was ultimately unsuccessful in those endeavors. Yet for all three kings, the occult and the stars were never far from their worlds.

The concern for regulating morality, as seen in Martí and Maria's early fifteenth-century legislation, continued well into that century. King

---

Anne J. Cruz (Berkeley: University of California Press, 1991), 105–24. For astrology in the early modern world, see, among others, Anthony Grafton, *Cardano's Cosmos: The Worlds and Works of a Renaissance Astrologer* (Cambridge, MA: Cambridge University Press, 1999); Paola Zambelli, ed., *"Astrologi hallucinati": Stars and the End of the World in Luther's Time* (Berlin: W. de Gruyter, 1986); Zambelli, "Profeti-astrologi sul medio periodo. Motivi pseudogioachimiti nel dibattito italiano e Tedesco sulla fine del mondo per la grande congiunzione del 1524," *Il profetismo gioachimita tra 400 e 500: Atti del III Congresso Internazionale di Studi Gioachimiti* (Geneva: Gian Luca Potestà, 1991), 273–86. For prophetic and apocalyptic expectations in early modernity, see Ottavia Niccoli, *Prophecy and People in Renaissance Italy*, trans. Lydia G. Cochrane (Princeton, NJ: Princeton University Press, 1990); Robert Aulotte, ed., *Prophètes et prophéties au XVIᵉ siècle* (Paris: Ecole Normal Superieure, 1998); Andrew Cunningham and Ole Peter Grell, *The Four Horsemen of the Apocalypse: Religion, War, Famine and Death in Reformation Europe* (Cambridge: Cambridge University Press, 2000).

Fernando of Aragon legislated against a host of unorthodox and immoral practices and gathered blasphemy, gambling, pimping, and sorcery under one mantle.[10] Queen Isabel of Castile, like Maria de Luna, also attempted to control her subjects' behavior; the principal duty of her *corregidores*, those representatives of the Crown who policed towns and cities in Castile, was to monitor morality at all levels of Castilian society.[11] If the ideas and actions of Maria and Martí continued well into the fifteenth century, it should thus come as no surprise that ideas surrounding millenarian, apocalyptic, and occult themes also persisted over the course of that century.

In addition to the increasing connection between the Iberian kingdoms of Castile and Aragon with the 1469 marriage between Isabel and Fernando, the fifteenth century also saw the completion of the seven-hundred-yearlong *Reconquista* of the Iberian Peninsula. In 1492 *los Reyes católicos*, the Catholic Sovereigns, conquered the Nasrid state of Granada, the last Muslim stronghold of al-Andalus. That same year also saw Christopher Columbus's arrival in the Americas and the closing of the *ecumene*, as Europeans and indigenous Americans encountered each other with globally momentous consequences.[12] One linkage between the two separate, but monumental, events was that the strain of messianic thought that percolated within European intellectual and cultural centers during the later Middle Ages took on a larger political and providential tone that applied to not just either the kingdom of Castile or of Aragon, but rather to all of Spain. The end of the *Reconquista* and the arrival of Iberians to American shores profoundly reinforced medieval Joachite expectations that the fulfillment of history and the advent of the presaged Third Age were at hand.

Medieval Europeans' exploration of the wider world and their encounters in the Americas were rooted in notions that drew upon apocalyptic,

10. Mark D. Meyerson, "Religion, Regionalism, and Royal Power," *Iberia and the Mediterranean World of the Middle Ages*, ed. Larry J. Simon (Leiden: Brill, 1995), 96–112, here 103.

11. Marvin Lunenfeld, *Keepers of the City: The Corregidores of Isabella I of Castile, 1474–1504* (Cambridge: Cambridge University Press, 1987), 118–20.

12. William D. Phillips Jr. and Carla Rahn Phillips, *The Worlds of Christopher Columbus* (Cambridge: Cambridge University Press, 1992). See also William H. McNeill, *Plagues and Peoples* (Garden City, NY: Anchor Books, 1976); and Alfred W. Crosby, *Ecological Imperialism: The Biological Expansion of Europe, 900–1900* (Cambridge: Cambridge University Press, 1986).

astrological, and occult ideas addressed throughout this book.[13] The Atlantic Ocean was no barrier to the transmission of late medieval and early modern European millenarianism and apocalypticism, but was rather a bridge; those ideas crossed the Atlantic, took root in the Americas, and circulated between intellectual centers in the Americas and Europe.[14] Early modern Franciscan missionaries were crucial to this process, as they carried those notions across the ocean and reread medieval apocalyptic notions by understanding and applying them in reaction to the experiences and peoples of the Americas.

One seminal figure for examining this transmission was the Genoese admiral Christopher Columbus. Columbus was the author of a prophetic and propagandistic work, the *Libro de las profecías*, in which he lauded Isabel of Castile and Fernando of Aragon, and the Spain over which they ruled, as occupying a providential place within Christian history.[15] Columbus portrayed himself as holding tremendous respect for the sovereigns and acting in concordance with both the temporal power of Ferdinand and Isabel and the spiritual power of Pope Alexander VI in Rome.[16] Like the fourteenth-century visionary John of Rupescissa, Columbus sought to be respectful of religious orthodoxy and secular authority in his work, especially since

13. Phillips and Phillips, *Worlds of Christopher Columbus*, 40. See also the 1372 purchase of an astrolabe in addition to a copy of Marco Polo's travel narrative by King Pere in Rubió i Lluch, *Documents*, 2:165–66.

14. Delno C. West, "Medieval Ideas of Apocalyptic Mission and the Early Franciscans in Mexico," *The Americas* 45, no. 3 (1989): 293–313.

15. Roberto Rusconi, ed., *The Book of Prophecies, edited by Christopher Columbus*, trans. Blair Sullivan, *Repertorium Columbianum*, vol. III (Berkeley: University of California Press, 1997); Delno C. West and August Kling, eds., *The Libro de las profecías of Christopher Columbus* (Gainesville: University of Florida Press, 1991); Djelal Kadir, *Columbus and the Ends of the Earth: Europe's Prophetic Rhetoric as Conquering Ideology* (Berkeley: University of California Press, 1992); Alain Milhou, *Colón y su mentalidad mesiánica en el ambiente franciscanista español* (Valladolid: Casa-Muséo de Colón, 1983). For the messianic and providentialist notions that surrounded the persons of King Ferdinand and Queen Isabel, see José Cepeda Adán, "El providencialismo en los cronistas de los Reyes Católicos," *Arbor* 17 (1950): 177–90; and Eulàlia Duran, "La cort reial com a centre de propaganda monàrquica: la participació morisca en l'exaltació mesiánica dels Reis Catòlics," *Pedralbes* 13 (1993): 505–14. Rusconi has suggested that "it seems reasonable to assume that the manuscript of the *Book of Prophecies* was never sent to the Spanish sovereigns and that Columbus took it with him on his fourth and last voyage," *Book of Prophecies*, 6.

16. Milhou, *Colón y su mentalidad mesiánica*, 470; Pauline Moffitt Watts, "Prophecy and Discovery: On the Spiritual Origins of Christopher Columbus's 'Enterprise of the Indies,'" *American Historical Review* 90 (1985): 73–102.

by "the final days of November 1500, [he] returned to Europe, ending his voyage to the Indies in chains rather than triumph."[17] Columbus wrote the *Libro de las profecías* to locate his discoveries in the Indies within a larger sequence of events that were crucial for the salvation of the human race and, in his opinion, which signified "the first step towards the liberation of Jerusalem and the Holy Land from Muslim domination."[18]

Columbus's arrival to the Americas did not occur in a vacuum, as he inherited an exploratory tradition that stretched back well into the medieval period.[19] The territorial conquests gained during the *Reconquista* required legislation to govern the new lands under Christian rule and to provide a stable environment that would foster sustained growth. Coupled with advances in technology and science, a result of the intellectual exchange between the Iberian worlds of the Dar al Islam and Christendom—especially in the realms of sidereal matters, as the stars were crucial for successful maritime navigation—Columbus was able to draw upon an extensive body of collective knowledge for his voyages.

Columbus himself occupies a unique space within the history of late medieval and early modern eschatology. A highly devout man, Columbus saw his role as an important one within the providential future of Spain. In his *Libro de las profecías* he personally addressed King Fernando and Queen Isabel and related to them how, like Rupescissa, through a sudden flash of divinely inspired insight he understood that all he experienced in his past had led him into his current state:

> At a very early age I began sailing the sea and have continued until now. This profession creates a curiosity about the secrets of the world. . . . During this time [of his training] I have studied all kinds of texts: cosmography, histories, chronicles, philosophy, and other disciplines. Through these writings, the hand of Our Lord opened my mind to the possibility of sailing to the Indies and gave me the will to attempt the voyage. . . . Who could doubt that this flash of understanding was the work of the Holy Spirit[?][20]

---

17. Rusconi, *Book of Prophecies*, iii.

18. Ibid., 5.

19. Felipe Fernández-Armesto, *Before Columbus: Exploration and Colonization from the Mediterranean to the Atlantic, 1229–1492* (Philadelphia: University of Pennsylvania Press, 1992); Valerie Irene Jane Flint, *The Imaginative Landscape of Christopher Columbus* (Princeton, NJ: Princeton University Press, 1992).

20. Columbus, *Book of Prophecies*, 67.

In light of late medieval thought about the end of the world, Columbus's encounter with the Americas was significant because it revealed that which was hidden and linked the early modern period with the ancient Christian past.[21] Read apocalyptically, Columbus's voyages were the penultimate episodes before Jerusalem's recapture, the event that would usher in the End Times. Because Iberian political unity had been achieved in name, Columbus believed that the prophecies of the Old Testament were coming to fruition, which announced the "unification of the ecumene under the standards of Christendom."[22] Columbus's work, intensely Joachite in nature, also appealed to the messianic and devout sensibilities of the king and queen, as he prophesized that "no one should be afraid to undertake any enterprise in the name of Our Savior, as long as it is just and appropriate to his holy service. . . . Remember, Your Highnesses, that with very little money you undertook the reconquest of the kingdom of Granada . . . [and] The Calabrian abbot Joachim [of Fiore] said that whoever was to rebuild the temple on Mount Zion would come from Spain."[23] Columbus, therefore, dwelled within a world that he understood as replete with messianic topoi.

Columbus struggled with his fame, to a degree. After his arrival to the Americas, he was proud to have achieved something significant and unique. Nevertheless, he struggled to check his pride, chief among the seven deadly sins, with humility. The result was a truly Columbine mixture of pride and humility that expressed itself through the motif of the rightly persecuted.[24] Columbus was also well aware of the Franciscans' role in missionary activities and viewed the Americas as a new arena in which proselytizing could take place. European missionaries who encountered indigenous Americans contextualized them within their own providential history as being the last people on earth whose ultimate conversion, along

---

21. Milhou, *Colón y su mentalidad mesiánica*, 471. See also Adriano Prosperi, "America e Apocalisse: Note sulla 'conquista spirituale' del Nuevo Mondo," *Critica Storica* 13 (1976): 1–61; Prosperi, "New Heaven and New Earth: Prophecy and Propaganda at the Time of the Discovery and Conquest of the Americas," *Prophetic Rome in the High Renaissance Period*, ed. Marjorie Reeves (Oxford: Clarendon Press, 1992), 279–303; and Leonard I. Sweet, "Christopher Columbus and the Millennial Vision of the New World," *Catholic Historical Review* 72 (1986): 372–81.

22. Milhou, *Colón y su mentalidad mesiánica*, 185.

23. Columbus, *Book of Prophecies*, 77.

24. Milhou, *Colón y su mentalidad mesiánica*, 42–45, 91.

with the restoration of the kingdom of Jerusalem, would usher in the End Times and fulfill medieval expectations of the future Apocalypse.[25]

In medieval and early modern Europe, visionary insight and recognizing the course of future events operated along multiple understandings. The writing, reading, and commenting on divinatory matters was experienced on many levels of late medieval European society. Yet attempting to foresee the future, albeit popular, was nevertheless inherently problematic within a medieval Christian framework. Harnessing the stars to this reckoning and using them in an attempt to provide additional elaboration and legitimacy to visionary insight further complicated the situation. The liminal space that astrology occupied, straddling magic and science, heresy and orthodoxy, and authority and dissent, convoluted the nature of revelatory insight. Because the Crown of Aragon was a premier center for astrological text production and commentary, whose kings themselves were interested in such matters, it was thus a kingdom of stargazers, filled with those who wrote, read, and understood these sidereal matters within a visionary framework and whose opinions were received, lauded, or rejected by others.

Attempting to glimpse the future, especially via astrology, is not simply the domain of the premodern past. Today's newspapers and websites offer their readers daily astrological predictions based on their natal star signs, and almanacs still make for popular reading. Checking one's daily horoscope may make for a harmless diversion, but there are those who still perceive astrology and divining the future as highly suspect, even diabolic. Moreover, when there is an undue interest in astrology at the highest echelons of state power, there are those who still raise a great clamor.

Take the 1988 disclosure from former White House chief of staff Donald Regan. Regan made headlines around the nation and the world when he revealed in his book, *For the Record*, that then-president Ronald Reagan and First Lady Nancy Reagan regularly consulted with an anonymous astrologer "friend." Donald Regan reported that Nancy Reagan periodically would schedule the president's public appearances and meetings only

---

25. John Leddy Phelan, *The Millennial Kingdom of the Franciscans in the New World*, 2nd ed. (Berkeley: University of California Press, 1970); and Edwin Edward Sylvest Jr., *Motifs of Franciscan Mission Theory in Sixteenth Century New Spain Province of the Holy Gospel* (Washington, DC: Academy of American Franciscan History, 1975).

after first consulting with her "friend," who suggested astrologically auspicious times and dates. This was especially the case after John Hinckley Jr.'s 1981 assassination attempt on President Reagan. The astrologer "friend" in question whom the Reagans consulted was the Nob Hill socialite Joan Quigley, and Regan's exposé suggested that the Reagans' dependence on astrology influenced other decisions of national and global import. The idea that the leader of the United States gave no small amount of credence to astrology was seen as risible by critics on the political left and as nigh horrific by the Reagans' politically conservative, especially Evangelical Christian, supporters. The controversy engendered by Regan's revelation was such that the cover story of the May 16, 1988, issue of *Time* magazine proclaimed, in a type size normally reserved for declarations of war, "Exclusive: Astrology in the White House," and featured a picture of Nancy Reagan staring up at the heavens as stars twinkled in the skies above the White House.[26] The criticism of astrology and its intersection with political authority thus still resonates some five hundred years after the end of the medieval era.

During the later Middle Ages, divination and astrology were not pastimes, but instead significant systems of thought used by people to access a body of information that was always tantalizingly out of reach. The edges of divinatory understanding were opaque, shifting, and fuzzy and eluded people's easy grasp, and the ways of divining the future were myriad and arcane. Some put their hopes in reading the patterns that the stars created as they wove a sidereal skein that blanketed the earth below. They held as much fascination for medieval people as they do for modern people today. The stars were, and still are, tempting oracles for people who seek to understand the meanings behind their cold beauty and to know better what information these silent harbingers had to offer about the future. Far from the fires of hearth and city, where the brilliantly cold light of an unfathomable quantity of stars bathed the intent observer, what quiet tales could the medieval stargazer create? What possible futures did he or she glimpse? And how many of those stories remain unavailable to scholars, having been

---

26. See also Barrett Seaman's article from the same May 16 issue, "Good Heavens! An Astrologer Dictating the President's Schedule?" *Time*, May 16, 1998, 24–25; and Newman and Grafton, *Secrets of Nature*, 2.

misplaced, permanently lost, or simply never recorded? Although attempting to divine the future is, by its very nature, a hazy endeavor, one thing is very clear. No matter how intently people tried to foresee the future by gazing at the glittering stars that wheeled and coursed throughout the nighttime skies above the medieval Crown of Aragon and the Mediterranean Sea, the stars themselves remained mute, indifferent to the events that occurred below and ever silent about those that were to come.

BIBLIOGRAPHY

Archival Sources and Manuscripts

Archival documents from the Arxiu Diocesà de Barcelona (ADB), Barcelona.

Archival documents from the Cancellería Real (CR), Archivo de la Corona de Aragón (ACA), Barcelona.

Beatus of Liébana. *Beato de Valladolid.* Valladolid: Universidad de Valladolid, 2002.

Beinecke Rare Book and Manuscript Library, Yale University, Mellon Collection of Alchemy and the Occult, MS 6.

Beinecke Rare Book and Manuscript Library, Yale University, Mellon Collection of Alchemy and the Occult, MS 12.

Carbonell, Pere Miquel. *Dança de Mort e de aquelles persones qui mal llur grat ab aquella ballen e dançen.* ACA, CR, Manuscritos Miscelánea, no. 26, ff. 140–162v., Barcelona.

Eiximenis, Francesc. *Art de Bé Morir.* Biblioteca de Catalunya (BC), Arxiu Fotogràfic Miquel i Planes (AFMP), 22, Barcelona.

Eymerich, Nicolau. *Contra astrologos imperitos.* BnF, MS lat. 3171, ff. 81–95v., Paris.

———. *Contra praefigentes certum terminum fini mundi.* Biblioteca Nacional de España (BNE), MS 6213, ff. 217r.–242r, Madrid.

———. *Contra praefigentes certum terminum fini mundi.* Bibliothèque nationale de France (BnF), MS lat. 3171, ff. 58–75, Paris.

Turmeda, Anselm. *P[ro]fecies q[ue] frare encelm turmeda feu el añy mccccv: En tunis de barberia/ço es de algunes cosses esdeuenidores (1405).* Biblioteca de Catalunya (BC), MS 485, ff. 259v.–261v., Barcelona.

Published Primary Sources

d'Ailly, Pierre. *De falsis prophetis.* In Jean Gerson, *Opera Omnia*, edited by L. E. du Pin. Antwerp: Sumptibus Societatis, 1706.

d'Alos, Ramón. "Les profecies de Turmeda." *Revue Hispanique* 24 (1911): 480–96.

Alverni, Guilielmi. *Opera Omnia.* 2 vols. Paris: Andream Pralard, 1674.

———. *De Legibus. Opera Omnia.* 2 vols. 1:67–84. Paris: Andream Pralard, 1674.

al-Andalusī, Ṣāʿid. *Science in the Medieval World: Book of the Categories of Nations.* Translated by Semaʿan I. Salem and Alok Kumar. Austin: University of Texas Press, 1991.

Aquinas, Thomas. *Summa Theologiae.* Translated by Blackfriars. 61 vols. London: Eyer and Spottiswoode, 1964.

Aristotle/Hermes. *Liber Antimaqvis.* Edited by Charles Burnett. In *Hermetis Trismegisti: Astrologica et Divinatoria*, 179–221.

Arnold, Ivor. Introduction to *L'Apparicion Maistre Jehan de Meun et le Somnium Super materia scismatis d'Honoré Bonet,* i–xi. Paris: Société d'Édition: Les Belles Lettres, 1926.

Augustine of Hippo. *The City of God against the Pagans.* Translated by R. W. Dyson. Cambridge: Cambridge University Press, 1998.

Bacon, Roger. *Fratris Rogeri Bacon, ordinis minorum, opus majus ad Clementem quartum, pontificem romanum: Ex MS codice Dubliniensi, cum aliis quibusdam collato, nunc primum editit S. Jebb, M.D.* London: William Bowyer, 1733.

———. *Secretum Secretorum cum glossis et notulis.* Opera hactenus inedita Rogeri Baconi, fasc. 5. Oxford: Clarendon Press, 1920.

Bakhouche, Béatrice, Frédéric Fauquier, and Brigitte Pérez-Jean, eds. *Picatrix: un traité de magie médiéval.* Turnhout, Belgium: Brepols, 2003.

Bohigas i Balaguer, Pere. "Profecies de fra Anselm Turmeda (1406)." *Estudis Universitaris Catalans* 9 (1915–1916): 173–81.

Bonner, Anthony. *Selected Works of Ramon Llull (1232–1316).* 2 vols. Princeton, NJ: Princeton University Press, 1985.

———, ed. and trans. *Doctor Illuminatus: A Ramon Llull Reader.* Princeton, NJ: Princeton University Press, 1993.

Cicero. *De Divinatione.* Translated by William Armistead Falconer. Cambridge, MA: Harvard University Press, 1927.

Colección de documentos inéditos del Archivo de la Corona de Aragón. Barcelona: J. E. Montfort, 1847–1910.

Conlon, Denis Joseph, ed. *"Li Romans de Witasse le Moine": Roman du treizième siècle.* Édité d'après le manuscrit, fonds français 1553, de la Bibliothèque nationale, Paris (Studies in the Romance Languages and Literatures, 126). Chapel Hill: University of North Carolina Press, 1972.

Constable, Olivia Remie, ed. *Medieval Iberia: Readings from Christian, Muslim, and Jewish Sources.* Philadelphia: University of Pennsylvania Press, 1997.

Coroleu, José. *Documents historichs catalans del sigle XIV.* Barcelona: Impr. la Renaixensa, 1889.

Corpus Iuris Canonici, Clementinarum V, I.1.26. Antwerp: Apud Ioannem and Iacobum Meursios, 1648.

Crapelet, Georges Adrien. *Proverbes et Dictons populaires, avec les dits du mercier et de marchands, et les Crieries de Paris, au XIIIe et XIV siècles.* Paris: Impr. de Crapelet, 1831.

Dante. *The Divine Comedy.* Translated by Charles Southward Singleton. 6 vols. Princeton, NJ: Princeton University Press, 1970–1975.

De Luanco, José Ramón, ed. *La Alquimia en España.* Madrid: Editorial "Tres, Catorce, Diecisiete," 1980.

Denifle, Henricus, and Aemilio Chatelain, eds. *Chartularium Universitatis Parisiensis.* Paris: Delalain Bros., 1889.

Desclot, Bernat. *Crònica.* Edited by Miquel Coll i Allentorn. Barcelona: Editorial Barcino, 1949–1951.

De Voragine, Jacobus. *The Golden Legend: Readings on the Saints.* Translated by William Granger Ryan. 2 vols. Princeton, NJ: Princeton University Press, 1993.

Eiximenis, Francesc. *Cercapou.* Edited by Guiseppe E. Sansone. 2 vols. Barcelona: Editorial Barcino, 1957–1958.

Elliott, J. K. *The Apocryphal New Testament: A Collection of Apocryphal Christian Literature in an English Translation.* Oxford: Clarendon Press, 1993.

Eymerich, Nicolau. *Diàleg contra els lul·listes.* Edited by Jaume de Puig i Oliver. Barcelona: Quadrens Crema, 2002.

Eymerich, Nicolau, and Francisco de la Peña. *Le manuel des inquisiteurs.* Translated by Louis Sala-Molins. Paris: Mouton Éditeur, 1973.

Franz, Adolf. *Die kirchlichen Benediktionen des Mittelalter.* 2 vols. Freiburg: M. Herder, 1909.

Girona i Llagostera, Daniel. *Itinerari de l'infant en Joan, primogènit del rei En Pere III, 1350–1387.* Valencia: Impremta de "Fill de F. Vives Mora," 1923.

———. *Itinerari del rei en Joan I.* Barcelona: Extret de la Revista D'Estudis Universitaris Catalans, 1931.

———. *Itinerari del rey en Martí (1396–1410).* Barcelona: Henrich y Compania, 1916.

Hanly, Michael, ed. and trans. *Medieval Muslims, Christians, and Jews in Dialogue: The Apparicion Maistre Jehan de Meun of Honorat Bovet: A Critical Edition with English Translation.* Tempe: Arizona Center for Medieval and Renaissance Studies, 2005.

al-Harīzī, Judah. *The Book of Tahkemoni.* Translated by David S. Segal. Portland, OR: Littman Library of Jewish Civilization, 2001.

Hermetis Trismegisti: Astrologica et Divinatoria. Edited by Gerrit Bos, Charles Burnett, Thérèse Charmasson, Paul Kunitzch, Fabrizio Lelli, Paolo Lucenti (Corpus Christianorum, Contiunatio Mediaeualis, CXLIV C). Turnhout, Belgium: Brepols, 2001.

Horrox, Rosemary, ed. *The Black Death.* Manchester Medieval Source Series. Manchester: Manchester University Press, 1994.

Isidore of Seville. *The Etymologies of Isidore of Seville*, trans. and ed. Stephen A. Barney, W. J. Lewis, J. A. Beach, and Oliver Berghof. Cambridge: Cambridge University Press, 2006.

Jaume I. *Crònica, o Llibre dels feits.* Edited by Ferran Soldevila. Barcelona: Edicions 62, 1982.

Kieckhefer, Richard. *Forbidden Rites: A Necromancer's Manual of the Fifteenth Century.* University Park: Pennsylvania State University Press, 1997.

Knight, Stephen, and Thomas H. Ohlgren, eds. *Robin Hood and Other Outlaw Tales.* Kalamazoo, MI: Medieval Institute Publications, 1997.

Levey, Martin, ed. "Medieval Arabic Toxicology: The Book of Poisons of ibn Wahshiya and Its Relation to Early Indian and Greek Texts." *Transactions of the American Philosophical Society*, New. Ser. 56, no. 7 (1966): 1–130.

Lucas, John Scott, ed. and trans. *Astrology and Numerology in Medieval and Early Modern Catalonia: The Tractat de Prenostication de la vida natural dels hòmens.* Leiden: Brill, 2003.

Maimonides, Moses. *The Guide of the Perplexed.* Translated by Shlomo Pines. 2 vols. Chicago: University of Chicago Press, 1963.

———. "Letter on Astrology." Translated by Ralph Lerner. In Ralph Lerner and Muhsin Mahdi, eds. *Medieval Political Philosophy*, 227–36. Ithaca, NY: Cornell University Press, 1972.

Manual de Novells Ardits vulgarment apellat Dietari del Antich Consell Barceloní. Edited by Frederich Schwartz y Luna and Francesch Carreras y Candi. 28 vols. Barcelona: Henrich y Companyía, 1892.

Manuel, Don Juan. *El Conde Lucanor o Libro de los enxiemplos del conde Lucanor et de Patronio.* Edited by José Manuel Blecua. Madrid: Clásicos Castalia, 1969.

Massó Torrents, Jaume. "Inventari dels Bens Mobles del Rey Martí d'Aragó." *Revue Hispanique* 12 (1905): 413–590.

Matton, Sylvain. "Le traité *Contre les alchimistes* de Nicholas Eymerich." *Chrysopoeia* 1 (1987): 93–136.

Metge, Bernat. *The Dream of Bernat Metge.* Translated by Richard Vernier. Burlington, VT: Ashgate, 2002.

———. *Lo somni*, Edited and translated by Lola Badia. Barcelona: Quaderns Crema, 1999.

Mézières, Philippe de. *Le Songe du Vieil Pelerin.* Edited by G. W. Coopland. 2 vols. Cambridge: Cambridge University Press, 1969.

Millás Vallicrosa, José María, ed. *Las tablas astronómicas del rey Don Pedro el Ceremonioso.* Madrid: Consejo Superior de Investigaciones Científicas, 1962.

Muntaner, Ramón. *Crònica.* Edited by J. F. Vidal Jové. Madrid: Alianzo Editorial, 1970.

Oresme, Nicole. *Nicole Oresme and the Astrologers: A Study of His Livre de Divinacions.* Translated by ·George William Coopland. Cambridge, MA: Harvard University Press, 1952.

Perarnau i Espelt, Josep. "La traducció catalana medieval del *Liber secretorum eventuum* de Joan de Rocatalhada: edició, estudi del text i apèndixs." *Arxiu de Textos Catalans Antics* 17 (1998): 7–219.

Pere el Cerimoniós. *Chronicle.* Edited and translated by Mary Hillgarth and Jocelyn N. Hillgarth. 2 vols. Toronto: Pontifical Institute of Mediaeval Studies, 1980.

Picatrix: The Latin Version of the Ghāyat Al-Hakīm. Edited by David Pingree. London: Warburg Institute, 1986.

Ptolemy, *Tetrabiblos.* Translated by F. E. Robbins. Cambridge, MA: Harvard University Press, 1940. Rev. ed., 2001.

Puig i Oliver, Jaume de. "El 'Dialogus contra lluistas,' de Nicolau Eimeric, O.P. Edició i estudi." *Arxiu de textos catalans antics* 19 (2000): 7–296.

Ritter, Hellmut, ed. *Ghayat al-hakim wa-ahaqq al-natijatayn bi-aitaqdim: Das Ziel des Weisen.* Berlin: B. G. Teubner, 1933.

Ritter, Hellmut, and Martin Plessner. *Picatrix: das Ziel des Weisen, von Pseudo-Magriti.* London: Warburg Institute, 1962.

Rubió i Lluch, Antonio. *Documents per a l'història de la cultura catalana medieval.* 2nd ed. 2 vols. Barcelona: Institut d'Estudis Catalans, 2000.

Rupescissa, Johannis de. *Liber ostensor quod adesse festinant tempora.* Edited by André Vauchez, Clémence Thévenaz Modestin, and Christine Morerod-Fattebert. Rome: École Française de Rome, 2005.

———. *Liber Secretorum Eventuum: Edition critique, traduction et introduction historique.* Edited and translated by Robert E. Lerner and Christine Morerod-Fattebert. Fribourg, Switzerland: Editions Universitaires, 1994.

Rusconi, Roberto, ed. *The Book of Prophecies, edited by Christopher Columbus.* Translated by Blair Sullivan. *Repertorium Columbianum,* vol. 3. Berkeley: University of California Press, 1997.

Salisbury, John of. *Policraticus: Of the Frivolities of Courtiers and the Footprints of Philosophers* Edited and translated by Cary J. Nederman. Cambridge: Cambridge University Press, 1990.

———. *Policraticus I–IV.* Edited by Katherine S. B. Keats-Rohan (Corpus Christianorum, Continuatio Mediaevalis, CXVIII). Turnholt, Belgium: Brepols, 1993.

Scott, Samuel Parsons, and Robert Ignatius Burns, eds. *Las Siete Partidas.* 5 vols. Philadelphia: University of Pennsylvania Press, 2001.

Segal, David S., ed. and trans. "Jewish Listeners and an Arab Astrologer." In Constable, ed. *Medieval Iberia,* 198–202.

Sextus Decretalium Liber. Antwerp: Apud Philippum Nutium sub Ciconlis, 1572.

Thorndike, Lynn, ed. *Latin Treatises on Comets between 1238 and 1368 A.D.* Chicago: University of Chicago Press, 1950.

Tresbéns, Bartomeu de. *Tractat d'Astrologia.* Edited by Juan Vernet Ginés and David Romano. Barcelona: Biblioteca catalana d'obres antigues, 1957.

Turmeda, Anselm. *Fray Anselm Turmeda ('Abdallah al-Taryuman) y su polémica islamocristiana: edición, traducción y estudio de la Tuhfa.* Edited and translated by Míkel de Epalza. Madrid: Hiperión, 1994.

———. *La disputa de los animals contra el hombre: Traducción del original árabe de La disputa del asno contra Fray Anselmo Turmeda.* Edited and translated by Emilio Tornero Poveda. Madrid: Editorial de la Universidad Complutense, 1984.

Veenstra, Jan R., ed. *Magic and Divination at the Courts of Burgundy and France: Text and Context of Laurens Pignon's "Contre le devineurs" (1411).* Leiden: Brill, 1998.

Villegas, Marcelino. *Picatrix: el fin del sabio y el mejor de los dos medios para avanzar.* Madrid: Editorial Nacional, 1982.

Waitz, G., ed. "Handschriften in Englischen Bibliotheken: Beilage zu dem Bericht über die Reise nach England." *Neues Archiv der Gesellschaft für ältere deutsche Geschichtskunde zur Beföderung einer Gesammtausgabe der Quellenschriften deutscher Geschichten des Mittelalters.* 4:2. Hannover: Hahn'sche Buchhandlung, 1879.

Wakefield, Walter L., and Austin P. Evans, eds. and trans. *Heresies of the High Middle Ages.* New York: Columbia University Press, 1991.

West, Delno C., and August Kling, eds. *The Libro de las profecías of* Christopher *Columbus.* Gainesville: University of Florida Press, 1991.

Williams, John. *The Illustrated Beatus: A Corpus of the Illustrations of the Commentary on the Apocalypse.* London: Harvey Miller, 1995–2005.

Secondary Sources

Aacheson, Eric. *A Gentry Community: Leicestershire in the Fifteenth Century, c. 1422– c. 1485.* Cambridge: Cambridge University Press, 1992.

d'Abadal y Vinyals, Ramón. "La vida politica y sus dirigentes." In Menéndez Pidal, ed. *España cristiana: Crisis de la reconquista luchas civiles: Historia de España.* 37 vols. Madrid: Espasa-Calpe, 1935–1984.

Abulafia, David. *A Mediterranean Emporium: The Catalan Kingdom of Majorca.* Cambridge: Cambridge University Press, 1994.

Alvarez, Lourdes María. "Anselm Turmeda: The Visionary Humanism of a Muslim Convert and Catalan Prophet." In Albrecht Classen, ed., *Meeting the Foreign in the Middle Ages,* 172–91. New York: Routledge, 2002.

———. "Beastly Colloquies: Of Plagiarism and Pluralism in Two Medieval Disputations between Animals and Men." *Comparative Literature Studies* 39, no. 3 (2002): 179–200.

d'Alverny, Marie-Thérèse. "La survivance de la magie antique." In Paul Wilpert, ed. *Miscellanea Medievalia, I: Antike und Orient im Mittelalter,* 154–78. Berlin: De Gruyter, 1962.

———. "Un adversaire de Saint Thomas: Petrus Iohannis Olivi." *St. Thomas Aquinas, 1274–1974. Commemorative Studies.* 2 vols., 179–218. Toronto: Pontifical Institute of Mediaeval Studies, 1974.

Ames, Christine Caldwell. "Does Inquisition Belong to Religious History?" *American Historical Review* 110, no. 1 (2005): 11–37.

———. *Righteous Persecution: Inquisition, Dominicans, and Christianity in the Middle Ages.* Philadelphia: University of Pennsylvania Press, 2009.

Anderson, Andrew Runni. *Alexander's Gate, Gog and Magog, and the Inclosed Nations.* Cambridge, MA: Medieval Academy of America, 1932.

Aulotte, Robert, ed. *Prophètes et prophéties au XVIᵉ siècle.* Paris: Ecole Normal Superieure, 1998.

Aurell, Martin. "Eschatologie, spiritualité, et politique dans la confédération catalano-Aragonese (1282–1412)." *Cahiers de Fanjeaux* (1992): 191–235.

———. "La fin du monde, l'enfer et le roi: une prophétie catalane du XVᵉ siècle." *Revue Mabillon* (1994): 143–77.

———. "Les Prophétes de la fin du monde." L'Histoire 206 (Jan., 1997): 50–54.

——. "Messianisme royal de la Couronne d'Aragon (XIVe–XVe s.)." *Annales. Histoire. Sciences Sociales* (1997): 119–55.

——. "Prophétie et messianisme politique: La Péninsule ibérique au miroir du *Liber ostensor* de Jean de Roquetaillade." *Mélanges de l'Ecole Française de Rome. Moyen Âge* 102 (1990): 317–61.

——, ed. *Convaincre et persuader: communication et propagande aux XII et XIIIe siècles.* Poitiers, France: Université de Poitiers, 2007.

d'Avout, Jacques. *La querelle des Armagnacs et de Bourguinons.* Paris: Gallimard, 1943.

Backman, Clifford R. "Arnau de Villanova and the Body at the End of the World." In Bynum and Freedman, eds., *Last Things*, 140–55.

Badia, Lola. "*Fa che tu scrive:* variaciones profanas sobre un motivo sagrado, de Ramon Llull a Bernat Metge." In *The Medieval Mind: Hispanic Studies in Honour of Alan Deyermond*, ed. Ian Macpherson and Ralph Penny, 3–20. London: Tamesis Books, 1997.

Bailey, Michael D. "A Late-Medieval Crisis of Superstition?" *Speculum* 84, no. 3 (2009): 633–61.

——. *Magic and Superstition in Europe: A Concise History from Antiquity to the Present.* Lanham, MD: Rowman and Littlefield, 2007.

——. "The Meanings of Magic." *Magic, Ritual, and Witchcraft* 1 (Summer 2006): 1–23.

Barnay, Sylvie. "Jean de Roquetaillade: Vie, Oeuvres, et Contexte Historique." In Rupescissa, *Liber ostensor quod adesse festinant tempora*, 1–4.

Barral i Altet, Xavier. *Vidrieras medievales de Cataluña.* Barcelona: Institut d'Estudis Catalans, 2000.

Beaune, Colette, and André Vauchez. "Recherches sur prophétisme en occidente." In J.-P. Genet, ed., *Genèse de l'état moderne: Bilans et perspectives*, 201–6. Paris: Editions du Centre national de la recherche scientifique, 1990.

Benedictow, Ole Jørgen. *The Black Death, 1346–1353: The Complete History.* Woodbridge, UK: Boydell Press, 2004.

Bernstein, Alan E. *Pierre d'Ailly and the Blanchard Affair: University and Chancellor of Paris at the Beginning of the Great Schism.* Leiden: Brill, 1978.

Bignami-Odier, Jeanne. *Études sur Jean de Roquetaillade.* Paris: Vrin, 1952.

——. "Jean de Roquetaillade (de Rupescissa)." *Histoire littéraire de la France* 41 (Paris, 1981): 75–240.

Biller, Peter. "A 'Scientific' View of Jews from Paris around 1300." *Micrologus: Natura, Scienze e Società Medievali* 9 (2001): 137–68.

Biraben, Jean-Noël. *Les hommes et la peste en France et dans les pays européens et mediterranéens.* 2 vols. Paris: Mouton, 1975–1976.

Bisson, Thomas N. *The Medieval Crown of Aragon: A Short History.* Oxford: Clarendon Press, 1986.

Blumenfeld-Kosinski, Renate. *Poets, Saints, and Visionaries of the Great Schism, 1378–1417.* University Park: Pennsylvania State University Press, 2006.

Bohigas i Balaguer, Pere. "Profecies catalanes dels segles xiv i xv: assaig bibliogràfic." *Butletí de la Biblioteca de Catalunya* 6, no. 9 (1920–1922): 24–49.

——. "Proficies de Merlí: Altres profecies contingudes en manuscrits catalans." *Butletí de la Biblioteca de Catalunya* 8 (1928–1932): 253–79.

————. "La 'Visión' de Alfonso X y las 'Profecías de Merlín.'" *Revista de Filología Española* 25 (1941): 383–98.

Bonner, Anthony, and Lola Badia. *Ramon Llull: Vida, pensament i obra literària*. Barcelona: Empúries, 1988.

Boswell, John. *The Royal Treasure: Muslim Communities under the Crown of Aragon in the Fourteenth Century*. New Haven, CT: Yale University Press, 1977.

Boudet, Jean-Patrice. *Entre science et nigromance: astrologie, divination et magie dans l'occident médiéval, XII^c–XV^c siècle*. Paris: Publications de la Sorbonne, 2006.

————. "Jean de Roquetaillade et l'Astrologie." In Rupescissa, *Liber Ostensor quod adesse festinant tempora*, 954–56.

————. "La papauté d'Avignon et l'astrologie." *Fin du monde et signes des temps: visionnaires et prophètes en France méridionale (fin XIII^c–début XV^c siècle)*. Cahiers de Fanjeux 27, 257–93. Toulouse: Privat, 1992.

————. "Simon de Phares et les rapports entre astrologie et prophetié à la fin du Moyen Âge." *Mélanges de l'École Française de Rome. Moyen Âge* 102 (1990): 617–48.

Bremmer, Jan N., ed. *The Apocryphal Acts of Peter: Magic, Miracles, and Gnosticism*. Leuven, Belgium: Peeters, 1998.

Burke, James. "Juan Manuel's Tabardíe and Golfín." *Hispanic Review* 44, no. 2 (1976): 171–78.

Burke, Peter. *Varieties of Cultural History*. Ithaca, NY: Cornell University Press, 1997.

————. *What Is Cultural History?* 2nd ed. Cambridge: Polity Press, 2008.

Burnham, Louisa A. *So Great a Light, So Great a Smoke: The Beguin Heretics of Languedoc*. Ithaca, NY: Cornell University Press, 2008.

————. "The Visionary Authority of Na Prous Boneta." In Alain Boureau and Sylvain Piron, eds., *Pierre de Jean Olivi (1248–1298)*, 319–39. Paris: Vrin, 1999.

Burns, Robert Ignatius, ed. "Stupor Mundi: Alfonso X of Castile, the Learned." In Burns, ed., *Emperor of Culture*, 1–13.

————, ed. *Emperor of Culture: Alfonso X the Learned of Castile and His Thirteenth-Century Renaissance*. Philadelphia: University of Pennsylvania Press, 1990.

Burr, David. "Apokalyptische Erwartung und die Entstehung der Usus-Pauper-Kontroverse: Zur Geschichte und Theologie des Franziskanerordens bei Petrus Johannis Olivi." *Wissenschaft und Weisheit* 47 (1984): 84–99.

————. "Bonaventure, Olivi, and Franciscan Eschatology." *Collecta Franciscana* 53 (1983): 23–40.

————. *Olivi and Franciscan Poverty: The Origin of the Usus Pauper Controversy*. Philadelphia: University of Pennsylvania Press, 1989.

————. "Olivi, Apocalyptic Expectation, and Visionary Experience." *Traditio* 41 (1985): 273–88.

————. "Olivi's Apocalyptic Timetable." *Journal of Medieval and Renaissance Studies* 11 (1981): 237–60.

————. *The Spiritual Franciscans: From Protest to Persecution in the Century after Saint Francis*. University Park: Pennsylvania State University Press, 2001.

Bynum, Caroline Walker, and Paul Freedman, eds. *Last Things: Death and the Apocalypse in the Middle Ages*. Philadelphia: University of Pennsylvania Press, 2000.

Calvet, Agustí. *Fray Anselmo Turmeda: Heterodoxo español*. Barcelona: Casa Editorial Estudio, 1914.

Carey, Hilary. "Astrology and Antichrist in the Later Middle Ages." In Gerhard Jaritz and Gerson Moreno-Riaño, eds., *Time and Eternity: The Medieval Discourse*, 477–535. Turnhout,Belgium: Brepols, 2003.

——. *Courting Disaster: Astrology at the English Court and University in the Later Middle Ages*. New York: St. Martin's, 1992.

Caro Baroja, Julio. *Vidas mágicas e inquisición*. 2 vols. Madrid: Taurus, 1967.

Carreras y Artau, Joaquín. "La pólemica gerundiense sobre el Antichristo entre Arnau de Villanova y los dominicos." *Anales del Instituto de Estudios Gerundenses* 5 (1950): 34–44.

Carrère, Claude. *Barcelone, centre économique à l'époque des difficultés, 1380–1462*. 2 vols. Paris: Mouton, 1967.

Cepeda Adán, José. "El providencialismo en los cronistas de los Reyes Católicos." *Arbor* 17 (1950): 177–90.

Chaytor, H. J. *A History of Aragon and Catalonia*. New York: AMS Press, 1969.

Chevalier, Jacques. *A Postmodern Revelation: Signs of Astrology and the Apocalypse*. Toronto: University of Toronto Press, 1997.

Clark, Charles. "The Zodiac Man in Medieval Medical Astrology." *Journal of the Rocky Mountain Medieval and Renaissance Association* 3 (1982): 13–38.

Corry, Jennifer M. *Perceptions of Magic in Medieval Spanish Literature*. Bethlehem, PA: Lehigh University Press, 2005.

Crosby, Alfred W. *Ecological Imperialism: The Biological Expansion of Europe, 900–1900*. Cambridge: Cambridge University Press, 1986.

Cuffel, Alexandra. *Gendering Disgust in Medieval Religious Polemic*. Notre Dame, IN: University of Notre Dame Press, 2007.

Cunningham, Andrew, and Ole Peter Grell. *The Four Horsemen of the Apocalypse: Religion, War, Famine, and Death in Reformation Europe*. Cambridge: Cambridge University Press, 2000.

Darby, George O. S. "Ibn Wahshīya in Medieval Spanish Literature." *Isis* 33, no. 4 (1941): 433–38.

Darlington, Oscar G. "Gerbert, the Teacher." *American Historical Review* 52, no. 3 (1947): 456–76.

Davies, Owen. *Grimoires: A History of Magic Books*. Oxford: Oxford University Press, 2009.

De Barcelona, Martí. *La cultura catalana durant el regnat de Jaime II*. Barcelona: Estudios Franciscanos, 1991.

Delaruelle, Étienne. *L'Église au temps du Grand Schisme et de la crise conciliaire*. 2 vols. Paris: Bloud and Gay, 1962.

De Montoliu, Manuel. *Ramon Llull i Arnau de Vilanova*. Barcelona: Editorial Alpha, 1958.

De Rubi, Basilio. "La escuela franciscana de Barcelona y su intervención en los decretos inmaculistas de la corona de Aragon." *Estudios franciscanos* 57 (1956): 363–405.

DeVun, Leah. "Human Heaven: John of Rupescissa's Alchemy at the End of the World." In Rachel Fulton and Bruce W. Holsinger, eds., *History in the Comic Mode:*

Medieval Communities and the Matter of Person, 251–61. New York: Columbia University Press, 2007.

———. *Prophecy, Alchemy, and the End of Time: John of Rupescissa in the Late Middle Ages.* New York: Columbia University Press, 2009.

Dienstag, Jacob I. "Maimonides' Letter on Astrology to the Rabbis of Southern France." *Kiryat Sefer* 61 (1987): 147–58.

Duby, Georges. *Women of the Twelfth Century: Volume 3: Eve and the Church.* Translated by Jean Birrell. Chicago: University of Chicago Press, 1998.

Duran, Eulàlia. "La cort reial com a centre de propaganda monàrquica: la participació morisca en l'exaltació mesiánica dels Reis Catòlics." *Pedralbes* 13 (1993): 505–14.

Dutton, Paul Edward. *Charlemagne's Mustache and Other Cultural Clusters of a Dark Age.* New York: Palgrave MacMillan, 2004.

———. *The Politics of Dreaming in the Carolingian Empire.* Lincoln: University of Nebraska Press, 1994.

Eamon, William. *Science and the Secrets of Nature: Books of Secrets in Medieval and Early Modern Culture.* Princeton, NJ: Princeton University Press, 1994.

Eliade, Mircea. "Some Observations on European Witchcraft." *History of Religions* 14, no. 3 (1975): 149–72.

Elliott, Dyan. *Fallen Bodies: Pollution, Sexuality, and Demonology in the Middle Ages.* Philadelphia: University of Pennsylvania Press, 1999.

———. "Seeing Double: John Gerson, the Discernment of Spirits, and Joan of Arc." *American Historical Review* 107, no. 1 (2002): 26–54.

Elliott, J. K., ed. *The Apocryphal New Testament: A Collection of Apocryphal Christian Literature in an English Translation.* Oxford: Clarendon Press, 1993.

Emmerson, Richard K. *Antichrist in the Middle Ages: A Study of Medieval Apocalypticism, Art, and Literature.* Seattle: University of Washington Press, 1981.

———. "'Coveitise to Konne,' 'Goddes Privetee,' and Will's Ambiguous Visionary Experience in *Piers Plowman*." In Míceál Vaughan, ed., *Suche Werkis to Weche: Essays on Piers Plowman in Honor of David C. Fowler*, 89–121. East Lansing, MI: Colleagues Press, 1993.

———. "The Secret." *American Historical Review* 104 (1999): 1603–14.

Emmerson, Richard K., and Ronald Herzman. *The Apocalyptic Imagination in Medieval Literature.* Philadelphia: University of Pennsylvania Press, 1992.

Emmerson, Richard K., and Suzanne Lewis. "Census and Bibliography of Medieval Manuscripts Containing Apocalypse Illustrations, ca. 800–1500." *Traditio* 40 (1984): 337–79; 41 (1985): 367–409; 42 (1986): 443–72.

Espantoso Foley, Augusta. *Occult Arts and Doctrine in the Theater of Juan Ruiz de Alarcón.* Geneva: Droz, 1972.

Esteban Mateo, León. *Cultura y prehumanismo en la curia pontificia del Papa Luna, 1394–1423.* Valencia: Universitat de Valencia, 2002.

Favier, Jean. *La guerre de Cent Ans.* Paris: Fayard, 1980.

Fernández-Armesto, Felipe. *Before Columbus: Exploration and Colonization from the Mediterranean to the Atlantic, 1229–1492.* Philadelphia: University of Pennsylvania Press, 1992.

Ferreiro, Alberto. *Simon Magus in Patristic, Medieval and Early Modern Traditions.* Leiden, The Netherlands: Brill, 2005.

Ferrer i Mallol, María Teresa. *Els Sarraïnes de la Corona Catalano-Aragonesa en el Segle XV: Segregació i Discrimació.* Barcelona: Consell Superior d'Investigacions Científiques, 1987.

Festugière, A.-J. *La Révélation d'Hermès Trismégiste.* Paris: Les Belles Lettres, 2006.

Fin du monde et signes des temps: visionnaires et prophètes en France méridionale (fin XIIIe–début XVe siècle). Cahiers de Fanjeux 27. Toulouse: Privat, 1992.

Fletcher, R. A. *The Quest for El Cid.* New York: Oxford University Press, 1989.

Flint, Valerie Irene Jane. *The Imaginative Landscape of Christopher Columbus.* Princeton, NJ: Princeton University Press, 1992.

——. *The Rise of Magic in Early Medieval Europe.* Princeton, NJ: Princeton University Press, 1991.

——. "The Transmission of Astrology in the Early Middle Ages." *Viator* 21 (1990): 1–27.

Fort i Cogul, Eufemià. *La Inquisició i Ramon Llull.* Barcelona: Rafael Dalmau, 1972.

Friedman, John Block. *Orpheus in the Middle Ages.* Syracuse, NY: Syracuse University Press, 2000.

Garbarino, Anna Maria. *Donne e medicina nel medioevo: la scuola medica salernitana.* Empoli, Italy: Ibiskos Editrice di Antonietta Risolo, 2005.

García Avilés, Alejandro. "Two Astromagical Manuscripts of Alfonso X." *Journal of the Warburg and Courtauld Institutes* 59 (1996): 14–23.

Gazulla, Faustino D. "Los reyes de Aragon y la Purísima Concepción de María." *Boletín de la Real Academia de Buenas Letras de Barcelona* 3 and 4 (1905–1906).

Gerwing, Manfred. *Vom Ende der Zeit: der Traktat des Arnald von Villanova über die Ankunft des Antichrist in der akademischen Auseinandersetzung zu Beginn des 14. Jahrhunderts.* Münster: Achendorff, 1996.

Gettings, Fred. *Dictionary of Occult, Hermetic, and Alchemical Sigils.* London: Routledge and Kegan Paul, 1981.

Gitlitz, David M. *Secrecy and Deceit: The Religion of the Crypto-Jews.* Albuquerque: University of New Mexico Press, 2002.

Gilson, Etienne. *History of Christian Philosophy in the Middle Ages.* New York: Random House, 1955.

Ginzburg, Carlo. *The Cheese and the Worms: The Cosmos of a Sixteenth-Century Miller.* Translated by John and Anne Tedeschi. Baltimore: Johns Hopkins University Press, 1980.

Grafton, Anthony. *Cardano's Cosmos: The Worlds and Works of a Renaissance Astrologer.* Cambridge, MA: Cambridge University Press, 1999.

Graus, František. *Pest—Geissler—Judenmorde: Das 14. Jahrhundert als Krisenzeit.* Göttingen: Vandenhoeck and Rupprecht, 1994.

Guillemain, Bernard. *Les Papes d'Avignon 1309–1376.* Paris: Les Éditions du CERF, 2000.

Gyug, Richard. *The Diocese of Barcelona during the Black Death. The Register Notule Communium 15 (1348–1349).* Toronto: Pontifical Institute of Mediaeval Studies, 1994.

Hamarneh, Sami. "Development of Arabic Medical Therapy in the Tenth Century." *Journal of the History of Medicine and Allied Sciences* 27, no. 1 (1972): 65–79.

Hanly, Michael, and Hélène Millet, "Les Batailles d'Honorat Bovet: Essai de biographie." *Romania* 114 (1996): 135–81.

Harmening, Dieter. *Superstitio: Überlieferung und theoriegeschichtliche Untersuchungen zur kirchlich-theologischen Aberglaubensliteratur des Mittelalters.* Berlin: E. Schmidt, 1979.

Heimann, Claudia. *Nicolaus Eymerich (vor 1320–1399)—pradicator veridicus, inquisitor intrepidus, doctor egregius: Leben und Werk Eines Inquisitors.* Münster: Aschendorff, 2001.

Hendrix, Scott E. *How Albert the Great's Speculum Astronomiae Was Interpreted and Used by Four Centuries of Readers: A Study in Late Medieval Medicine, Astronomy, and Astrology.* Lewiston, NY: Edwin Mellen Press, 2010.

Hillgarth, Jocelyn N. *The Spanish Kingdoms, 1250–1516.* 2 vols. Oxford: Clarendon Press, 1976–1978.

Hobbins, Daniel. *Authorship and Publicity before Print: Jean Gerson and the Transformation of Late Medieval Learning.* Philadelphia: University of Pennsylvania Press, 2009.

———. "The Schoolman as Public Intellectual: Jean Gerson and the Late Medieval Tract." *American Historical Review* 108, no. 5 (2003): 1308–35.

Hsia, R. Po-chia. *The Myth of Murder: Jews and Magic in Reformation Germany.* New Haven, CT: Yale University Press, 1988.

Hughes, Kevin L. *Constructing Antichrist: Paul, Biblical Commentary, and the Development of Doctrine in the Early Middle Ages.* Washington, DC: Catholic University of America Press, 2005.

Infantes, Víctor. *Las Danzas de la Muerte: Génesis y desarrollo de un género medieval (siglos XIII–XVII).* Salamanca: Ediciones Universidad de Salamanca, 1997.

Ivars Andrés, P. "Franciscanismo de la reina de Aragon doña Maria de Luna (1396–1406)." *Archivo Ibero-americano* 34 (1931): 568–94.

———. "La 'indiferencia' de Pedro IV de Aragon en el Gran Cisma de Occidente." *Archivo ibero-americano* 29 (1928): 21–97 and 161–86.

Johnston, Mark D. *The Evangelical Rhetoric of Ramon Llull: Lay Learning and Piety in the Christian West around 1300.* New York: Oxford University Press, 1996.

———. *The Spiritual Logic of Ramon Llull.* Oxford: Oxford University Press, 1987.

Jolly, Karen. "Medieval Magic: Definitions, Beliefs, Practices." In Bengt Ankarloo and Stuart Clark, eds., *Witchcraft and Magic in Europe.* 6 vols. 3:1–71. Philadelphia: University of Pennsylvania Press, 2002.

Joosse, N. Peter. "An Example of Medieval Arabic Pseudo-Hermetism: The Tale of Salāmān and Absāl." *Journal of Semitic Studies* 38, no. 2 (1993): 279–93.

Jordan, William Chester. *The Great Famine: Northern Europe in the Early Fourteenth Century.* Princeton, NJ: Princeton University Press, 1996.

Kadir, Djelal. *Columbus and the Ends of the Earth: Europe's Prophetic Rhetoric as Conquering Ideology.* Berkeley: University of California Press, 1992.

Kagan, Richard L. *Lucrecia's Dreams: Politics and Prophecy in Sixteenth-Century Spain.* Berkeley: University of California Press, 1990.

———. "Politics, Prophecy, and the Inquisition in Late Sixteenth-Century Spain." In Mary Elizabeth Perry and Anne Cruz, eds., *Cultural Encounters: The Impact of the Inquisition in Spain and the New World*,105–24. Berkeley: University of California Press, 1991.

Kagay, Donald. "Poetry in the Dock: The Court Culture of Joan I on Trial (1396–1397)." Conference paper, 36th Annual International Congress on Medieval Studies, Western Michigan University, Kalamazoo, MI, May 5, 2001.

Kaminsky, Howard. "From Lateness to Waning to Crisis: The Burden of the Later Middle Ages." *Journal of Early Modern History* 4, no. 1 (2000): 85–125.

Kaye, Joel. "Law, Magic, and Science: Constructing a Border Between Licit and Illicit Knowledge in the Writings of Nicole Oresme." In Ruth Mazo Karras, Joel Kaye, and E. Ann Matter, eds., *Law and the Illicit in Medieval Europe*, 225–37. Philadelphia: University of Pennsylvania Press, 2008.

Kellner, Menachem. *Maimonides on the "Decline of Generations" and the Nature of Rabbinic Authority.* Albany: SUNY Press, 1996.

———. "On the Status of the Astronomy and Physics in Maimonides' Mishneh Torah and Guide of the Perplexed: A Chapter in the History of Science." *British Journal for the History of Science* 24, no. 4 (1991): 453–63.

Kelly, Henry Ansgar. "Inquisition and the Prosecution of Heresy: Misconceptions and Abuses." *Church History* 58 (1989): 439–51.

Kieckhefer, Richard. *European Witch Trials: Their Foundations in Popular and Learned Culture, 1300–1500.* Berkeley: University of California Press, 1976.

———. "The Holy and the Unholy: Sainthood, Witchcraft, and Magic in Late Medieval Europe." In Scott Waugh and Peter Diehl, eds., *Christendom and Its Discontents*, 310–37. Cambridge: Cambridge University Press, 1996.

———. *Magic in the Middle Ages.* Cambridge: Cambridge University Press, 1989.

———. "The Office of Inquisition and Medieval Heresy: The Transition from Personal to Institutional Jurisdiction." *Journal of Ecclesiastical History* 46 (1995): 36–61.

———. *Repression of Heresy in Medieval Germany.* Philadelphia: University of Pennsylvania Press, 1979.

Kraditor, Aileen. "American Radical Historians on Their Heritage." *Past and Present* 56 (Aug. 1972): 136–53.

Kreisel, H. "Maimonides' Approach to Astrology." *Proceedings of the Eleventh World Congress of Jewish Studies, Division C*, 2 vols. Jerusalem: World Union of Jewish Studies, 1994, 2:25–32.

Kruger, Steven F. *Dreaming in the Middle Ages.* Cambridge: Cambridge University Press, 1992.

Lambert, Malcolm. *Medieval Heresy: Popular Movements from the Gregorian Reform to the Reformation.* 3rd ed. Oxford: Blackwell, 2002.

Lang, Justin. *Die Christologie bei Heinrich von Langenstein.* Freiburg: Herder, 1966.

Langermann, Y. Tzvi. "Maimonides' Repudiation of Astrology." *Maimonidean Studies* 2 (1991): 123–58.

Lea, Henry Charles. *History of the Inquisition.* 3 vols. New York: Macmillan, 1887–1922.

Lee, Harold. "*Scutamini Scripturas:* Joachimist Themes and *Figurae* in the Early Religious Writing of Arnold of Villanova." *Journal of the Warburg and Courtauld Institutes* 37 (1974): 33–56.

Lee, Harold, Marjorie Reeves, and Giulio Silano. *Western Mediterranean Prophecy: The School of Joachim of Fiore and the Fourteenth-Century Breviloquium.* Toronto: Pontifical Institute of Mediaeval Studies, 1989.

Leff, Gordon. *Heresy in the Later Middle Ages: The Relation of Heterodoxy to Dissent, ca. 1250–ca. 1450.* 2 vols. Manchester: Manchester University Press, 1967.

LeGoff, Jacques. *The Birth of Purgatory.* Translated by Arthur Goldhammer. Chicago: University of Chicago Press, 1984.

Lehrich, Christopher I. *The Occult Mind: Magic in Theory and Practice.* Ithaca, NY: Cornell University Press, 2007.

Lerner, Robert E. "Aspects of the Fourteenth-Century Iconography of Death and the Plague." In Daniel Williman, ed., *The Black Death: The Impact of the Fourteenth-Century Plague: Papers of the Eleventh Annual Conference of the Center for Medieval and Renaissance Studies,* 77–105. Binghamton, NY: Center for Medieval and Early Renaissance Studies, 1982.

———. "The Black Death in Western European Eschatological Mentalities." *American Historical Review* 86 (1981): 533–52.

———. "Frederick II, Alive, Aloft, and Allayed, in Franciscan-Joachite Eschatology." In Verbeke, Verhelst, and Welkenhuysen, eds., *Use and Abuse of Eschatology,* 358–84.

———. "Historical Introduction." In Rupescissa, *Liber Secretorum Eventuum,* ed. Lerner and Morerod-Fattebert, 13–85.

———. "Popular Justice: Rupescissa in Hussite Bohemia," *Eschatologie und Hussitismus: Internationales Kolloquium Prag 1.–4. September 1993.* Prague: Historiches Institut, 1993, 39–52.

———. *The Powers of Prophecy: The Cedar of Lebanon Vision from the Mongol Onslaught to the Dawn of the Enlightenment.* Berkeley: University of California Press, 1983. Reprt. Ithaca, NY: Cornell University Press, 2008.

Lima, Robert. *Stages of Evil: Occultism in Western Theater and Drama.* Lexington: University Press of Kentucky, 2005.

Little, Lester K. *Religious Poverty and the Profit Economy in Medieval Europe.* Ithaca, NY: Cornell University Press, 1983.

Lucas, John Scott. "Tempting Fate: The Case against Astrology and the Catalan Response." *Catalan Review* 17, no. 2 (2003): 123–37.

Lunenfeld, Marvin. *Keepers of the City: The Corregidores of Isabella I of Castile, 1474–1504.* Cambridge: Cambridge University Press, 1987.

Magdalino, Paul, and Maria Mavroudi. Introduction to Magdalino and Mavroudi, eds. *The Occult Sciences in Byzantium,* 11–37. Geneva: La Pomme d'or, 2006.

Manselli, Raoul. "La religiosità d'Arnaldo da Villanova." *Bullettino dell'Istituto Storico per il Medio Evo e Archivio Muratoriano* 63 (1951): 13–14.

Masià de Ros, Àngels. *El Dissortat Comte d'Urgell.* Barcelona: Rafael Dalmau, 1960.

McCluskey, Stephen C. *Astronomies and Cultures in Early Medieval Europe.* Cambridge: Cambridge University Press, 1998.

McGinn, Bernard. *Antichrist: Two Thousand Years of the Human Fascination with Evil.* New York: Harper Collins, 1994.

——. *Apocalypticism in the Western Tradition.* Brookfield, VT: Variorum, 1994.

——. *The Calabrian Abbot: Joachim of Fiore in the History of Western Thought.* New York: Macmillan, 1985.

——. *Visions of the End: Apocalyptic Traditions in the Middle Ages.* New York: Columbia University Press, 1979.

McNeill, William H. *Plagues and Peoples.* Garden City, NY: Anchor Books, 1976.

McVaugh, Michael R. *Medicine before the Plague: Practitioners and Their Patients in the Crown of Aragon, 1285–1345.* Cambridge: Cambridge University Press, 1993.

Mebane, John S. *Renaissance Magic and the Return of the Golden Age: The Occult Tradition and Marlowe, Jonson, and Shakespeare.* Lincoln: University of Nebraska Press, 1989.

Menéndez y Pelayo, Marcelino. *Historia de los heterodoxos españoles.* Madrid: Librería católica de San José, gerente V. Sancho-Tello, 1880–1881.

Menéndez Pidal, Ramón. *La España del Cid.* Madrid: Editorial Plutarco, 1929.

Mensa i Valls, Jaume. *Arnau de Vilanova, espiritual: guia bibliogràfica.* Barcelona: Institut d'Estudis Catalans, 1994.

——. *Arnau de Villanova (c. 1240–1311).* Madrid: Ediciones del Oro, 2000.

——. *Les raons d'un anunci apocalíptic: La polèmica escatològica entre Arnau de Villanova i els filòsofs i teòlegs professionals (1297–1305): anàlisi dels arguments i de les argumentacions.* Barcelona: Facultat de Teologia de Catalunya, 1998.

Mentgen, Gerd. *Astrologie und Öffentlichkeit im Mittlealter.* Stuttgart: Hiersemann, 2005.

Meyerson, Mark D. "Religion, Regionalism, and Royal Power." In Larry J. Simon, ed., *Iberia and the Mediterranean World of the Middle Ages: Studies in honor of Robert I. Burns,* 96–112. Leiden, Netherlands: Brill, 1995.

Milhou, Alain. *Colón y su mentalidad mesiánica en el ambiente franciscanista español.* Valladolid: Casa-Museo de Colón, 1983.

Millás Vallicrosa, José María. *Assaig d'història de les idees físiques i matèmatiques a la Catalunya medieval.* Barcelona: Institució Patxot, 1931.

——. *Estudios sobre historia de la ciencia española.* Barcelona: Consejo Superior de Investigaciones Científicas, 1949.

——. *Nuevos estudios sobre historia de la ciencia española.* Barcelona: Consejo Superior de Investigaciones Científicas, 1960.

Millet, Hélène. "Le grande schisme d'Occident selon Eustache Deschamps: un monstre prodigieux." *Miracles, prodiges et mervielles au Moyen Age: Actes du XXVe Congrès de la Société des Historiens Médiévistes de l'Enseignement Supérieur Public Orleáns, juin 1994,* 215–26. Paris: Publications de la Sorbonne, 1995.

Milner, Stephen J. "Exile, Rhetoric, and the Limits of Discourse." In Stephen J. Milner, ed., *At the Margins: Minority Groups in Premodern Italy,* 162–91. Minneapolis: University of Minnesota Press, 2005.

Mitjà, Marina. "Procés contra els consellers, domèstics i curials de Joan I, entre ells Bernat Metge." *Boletín de la Real Academia de Buenas Letras de Barcelona* 27 (1957–1958): 375–417.

Mollat, Guillaume. *Les Papes d'Avignon 1305–1378.* Paris: Letouzey and Ané, 1949.

Moorman, John. *A History of the Franciscan Order from Its Origins to the Year 1517.* Oxford: Oxford University Press, 1968.

Mormando, Franco. *The Preacher's Demons: Bernardino of Siena and the Social Underworld of Early Renaissance Italy.* Chicago: University of Chicago Press, 1999.

Mott, Lawrence V. *Sea Power in the Medieval Mediterranean: The Catalan-Aragonese Fleet in the War of the Sicilian Vespers.* Gainesville: University of Florida Press, 2003.

Neufeld, Christine M. "Hermeneutical Perversions: Ralph of Coggeshall's 'Witch of Rheims.'" *Philological Quarterly* 85, no. 1/2 (2006): 1–23.

Newman, Barbara. *God and the Goddesses: Vision, Poetry, and Belief in the Middle Ages.* Philadelphia: University of Pennsylvania Press, 2003.

Newman, William R. *Promethean Ambitions: Alchemy and the Quest to Perfect Nature.* Chicago: University of Chicago Press, 2004.

Newman, William R., and Anthony Grafton, eds. *Secrets of Nature: Astrology and Alchemy in Early Modern Europe.* Cambridge: MIT Press, 2001.

Niccoli, Ottavia. *Prophecy and People in Renaissance Italy.* Translated by Lydia G. Cochrane. Princeton, NJ: Princeton University Press, 1990.

Nirenberg, David. *Communities of Violence: Persecution of Minorities in the Middle Ages.* Princeton, NJ: Princeton University Press, 1996.

O'Callaghan, Joseph F. *A History of Medieval Spain.* Ithaca, NY: Cornell University Press, 1975.

O'Connor, Edward D., ed. *The Dogma of the Immaculate Conception: History and Significance.* Notre Dame, IN: University of Notre Dame Press, 1958.

Olivar Bertrand, Rafael. *Bodas reales entre Francia y la Corona de Aragón: política matrimonial de los príncipes de Aragón y Cataluña, con respecto a Francia, en el siglo XIV.* Barcelona: Editorial Alberto Martín, 1947.

Ouy, Gilbert. "Honoré Bovet (appelé à tort Bonet), prieur de Selonnet." *Romania* 85 (1959): 255–59.

Owst, G. R. "Sortilegium in English Homiletic Literature of the Fourteenth Century." In Davies, ed., *Studies Presented to Sir Hilary Jenkison*, 272–303. London: Oxford University Press, 1957.

La papauté d'Avignon et le Languedoc 1316–1342. Cahiers de Fanjeaux 26. Toulouse: Édouard Privat and Centre d'études historiques de Fanjeaux, 1991.

Paniagua, Juan. *Estudios y notas sobre Arnau de Vilanova.* Madrid: Consejo Superior de Investigaciones Científicas, 1963.

Park, George K. "Divination and Its Social Contexts." *The Journal of the Royal Anthropological Institute of Great Britain and Ireland* 93, no. 2 (1963): 195–209.

Pascoe, Louis B. *Church and Reform: Bishops, Theologians, and Canon Lawyers in the Thought of Pierre d'Ailly (1351–1420).* Leiden: Brill, 2005.

Patai, Raphael. *The Jewish Alchemists.* Princeton, NJ: Princeton University Press, 1994.

Pederson, Olaf. "Astronomy." In David C. Lindberg, ed., *Science in the Middle Ages*, 303–37. Chicago: University of Chicago Press, 1978.

Pegg, Mark Gregory. *The Corruption of Angels: The Great Inquisition of 1245–1246.* Princeton, NJ: Princeton University Press, 2001.

Pelikan, Jaroslav. *The Growth of Medieval Theology (600–1300)*. 3 vols. Chicago: University of Chicago Press, 1978.

Perarnau, Josep. "Opere di Fr. Petrus Johannis in processi catalane d'inquisizione della prima metà del XIV secolo." *Archivum franciscanum historicum* 91 (1998): 505–16.

Pérez Jiménez, Aurelio, ed. *Astronomía y astrología: de los orígenes al Renacimiento*. Madrid: Ediciones Clásicas, 1994.

Peters, Edward. *Heresy and Authority in Medieval Europe*. Philadelphia: University of Pennsylvania Press, 1980.

———. *Inquisition*. Berkeley: University of California Press, 1988.

———. *The Magician, the Witch, and the Law*. Philadelphia: University of Pennsylvania Press, 1978.

———. "The Magical Church and State on Superstition, Magic and Witchcraft: From Augustine to the Sixteenth Century." In Bengt Ankarloo and Stuart Clark, eds., *Witchcraft and Magic in Europe*, 6 vols. 3:175–272. Philadelphia: University of Pennsylvania Press, 2002.

———. "*Quoniam abundavit iniquitas:* Dominicans as Inquisitors, Inquisitors as Dominicans." *Catholic Historical Review* 91, no. 1 (2005): 105–21.

Phelan, John Leddy. *The Millennial Kingdom of the Franciscans in the New World*. 2nd rev. ed. Berkeley: University of California Press, 1970.

Phillips, William D., Jr. "*Peste Negra:* The Fourteenth-Century Plague Epidemics in Iberia." In Donald Kagay and Theresa Vann, eds., *On the Social Origins of Medieval Institutions: Essays in Honor of Joseph F. O'Callaghan*, 47–62. Leiden, The Netherlands: Brill, 1998.

Phillips, William D., Jr., and Carla Rahn Phillips. *The Worlds of Christopher Columbus*. Cambridge: Cambridge University Press, 1992.

Pingree, David. "Between the *Ghāya* and *Picatrix* I: The Spanish Version." *Journal of the Warburg and Courtauld Institutes* 44 (1981): 27–56.

Platzeck, Erhard-Wolfram. *Raimund Lull, sein Leben, seine Werke, die Grundlagen seines Denkens (Prinzipienlehre)*. 2 vols. Düsseldorf: L. Schwann, 1962–1964.

Potter, David. *Prophets and Emperors: Human and Divine Authority from Augustus to Theodosius*. Cambridge, MA: Harvard University Press, 1994.

Pou i Martí, Josep Maria. *Visionarios, Beguinos y Fraticelos Catalanes (Siglos XIII–XV)*. Alicante, Spain: Instituto de Cultura "Juan Gil-Albert" Diputación-Provincial de Alicante, 1996.

Procter, Evelyn S. "The Scientific Works of the Court of Alfonso X of Castille: The King and His Collaborators." *Modern Language Review* 40, no. 1 (1945): 12–29.

Prosperi, A. "America e Apocalisse: Note sulla 'conquista spirituale' del Nuevo Mondo." *Critica Storica* 13 (1976): 1–61.

———. "New Heaven and New Earth: Prophecy and Propaganda at the Time of the Discovery and Conquest of the Americas." In Marjorie Reeves, ed., *Prophetic Rome in the High Renaissance Period*, 279–303. Oxford: Clarendon Press, 1992.

Prügl, Thomas. "Der häertische Papst und seine Immunität im Mittelalter." *Münchener theologische Zeitschrift* 47, no. 3 (1996): 197–215.

Puig i Oliver, Jaume de. "Documents inèdits referents a Nicolau Eimeric i el Lul·lisme." *Arxiu de Textos Catalans Antics* 2 (1983): 319–46.

———. "El pagament dels inquisidors en la Corona d'aragó els segles XIII i XIV." *Arxiu de Textos Catalans Antics* 22 (2003): 175–222.

———. "El procés dels lul·listes valencians contra Nicolau Eimeric en el marc del Cisma d'Occident." *Boletín de la Sociedad Castellonese de Cultura* 56 (1980): 319–463.

———. "La 'Sentència definitive' de 1419 sobre l'ortodòxia lul·liana: Contextos, protagonistes, problemes." *Arxiu de textos catalans antics* 19 (2000): 297–388.

Pumfrey, Stephen, Paolo L. Rossi, and Maurice Slawinski, eds. *Science, Culture, and Popular Belief in Renaissance Europe.* Manchester: Manchester University Press, 1994.

Redondo, Augustin, ed. *La Prophétie comme arme de guerre des pouvoirs, XVe–XVIIe siècles.* Paris: Presses de la Sorbonne Nouvelle, 2000.

Reeves, Marjorie. *The Influence of Prophecy in the Later Middle Ages: A Study in Joachimism.* Oxford: Oxford University Press, 1969.

———. *The Prophetic Sense of History in Medieval and Renaissance Europe.* Brookfield, VT: Ashgate, 1999.

Reeves, Marjorie, and Beatrice Hirsch-Reich. *The Figurae of 'Joachim' of Fiore.* Oxford: Clarendon Press, 1972.

Roca i Heras, José María. *Johan I d'Aragó.* Barcelona: Institució Patxot, 1929.

———. "Johan I y les supersticions." *Boletín de la Real Academia de Buenas Letras de Barcelona* 10 (1921): 125–69.

Roca Traver, Francisco A. "Un siglo de vida mudéjar en la Valencia medieval (1238–1338)." *Estudios de Edad Media de la Corona de Aragon* 5 (1952): 115–208.

Roubaud, Sylvia. "La prophétie merlinienne en Espagne: des rois de Grande-Bretagne aux rois de Castille." In Redondo, ed., *La Prophétie comme arme de guerre des pouvoirs*, 159–73.

Rubin, Miri. *Gentile Tales: The Narrative Assault on Late Medieval Jews.* New Haven, CT: Yale University Press, 1999.

Ruiz, Teofilo. *Spain's Centuries of Crisis, 1300–1474.* Malden, MA: Blackwell, 2007.

Ruiz-Gálvez Priego, Estrella. " 'Fállase por profecía': les prophètes, les prophéties et la projection sociale: Le *Rimado o Cancionero* de Pedro Marcuello et la prophétisme de la fin du XVe siècle." In Redondo, ed., *La Prophétie comme arme de guerre des pouvoirs*, 75–95.

Runciman, Steven. *The Sicilian Vespers: A History of the Mediterranean World in the Later Thirteenth Century.* Cambridge: Cambridge University Press, 1958.

Rusconi, Roberto. *L'attesa della fine: crisi della società, profezia ed Apocalisse in Italia al tempo del grande scisma d'Occidente.* Rome: Istituto storico italiano per il Medio Evo, 1979.

Russell, J. C. "Chroniclers of Medieval Spain." *Hispanic Review* 6, no. 3 (1938): 218–35.

Russell, Jeffrey Burton, and Douglas W. Lumsden. *A History of Medieval Christianity: Prophecy and Order.* New York: P. Lang, 2000.

Rutkin, H. Darrel. "Astrological Conditioning of Same-Sexual Relations in Girolamo Cardano's Theoretical Treatises and Celebrity Genitures." In Kenneth Borris and George Rousseau, eds., *The Sciences of Homosexuality in Early Modern Europe*, 183–99. New York: Routledge, 2008.

Ryan, Michael A. "Byzantium, Islam, and the Great Western Schism." In Jöelle Rollo-Koster and Thomas Izbicki, eds., *A Companion to the Great Western Schism (1378–1417)*.197–238. Leiden, The Netherlands: Brill, 2009.

———. "Nicolau Eymerich and Discerning the End of Days." In Peter Dendle and Richard Raiswell, eds., *The Devil in Premodern Society*. Toronto: CRRS Publications, forthcoming.

———. "Power and Pilgrimage: The Restriction of *Mudéjares'* Pilgrimage in the Kingdom of Valencia." *Essays in Medieval Studies* (2008): 115–28.

———. "Sidereal Remedies: Healing and the Stars in Newberry Library Ayer 746." *AVISTA Forum Journal of Medieval Science, Technology, and Art* 17, no. 1/2 (2007): 8–20.

———. "To Condemn a King: The Dream of Bernat Metge and King Joan's Ties with the Occult." *Magic, Ritual, and Witchcraft* (Winter 2008): 158–86.

Samsó, Julio. *Astronomy and Astrology in al-Andalus and the Maghrib*. Burlington, VT: Ashgate, 2007.

———. *Islamic Astronomy and Medieval Spain*. Brookfield, VT: Variorum, 1994.

Sansone, Guiseppe E. "Un nuovo manoscritto di Francesc Eiximenis e la questione del Cercapou." *Filología Romanza* 3, no. 9 (1956): 11–29.

Saugnieux, Joël. *Les Danses Macabres de France et d'Espagne et leurs prolongements littéraires*. Lyon: Emmanuel Vitte, 1972.

Savage-Smith, Emilie, ed. *Magic and Divination in Early Islam*. Aldershot, UK: Ashgate, 2004.

Savage-Smith, Emilie, and Marion B. Smith. "Islamic Geomancy and a Thirteenth-Century Divinatory Device: Another Look." In Savage-Smith, ed., *Magic and Divination*, 211–76.

Schechner, Sara J. *Comets, Popular Culture, and the Birth of Modern Cosmology*. Princeton, NJ: Princeton University Press, 1997.

Schuster, Peter. "Krise des Spätmittelalters: Zur Evidenz eines sozial- und wirtschaftsgeschichtlichen Paradigmas in der Geschichtsschreibung des 20. Jahrhunderts." *Historisches Zeitschrift* 269 (1999): 19–56.

Schwartz, Dov. *Studies on Astral Magic in Medieval Jewish Thought*. Translated by David Louvish and Batya Stein. Leiden: Brill, 2005.

Seaman, Barrett. "Good Heavens! An Astrologer Dictating the President's Schedule?" *Time*, May 16, 1988, 24–25.

Silleras-Fernández, Núria. *Power, Piety, and Patronage in Late Medieval Queenship*. New York: Palgrave Macmillan, 2008.

———. "Spirit and Force: Politics, Public and Private in the Reign of Maria de Luna (1396–1406)." In Theresa Earenfight, ed., *Queenship and Political Power in Medieval and Early Modern Spain*, 78–90. Burlington, VT: Ashgate, 2005.

Simons, Walter. *Cities of Ladies: Beguine Communities in the Medieval Low Countries, 1200–1565*. Philadelphia: University of Pennsylvania Press, 2001.

Smoller, Laura Ackerman. "Of Earthquakes, Hail, Frogs, and Geography: Plague and the Investigation of the Apocalypse in the Later Middle Ages." In Bynum and Freedman, eds., *Last Things*, 156–87.

——. *History, Prophecy, and the Stars: The Christian Astrology of Pierre d'Ailly, 1350–1420.* Princeton, NJ: Princeton University Press, 1994.

Sobré, Josep Miquel. *L'èpica de la realitat: l'escriptura de Ramón Muntaner i Bernat Desclot.* Barcelona: Curial Edicions Catalanes, 1978.

Soldevila, Ferran. *Les quatre grans cròniques.* Barcelona: Selecta, 1971.

Sondheim, Moriz. "Shakespeare and the Astrology of His Time." *Journal of the Warburg Institute* 2, no. 3 (1939): 243–59.

Starn, Randolph. "Historians and 'Crisis.'" *Past and Present* 52 (Aug. 1971): 3–22.

Stephens, Walter. *Demon Lovers: Witchcraft, Sex, and the Crisis of Belief.* Chicago: University of Chicago Press, 2002.

Stock, Brian. "Science, Technology, and Economic Progress in the Early Middle Ages." In Lindberg, ed., *Science in the Middle Ages*, 1–51.

Strauss, Leo. "How to Begin to Study *The Guide of the Perplexed.*" In Maimonides, *Guide of the Perplexed*, 1: xi–lvi.

Suárez Fernández, Luis. *Intervención de Castilla en la Guerra de los Cien Años.* Valladolid: Industrias Gráficas ESPE, 1950.

Sumption, Jonathan. *The Hundred Years' War.* 2 vols. London: Faber and Faber, 1999.

Swanson, Robert Norman. "A Survey of Views on the Great Schism, c. 1395." *Archivum Historiae Pontificiae* 21 (1983): 79–103.

Sweet, Leonard I. "Christopher Columbus and the Millennial Vision of the New World." *Catholic Historical Review* 72 (1986): 372–81.

Sylvest, Edwin Edward, Jr. *Motifs of Franciscan Mission Theory in Sixteenth Century New Spain Province of the Holy Gospel.* Washington, DC: Academy of American Franciscan History, 1975.

Tachau, Katherine. "God's Compass and *Vana Curiositas:* Scientific Study in the Old French *Bible Moralisée.*" *Art Bulletin* 80 (1998): 7–33.

Tarré, José. "Las profecías del sabio Merlín y sus imitaciones." *Analecta Sacra Taraconensia* 16 (1943): 135–71.

Tasis i Marca, Rafael. *Pere el Cerimoniós i els seus fills.* Barcelona: Editorial Teide, 1957.

Tester, S. Jim. *A History of Western Astrology.* Woodbridge, UK: Boydell Press, 1987.

Theseider, Eugenio Dupré. "L'attesa escatologica durante il periodo Avignonese." *L'attesa dell'età nuova nella spiritualità della fine del medioevo*, 67–126. Todi, Italy: Presso l'Accademia Tudertina, 1962.

Thijssen, J. M. M. H. *Censure and Heresy at the University of Paris, 1200–1400.* Philadelphia: University of Pennsylvania Press, 1998.

Thomas, Keith. *Religion and the Decline of Magic: Studies in Popular Beliefs in Sixteenth and Seventeenth Century England.* New York: Oxford University Press, 1971.

Thompson, Guy Llewelyn. *Paris and Its People under English Rule: The Anglo-Burgundian Regime, 1420–1436.* Oxford: Oxford University Press, 1991.

Thorndike, Lynn. *The History of Magic and Experimental Science.* 8 vols. New York: Macmillan, 1923–1958.

——. "Introduction and Canon by Dalmatius to Tables of Barcelona for the Years 1361–1433." *Isis* 26, no. 2 (1937): 310–20.

Tobienne, François, Jr. *The Position of Magic in Selected Medieval Spanish Texts.* Cambridge: Cambridge Scholars Publishing, 2008.

Torrents Bertran, Ricard. "La peregrinatio accademica de Gerbert d'Orlhac (Silvestre II)." In Imma Ollich i Castanyer, ed., *Actes del Congrés Internacional Gerbert d'Orlhac i el seu temps: Catalunya i Europa a la fi del Iʳ mil·leni, Vic-Ripoll, 10–13 de novembre de 1999*, 13–16. Vic, Spain: Eumo Editorial, 1999.

Torres Amat, Félix. *Memorias para ayudar a formar un diccionario critico de los escritores catalanes.* Barcelona: Impr. de J. Verdaguer, 1836.

Tuchman, Barbara. *A Distant Mirror: The Calamitous 14th Century.* New York: Knopf, 1978.

Ullmann, Walter. *The Origins of the Great Schism: A Study in Fourteenth-Century Ecclesiastical History.* Hamden, CT: Archon Books, 1967.

Vale, Malcolm. *The Princely Court: Medieval Courts and Culture in North-West Europe.* Oxford: Oxford University Press, 2001.

Valois, Noël. *La France et le Grand Schisme d'Occident.* 4 vols. Paris: A. Picard et fils, 1896–1902.

———. "Un ouvrage inédit d'Honoré Bonet, Prieur de Salon." *Annuaire-Bulletin de la Société de l'Histoire de France* 27 (1890): 193–228.

Vauchez, André. "Jean de Roquetaillade (†1366 ca.). Bilan des recherches et état de la question." *Eschatologie und Hussitismus. Internationales Kolloquium Prag 1.–4. September 1993,* 25–37. Prague: Historiches Institut, 1993.

———. *Sainthood in the Middle Ages.* Translated by Jean Birrell. Cambridge: Cambridge University Press, 1997.

———. *Saints, prophètes et visionnaires: Le pouvior surnaturel au Moyen Age.* Paris: Albin Michel, 1999.

———. "Les théologiens face aux prophéties à l'époque des papes d'Avignon et du Grand Schisme." *Mélanges de l'Ecole Française de Rome. Moyen Age* 102, no. 2 (1990): 577–88.

Verbeke, Werner, D. Verhelst, and Andries Welkenhuysen, eds. *The Use and Abuse of Eschatology in the Middle Ages.* Louvain: Louvain University Press, 1988.

Verger, Jacques. "Different Values and Authorities." In Robert Fossier, ed., *The Cambridge Illustrated History of the Middle Ages III, 1250–1520,* translated by Sarah Hanbury Tenison, 119–91. Cambridge: Cambridge University Press, 1986.

Verlinden, Charles. "La Grande Peste de 1348 en Espagne: Contribution à l'étude de ses conséquences économiques et sociales." *Revue belge de Philologie et d'Histoire* 17 (1938): 101–46.

Viera, David J. "Foreword: Astrology in the Thirteenth- and Fourteenth-Century Kingdom of Aragon." In John Scott Lucas, *Astrology and Numerology in Medieval and Early Modern Catalonia: The Tractat de prenostication de la vida natural dels hòmens,* xi–xxvii. Leiden: Brill, 2003.

Walker, D. P. "Orpheus the Theologian and Renaissance Platonists." *Journal of the Warburg and Courtauld Institutes* 16, no. 1/2 (1953): 100–120.

Watts, Pauline Moffitt. "Prophecy and Discovery: On the Spiritual Origins of Christopher Columbus's 'Enterprise of the Indies.'" *American Historical Review* 90 (1985): 73–102.

Waxman, Samuel M. *Chapters on Magic in Spanish Literature.* PhD diss., Harvard University, 1912.

Webster, Jill. *Els Menorets: The Franciscans in the Realms of Aragon from St. Francis to the Black Death*. Toronto: Pontifical Institute of Mediaeval Studies, 1993.

Wedel, Theodore Otto. *The Mediaeval Attitude toward Astrology, Particularly in England*. Hamden, CT: Archon Books, 1968.

Wei, Ian P. "Predicting the Future to Judge the Present: Paris Theologians and Attitudes to the Future." In J. A. Burrow and Ian P. Wei, eds., *Medieval Futures: Attitudes to the Future in the Middle Ages*, 19–36. Woodbridge, Suffolk: Boydell Press, 2000.

West, Delno C. "Medieval Ideas of Apocalyptic Mission and the Early Franciscans in Mexico." *The Americas* 45, no. 3 (1989): 293–313.

West, Delno C., and Sandra Zimdars-Swartz. *Joachim of Fiore: A Study in Spiritual Perception and History*. Bloomington: Indiana University Press, 1983.

Whalen, Brett. *Dominion of God: Christendom and Apocalypse in the Middle Ages*. Cambridge, MA: Harvard University Press, 2009.

———. "Joachim of Fiore and the Division of Christendom." *Viator* 34 (2003): 89–108.

Whyte, Florence. *The Dance of Death in Spain and Catalonia*. New York: Arno Press, 1977.

Williams, Steven J. *The Secret of Secrets: The Scholarly Career of a Pseudo-Aristotelian Text in the Latin Middle Ages*. Ann Arbor: University of Michigan Press, 2003.

Witte, Maria Magdalena. *Elias und Henoch als Exempel, typologische Figuren und apokalyptische Zeugen: Zu Verbindungen von Literatur und Theologie im Mittlealter*. Frankfurt: Lang, 1987.

Wright, Rosemary Muir. *Art and Antichrist in Medieval Europe*. Manchester: Manchester University Press, 1995.

Zambelli, Paola. "Profeti-astrologi sul medio periodo. Motivi pseudogioachimiti nel dibattito italiano e Tedesco sulla fine del mondo per la grande congiunzione del 1524." *Il profetismo gioachimita tra 400 e 500. Atti del III Congresso Internazionale di Studi Gioachimiti*, 273–86. Geneva: Gian Luca Potestà, 1991.

———, ed. *"Astrologi hallucinati." Stars and the End of the World in Luther's Time*. Berlin: W. de Gruyter, 1986.

Ziegler, Joseph. *Medicine and Religion c. 1300: The Case of Arnau de Villanova*. Oxford: Oxford University Press, 1998.

Index